Next *of* Kin

A book in the series
LATIN AMERICA OTHERWISE:
LANGUAGES, EMPIRES, NATIONS

A series edited by
Walter D. Mignolo, Duke University
Irene Silverblatt, Duke University
Sonia Saldívar-Hull, University of Texas,
San Antonio

Next *of* Kin

The Family in Chicano/a Cultural Politics

Richard T. Rodríguez

DUKE UNIVERSITY PRESS   DURHAM AND LONDON   2009

© 2009 Duke University Press

All rights reserved

Printed in the United States of America
on acid-free paper ∞

Designed by Heather Hensley

Typeset in Warnock Pro by Achorn
International

Library of Congress Cataloging-in-
Publication Data appear on the last
printed page of this book.

About the Series

Latin America Otherwise: Languages, Empires, Nations is a critical series. It aims to explore the emergence and consequences of concepts used to define "Latin America" while at the same time exploring the broad interplay of political, economic, and cultural practices that have shaped Latin American worlds. Latin America, at the crossroads of competing imperial designs and local responses, has been construed as a geocultural and geopolitical entity since the nineteenth century. This series provides a starting point to redefine Latin America as a configuration of political, linguistic, cultural, and economic intersections that demands a continuous reappraisal of the role of the Americas in history and of the ongoing process of globalization and the relocation of people and cultures that have characterized Latin America's experience. Latin America Otherwise: Languages, Empires, Nations is a forum that confronts established geocultural constructions, rethinks area studies and disciplinary boundaries, assesses convictions of the academy and of public policy, and correspondingly demands that the practices through which we produce knowledge and understanding about and from Latin America be subject to rigorous and critical scrutiny.

As both an idea and an institution, the family has been at the heart of Chicano/a cultural politics since the beginnings of the Chicano movement in the 1960s and 1970s. In *Next of Kin* Richard T. Rodríguez reviews the history of "la familia" within the movement and analyzes the politics around it, the ways it has been entangled with ideas of the community and the extended kinship network of people with whom one shares a cultural and spiritual identity ("la raza"), and in particular the ways it has been mobilized by heteronormative and patriarchal discourses. He critiques the genealogy of the family in much the same way as Foucault critiques the genealogy of history—by interrupting and retelling a purportedly continuous process and absolute paradigm—particularly in the context of economic exploitation, racism, sexism, and homophobia. He argues that as minority nationalisms endeavor to liberate their purported constituencies from the subordinating forces of the state, they must relinquish their dependence on exclusionary kinship relations.

Next of Kin reaffirms the role of machismo in the creation of the Mexican American civil rights and cultural empowerment movement known as the Chicano movement. Machismo permeated the movement's internal politics, which was a major catalyst in the development of contemporary Chicana feminism. In examining the origins of this movement, Rodríguez begins by reviewing the discourses that have laid the foundation on which the family became an organizing strategy for communitarian politics, assessing why the family was of such fundamental importance to movement intellectuals and writers. He does so by foregrounding the emergent nationalist consciousness adopted by Chicanos in relation to the U.S. nation state. By looking at drawings and paintings of the family-portrait type (posters, periodical and book covers and illustrations, murals, postcards), he uncovers the powerful role of masculinity as a normalizing force. Turning to film, video, and television, then later to Chicano rap music and hip-hop culture, he examines the ways the family is articulated in calls for collective struggle and finds that while Chicano rap may challenge state violence around issues of racism and police hostility, it often relies on articulations of community as dominated by men. Focusing next on Chicano gay men involved in cultural production, Rodríguez illustrates the ways male homosexuality has been cast in antifamily terms, and he identifies the popular culture arena of car customizing as an area in which gay male subjects have emerged to challenge beliefs about their closeted identities. He concludes by suggesting the importance of reimagining new communities while maintaining biological kinship ties, highlighting the ways queers have forged alternative kinship networks that also incorporate their own families.

Given the complexities and contradictions in such queer networks, the author cautions that even queer communities, especially those dominated by men, can reproduce gender inequalities characteristic of the patriarchal hierarchies of the movement era.

Contents

Acknowledgments

Although it is impossible to acknowledge every single person who has lavished on me the motivation and sense of purpose required to write this book, thanks are due to those who assisted in enabling its completion.

First I wish to thank James Clifford, Teresa de Lauretis, and Kirsten Silva Gruesz for their critical feedback and mentorship that profoundly shaped the thinking that went into this project in its initial incarnation as a dissertation. While a graduate student in History of Consciousness at the University of California, Santa Cruz, I also benefited from the invaluable guidance of José David Saldívar, Angela Y. Davis, Lourdes Martínez-Echazábal, Susan Gillman, Hayden White, Chris Connery, and Patricia Zavella.

Many scholars have graciously given their time and support, which made the book possible. For their generosity and timely interventions, I am particularly thankful to Sonia Saldívar-Hull, Jorge Mariscal, John Carlos Rowe, José Esteban Muñoz, Judith Halberstam, Alfred Arteaga, David Lloyd, Alicia Gaspar de Alba, Genaro Padilla, Norma E. Cantú, Rafael Pérez-Torres, Francisco Balderrama, Ricardo L. Ortíz, Curtis Márez, Alicia Arrizón, Marta López-Garza, Tomás Ybarra-Frausto, Marilyn Elkins, Carlos Muñoz, Jr., Lionel Maldonado, Norma Alarcón, Chon Noriega, and Vicki Ruíz. In addition, Pete Sigal, Catrióna Rueda Esquibel, Luz Calvo, Ernesto Chávez, Jerry Miller, José Alamillo, Ellie D. Hernández, Talia Bettcher, Michael Hames-García, Ernesto J. Martínez, Lilia Fernández, John Ramírez, David Hernández, Catherine Ramírez, Karen Tongson, Ramón García, and Wendy White have given the gift of collegiality fused with intellectual insight, critical feedback, laughter, and breathtaking wit. Dionne Espinoza is my confidant, coconspirator, and brilliant friend for whom I'm always appreciative. Lily Castillo-Speed is every Chicano/a studies scholar's reference savior.

At the University of Illinois, Urbana-Champaign and in the Midwest in general many people helped me reassess and strengthen this project. For offering repeated doses of insight, support, and friendship, I am most indebted to Arlene Torres, Martin Manalansan, Siobhan Somerville, Lisa Cacho, David Coyoca, Isabel Molina, Junaid Rana, Mirelsie Velázquez, Veronica Kann, Aidé Acosta, Abel Correa, Rigoberto González, Johanna Galarte, Maria del Mar González-González, Wanda Pillow, Laurence Parker, Robert Dale Parker, Michael Rothberg, Dale Bauer, Gordon Hutner, Lauren Goodlad, Sandy and Martin Camargo, Ariana Ruíz, Natalie Havlin, Isabel Quintana-Wulf, Kim O'Neill, Rudy Aguilar, Antonia Darder, Brian Montes, Alicia P. Rodríguez, Victoria González, Olga Sofer, Amelia Montes, Rolando J. Romero, Curt McKay, and Laura Castañeda.

One can tell by perusing this book that the work of numerous writers, artists, and cultural workers enabled the generation of my ideas and arguments. For this I am grateful, but I would be remiss not to mention that they have repeatedly shaped and reshaped my worldviews. I especially want to thank Eugene Rodríguez, Harry Gamboa Jr., Barbara Carrasco, Jesús Salvador Treviño, Augie Robles, Gronk, Aurora Sarabia, Dan Guerrero, Deadlee, and Héctor Silva.

Then there are the friends who have stuck with me through the thick and the very thin. They include Francisco J. Ceja, Alejandro Lara, Miguel Ramírez, Alberto Vaca, Vanessa Alvarado, Keri Castañeda, Monica López, Enrique Orozco, Juan Chávez, Angel Carrillo, Susana Martínez, Obiel Leyva, Javier Vásquez, Marcus Cordero, Larry Padua, Mario A. Hernández, Carlos Moreno, Fred Wells, Alex Espinosa, and Carlos Samaniego.

Over the years, my students have bestowed upon me innumerable intellectual gifts, and indeed their interventions and provocations never ceased to make an indelible mark on my commitment to teaching, my relationship to academia, and, of course, my scholarship of which this book is representative. While Luis E. Ramírez, Sonia A. Rodríguez, Luis Benavides, Steven Rosado, David Orta, Will García, Natalie Lira, Brenda Rodríguez, Andy Robledo, Anona Whitley, Christopher Garibay, Joe and Jesse Palencia, Jaime Olmos, Diana Rodríguez, Albert Flores, Nathan McKeown, David Rodríguez, Oscar Rivera, Lucas McKeever, Tim Meyers, Berenice Vargas, Pearce Durst, Eric Téllez, Daniel Nuñez, Juan López,

Miguel Saucedo, Victor Benitez, Rubén Martínez, Carlos Lazaro, Jessica Guzmán, Pablo Quintana, and Tiana Carrillo quickly come to mind, there are additional luminaries who have enrolled in my courses and with whom I have worked in various capacities that warrant my gratitude.

At Duke University Press I am thankful to J. Reynolds Smith and Sharon Torian for their unflagging dedication and patience. To G. Neal McTighe and Michael Wakoff, thanks are due for their meticulous editorial skills. I also wish to thank the anonymous readers of the manuscript who helped kick it into shape.

A portion of chapter 1 was published as "Serial Kinship: Representing La Familia in Early Chicano Publications," *Aztlán: A Journal of Chicano Studies* 27 (spring 2002): 123–38, and is reproduced with permission. Portions of chapter 3 appeared as "The Verse of the Godfather: Signifying Family and Nationalism in Chicano Rap and Hip-Hop Culture," in *Velvet Barrios: Popular Culture and Chicana/o Sexualities*, ed. Alicia Gaspar de Alba, copyright 2003 by Palgrave Macmillan, and are reproduced with permission of Palgrave Macmillan.

Truth be told, I couldn't have gone very far without my family. I therefore thank all my cousins, aunts, and uncles who have sustained me for as far back as I can remember. My grandmother Mary Valdez and my late grandfather Sam F. Valdez have taught me so much about unconditional support. My sister Renée Rodríguez-Merino and my brother-in-law Eddie Merino are both kin and political allies. And last but never least, my parents, Richard Rodríguez and Diane Valdez, have given me so much for which I will always be grateful. With all of my heart, I love them.

Introduction Staking Family Claims

> The family is the place where, for better or worse, we learn how
> to love.
>
> • • • Cherríe Moraga, *Loving in the War Years: Lo que nunca pasó por*
> *sus labios* (1983)

In her "Introduction" to the collection *Chicana Feminist Thought: The*
Basic Historical Writings, sociologist Alma M. García notes how intersecting discourses of nationalism, family, and machismo provoked
Chicana feminism in the late 1960s and 1970s, the historical moment that
gave way to organized struggles for Mexican American civil rights and
cultural empowerment known as the Chicano movement.

> Although many issues contributed to the development of Chicana feminist
> thought, the ideological critique of sexism or *machismo*, the term most fre-
> quently used within a Chicano context, contributed significantly to the for-
> mation of Chicana feminism. Chicana feminists, as active participants in the
> Chicano movement, experienced the immediate constraints of male domina-
> tion in their daily lives. Their writings express their concern with traditional
> gender roles within Chicano families that relegated women into secondary
> roles. Chicana feminists challenged the portrait of the so-called "Ideal Chi-
> cana" drawn by Chicano cultural nationalists. (A. García 1997, 5)

Furthermore, within various movement contexts, strands of Chicano cultural nationalism tethered to machismo promoted a family ideal that, extrapolating from Christopher Lasch, García identifies as a "safe 'haven in
a heartless world.'" In this romanticized haven—a "nation" defined within

the contours of domesticity—the archetypal Chicana would necessarily provide a feminine spirit of maternal consolation (in spite of her suffering) while ensuring the procreation, hence survival, of Chicano culture.

Writing about feminine space within the context of Indian nationalism (in terms that fittingly apply to Chicano movement contexts), Partha Chatterjee argues, "the crucial requirement was to retain the inner spirituality of indigenous social life" by way of locating "the home" as "the principal site for expressing the spiritual quality of the national culture." Women "must take the main responsibility of protecting and nurturing this quality." Thus, "no matter what the changes in the external conditions of life for women, they must not lose their essentially spiritual (i.e., feminine) virtues" (Chatterjee 1990, 243). Chicana feminist criticism, upon which I will soon elaborate, unravels the threads that bind *la familia* (the family) with *la raza* (the people), an often-taken-for-granted, naturalized site, where cohesion presupposes not only the fixity of gender roles but, by extension, a continuum between male authority and heterosexual presumption.

Building on the Chicana feminist critique and extending its objectives, *Next of Kin: The Family in Chicano/a Cultural Politics* critically examines both discursive and material configurations of la familia. If there is a single issue almost always at stake in Chicano/a cultural politics since the Chicano movement of the 1960s and 1970s, it is the family in some shape, form, or fashion. Indeed, the family is a crucial symbol and organizing principle that by and large frames the history of Mexican Americans in the United States.[1] In plotting a Chicano/a cultural history that encompasses the 1960s to the present, this book examines kinship and the family as, simultaneously, ideologies adopted by heteronormative and patriarchal discourses—or what Roderick A. Ferguson (2004) has importantly termed heteropatriarchy—and as crucial sites for political struggle when informed by egalitarian possibility.[2] In the book, la familia is analyzed as framing and underscoring a genealogy of Chicano/a cultural texts—poems, manifestos, drawings, paintings, murals, music, film, video, and television—informed by the imperatives of the Chicano movement in conjunction with the influence of gender and sexuality on kinship formations. At root this project serves as an interrogation of heteropatriarchal articulations of cultural nationalism by scrutinizing who and what counts as la familia in the name of Chicano/a cultural politics.[3]

Departing from fixed notions of family, the texts gathered and analyzed here—constituting both an archive formed by Chicano movement principles and my desire to conjoin sources that fall outside traditional disciplinary locations or historical mappings—illustrate la familia as a genealogical tradition that entails successive shifts contingent upon changing kinship discourses and formations. Extrapolating from Michel Foucault's essay "Nietzsche, Genealogy, History" (1984), the genealogy I track critiques family much as Foucault critiques "History," by interrupting and retelling a purportedly continuous process and absolute paradigm. Considering how historical "truth" reflects a process of systematic domination suppressing discrepant narratives, Foucault argues that the task of the historian is to undo History as an ideal schema, displacing the authority that assures its smooth continuity. In turn, history and genealogy are understood as sites of struggle and contestation, "a profusion of entangled events" (Foucault 1984, 89). History and its constitution, in the conventional sense, is akin to conventional kinship arrangements in that they purport to produce monumental narratives based on "the inviolable identity of their origin" (79). Emphasizing genealogy in such terms thus allows this book to construe the family as both symbol and social category whose signification is not necessarily foreordained by blood, circumstance, and monologic notions such as "History." We can thus reimagine what family has been and, especially, what it could be for those who fall outside its otherwise regulatory borders.

Although *Next of Kin* interrupts those discourses intimately linking nationalism and heteropatriarchy as underpinnings of a compulsory normative Chicano family romance, it does not result in its dismissal. Ultimately, the critique carried out points to a return, not transcendence. The book necessarily considers the crucial familial attachments—attachments predicated upon diverse modes of kinship by various constituencies—maintained by Chicanos and Chicanas at historical moments in which economic exploitation, racism, sexism, and homophobia persist. As Foucault does not aim to dissolve "History" but instead calls for its reconfiguration as genealogy (making it available to refashioned subjects and projects), numerous cultural workers have revised la familia as alternative kinship relations. I thus foreground these "reinventions" of family in forms and practices that displace its otherwise normatively domesticating effects.

The connections between masculinity, nationalism, and the family are hardly exclusive to Chicanos and Chicanas. Indeed, their interlocking connections typify a broad range of historical moments, geographies, and cultural practices. When Anne McClintock (1995, 357) suggests in *Imperial Leather: Race, Gender, and Sexuality in the Colonial Contest* that nationalism is "frequently figured through the iconography of familial and domestic space," for example, she is drawing from Frantz Fanon's observation in *Black Skin, White Masks* that "there are close connections between the structure of the family and the structure of the nation" (360). McClintock observes that nationalism, as Fanon similarly elaborates, is "constituted from the very beginning as a gendered discourse and cannot be understood without a theory of gender power" (355). Conversantly, in *Bananas, Beaches, and Bases: Making Feminist Sense of International Politics*, Cynthia Enloe argues that

> nationalist movements have rarely taken women's experiences as the starting point for an understanding of how a people becomes colonized or how it throws off the shackles of that material and psychological domination. Rather, nationalism typically has sprung from masculinized memory, masculinized humiliation and masculinized hope. Anger at being 'emasculated'—or turned into 'a nation of busboys'—has been presumed to be the natural fuel for igniting a nationalist movement. (1989, 44)

I take seriously these observations for understanding Chicano cultural nationalism as conceived by many thinkers whose work emerged from the movement of the 1960s and 1970s. The demand for particular monologic versions of the family by these mostly male thinkers confirms McClintock's observation of a "gender difference between women and men [that] serves to symbolically define the limits of national difference and power between men" (1995, 354). Such definitions meant keeping women from occupying positions of power in regimes of male-determined nationalism.[4]

Yet the insistence upon adhering to such family formations is not a phenomenon to be relegated to the recent past of the 1960s and 1970s but one that continues to surface in recent Chicano/a cultural politics. The metaphorization of family as a unit governed by men has been recently expressed by Ignacio M. García (1996) in his essay "Juncture in the Road: Chicano Studies since 'El Plan de Santa Barbara.'" While making important observations on the present status of Chicano studies in light of its historical development, García's overall embattled view of the discipline mirrors his frustration with the shifting terms of what counts as family (especially those articulated by lesbians). Pondering the early goals of the Chicano movement, García investigates Chicano studies in its recent manifestations and questions its impact on nonacademic communities and its overall impetus for social change. García (1996,190) laments, "The academy has become the only world for some of these [Chicana lesbian] scholars, because they have redefined the concept of community." Furthermore, he writes, "These new definitions reduce the community to single females, or single-parent families led by females, who are poor and abused. There is very little vibrancy in that community beyond the mother-daughter relationship. Their definition of community stands in stark contrast with the community most Chicano/a scholars know" (202). García asserts there is very little vibrancy in communities or families that do not include men—and perhaps, by implication, in those not controlled by them. Thus his anxiety may be over the refusal to maintain a stable family dynamic that is decidedly heterosexual, procreative, and male dominated.

García's claims are not unlike those presented in Christopher Lasch's *Haven in a Heartless World: The Family Besieged* (1977), a book widely repudiated by many feminist scholars exploring the subject of the family. Yet as I find value in García's position (that is, I agree that Chicano scholarship should speak to, and connect with, the life experiences of Chicanos and Chicanas outside the academy), I see Lasch's work as articulating important observations about the family's significance as a social institution. The stakes are especially high when one considers the importance of family in countering the subordinating forces of racism and economic exploitation. Unfortunately both García and Lasch rely upon a patriarchal order that entails a dismissal—if not vilification—of feminism, thus limiting the terms by which kinship might be understood in more socially and historically grounded ways.

The lives that comprise those women's families García condemns are often based on common kinship networks, patterns of connection imposed perhaps by choice, perhaps by circumstance. These families, however, are not merely "academically" redefined communities but also reflect the material realities of many working-class women. An abundance of historical documentation fortifies this point. In fact, the social and historical significance of divergent kinship networks encompasses an extensive time frame that predates and exceeds narrow renditions of la familia in the movement era. Take, for example, Vicki L. Ruíz's study on California Chicana cannery workers from the 1930s to the 1950s that details the "extended kin networks within the [cannery] plants [that] reaffirmed a sense of family and cultural traditions" (1987, 19). According to Ruíz, such networks "nurtured the development of a closely knit work environment, one which eased [women's] adjustment to the routines and conditions of labor particular to canneries and packing houses" (20). In another premovement context, consider the groundbreaking historical work of George J. Sánchez that reveals how, in the 1920s, "Family life in the barrios of Los Angeles ranged from conventional to experimental" (1993, 143). "Rigid gender roles," he writes, "could hardly be maintained under [particular] circumstances" since "female-headed households . . . were not uncommon at the turn of the century" (132). In short, both Ruíz and Sánchez provide images of nonstandard, effective, family structures that defy the "nuclear" norm inscribed within many movement scripts. One might find it revealing that Ignacio García (1996, 202) berates such woman-dominant families, families who cannot move beyond "the mother-daughter relationship," for not being "the community most Chicano/a scholars know," a middle-class contingent at the very least. Thus García's quest to unveil elitism in Chicana studies becomes more of a confirmation of his struggle to keep the "o" in Chicano studies—maintaining a presumed family "most Chicano/a scholars know" (202)—firmly intact. To be sure, García's concept of la familia is a normative gesture that simplifies and disciplines a wider range of possibilities and strategies for imagining alliances and constituting a more elaborate genealogical enterprise. In charging Chicana lesbians with the creation of narrow kinship networks, he unveils a restricted understanding of la familia that is hopelessly romantic on the one hand and heteropatriarchal on the other. Quite similar to opponents of gay marriage, García's logic conforms to the belief that, in the words of Judith Butler (2004, 102), "kinship does not work, or does not qualify as kinship, unless it assumes a recognizable family form."

From *Loving in the War Years* (1983) to *Waiting in the Wings: Portrait of a Queer Motherhood* (1997), Chicana lesbian writer Cherríe Moraga's work attempts to establish la familia as a site of resistance to power, namely community fragmentation vis-à-vis racial discrimination, economic disenfranchisement, and the subordination of gender and sexual difference. In Moraga's estimation, the family is a collective consciousness premised on a shared opposition to such oppressions all the while contesting heteropatriarchal kinship relations. She does not desire the repudiation of masculinist nationalisms simply to appeal to a prescriptive antiessentialism that makes all community traditions suspect. On the contrary, Moraga's alternative rendering of la familia strives toward a utopian space that is able to critique yet sustain Chicano/a community formation.

Concerned as I am with the specific politics and functions (ranging from the pitfalls and affirmative moments) of Chicano cultural nationalism and its familial ties, it is essential to distinguish between subaltern (a category under which I situate Chicano cultural politics) and state-marshaled nationalisms.[5] Along with disseminating a rhetoric of "family values" that passes as truth in narratives transmitted by the dominant culture, official nationalisms also articulate with and against subaltern forms in the struggle for a hegemonic "common sense." Indeed, it is imperative to comprehend the existence of nationalisms that rail against the state, for example, while recognizing that many brands of nationalism— be they minor or major—adhere to similar ideologies around gender and sexuality.

I maintain, then, that if minority nationalisms endeavor to liberate their purported constituencies from the subordinating forces of the state, they must relinquish their dependency on exclusionary kinship relations. Furthermore, unlike the now-common move in Chicano/a and other ethnic studies scholarship to heavy-handedly render cultural nationalism the enemy that inherently generates sexism and homophobia, the project registers the political import it may serve for potentially inclusive orchestrations. As Moraga (1993b, 148–49) succinctly puts it, "What was right about Chicano Nationalism was its commitment to preserving the integrity of the Chicano people. A generation ago, there were cultural, economic, and political programs to develop Chicano consciousness, autonomy, and self-determination. What was wrong about Chicano

Nationalism was its institutionalized heterosexism, its inbred machismo, and its lack of a cohesive national political strategy." In keeping with this assessment, she formulates the idea of "Queer Aztlán," a "progressive" cultural nationalist strategy that embraces all Chicanos and Chicanas, especially women and queers. Moraga (150) "cling[s] to the word 'nation' because without the specific naming of the nation, the nation will be lost (as when feminism is reduced to humanism, the woman is subsumed). Let us retain our radical naming but expand it to meet a broader and wiser revolution."

Here Moraga is understood as arguing that the movement and the cultural nationalist sentiment emanating from it played a crucial role for consciousness raising and mobilization efforts around the multilayered issues impacting Chicano/a communities. Seizing the radical actions and potentials offered by it while insisting upon a critique of the sexism and heteronormative thinking wielded in its name, Moraga disputes the belief that the movement did more damage than good and thus calls into question its status as a monolithic entity away from which progressive thought has moved. Indeed, as Jorge Mariscal (2002, 59) writes, "By misrepresenting the multiple ideologies that informed the Chicano movement as a single current of reactionary cultural nationalism or 'identity politics' riddled by sexism, internal dissension, 'anti-Americanism,' and 'reverse racism,' revisionist historians (some of Mexican American descent) have deprived future generations of a complete portrayal of Chicano/a activism in one of the most revolutionary periods in American history."[6]

Moraga would no doubt concur with Mariscal, especially in light of conservative politicians like Patrick J. Buchanan who have identified Chicano cultural nationalism not only as anti-American but also (along with homosexuality and feminism) a threat to the family values that he and others of his ilk promote. In his books *The Death of the West: How Dying Populations and Immigrant Invasions Imperil Our Country and Civilization* (2002) and *State of Emergency: The Third World Invasion and Conquest of America*, Buchanan (2006, 109) cites passages from the movement manifesto *El Plan Espiritual de Aztlán* (misnamed *El Plan de Aztlan* and further discussed in chapter 1) to argue that the student organization MEChA (Movimiento Estudiantil Chicano de Aztlán) "is the Chicano version of the white-supremacist Aryan Nation." Most revealing for the context at hand is Buchanan's quotation of the following passage

from *El Plan*: "Political Liberation . . . can only come through independent action on our part, since the two-party system is the same animal
with two heads that feed from the same trough. Where we are a majority we will control; where we are a minority we will represent a pressure
group; nationally we represent one party: *La Familia de La Raza*." Here
the articulation of Chicano cultural nationalism vis-à-vis la familia that
inspires Buchanan's anxiety is two-pronged: not only does it serve to
generate—as he would put it—a dying West in light of immigration (not
recognizing that Chicanos are not always immigrants) but it also threatens an idealized "American" family that must fundamentally be white and
heteropatriarchal.[7]

CHICANO/A STUDIES, CULTURAL STUDIES

To fulfill its goals this book utilizes cultural studies paradigms, many of
which are formed as a result of transnational scholarly exchange. Since
cultural studies is a broad field of inquiry that evokes manifold meanings,
let me identify more specifically what I mean when I make reference to it.
For Stuart Hall (1990, 11), "Cultural studies is not one thing, it has never
been one thing." In the introduction to their foundational anthology (appropriately titled *Cultural Studies*), Lawrence Grossberg, Cary Nelson,
and Paula Treichler draw from Hall to argue:

> Even when cultural studies is identified with a specific national tradition like
> British cultural studies, it remains a diverse and often contentious enterprise,
> encompassing different positions and trajectories in specific contexts, address-
> ing many questions, drawing nourishment from multiple roots, and shaping
> itself within different institutions and locations. The passage of time, encoun-
> ters with new historical events, and the very extension of cultural studies into
> new disciplines and national contexts will inevitably change its meanings
> and uses. Cultural studies needs to remain open to unexpected, unimagined,
> even uninvited possibilities. No one can hope to control these developments.
> (1992, 3)

Cultural studies makes no particular claims to belonging to, or developing from, any particular discipline. Although some would stress cultural studies' anchoring in sociology or literary studies, it also folds into,
among other fields, media studies, history, women's studies, anthropology, and ethnic studies. Cultural studies, as I see it, enables the space for

addressing various social phenomena by employing multiple disciplines, methodologies, and discourses that speak to specific issues or concerns. Indeed, "it is interdisciplinary in the sense that it recognises that questions of culture and power must lead one beyond the realm of culture into fields of inquiry normally constitutive of a number of other disciplines" (Grossberg 1997, 7).[8]

One influential genealogy of cultural studies begins with the class-based cultural analysis of the "founding fathers" Richard Hoggart, E. P. Thompson, and Raymond Williams (Turner 1992). Stuart Hall extends these approaches into sociological studies of race and ethnicity. As director of the Centre for Contemporary Cultural Studies at Birmingham during the 1970s, he facilitated the creation of a context for the emergence of what is loosely known as "Black Cultural Studies," exemplified by the work of his former students Hazel Carby, Kobena Mercer, and Paul Gilroy. The critical interventions of these three scholars, among others, stake their claims at the crossroads of race, class, gender, and sexuality. This is the strand of cultural studies upon which I most consistently draw. So while some would stress its indebtedness to history (Thompson), literary studies (Williams), or sociology (Hall), this project hinges on cultural studies' overall consideration of multiple, overlapping discourses that enable fleshing out the theoretical and material impulses uncontainable by disciplinary boundaries.

For example, in his pioneering book *The Black Atlantic: Modernity and Double Consciousness*, Paul Gilroy (1993a) provides a historical mapping of black diaspora culture in the advent of modernism by simultaneously harmonizing fiction, music, and philosophy. With Gilroy as conductor, they speak in concert about the theme of the "history of the black Atlantic" that "yields a course of lessons as to the instability and mutabilities of identities which are always unfinished, always being made" (Gilroy 1993a, xi). On one level, I see the *The Black Atlantic* operating from an interdisciplinary base that enables a project acutely organized around a particular theme while drawing upon a variety of cultural forms and critical frameworks. On another level, Gilroy's black Atlantic diaspora, according to James Clifford (1997, 267), "tactically defines a map/history in ways that may best be seen as 'anti-antiessentialist,' the double negative not reducible to a positive." The anti-antiessentialist position, however, has been met with criticism by scholars such as Kobena Mercer who, in his critique of it in "Black Art and the Burden of Representation" (1990), accuses Gilroy of resituating blackness within foundationalist frames of reference. While I appreciate Mercer's critique—especially in view of his explicit concern with issues of sexuality and gender, issues that are largely absent from Gilroy's analyses—the antiessentialist position might too easily consign anything historical that smells of essentialism to the graveyard of bad essences, a move that, Clifford (1997, 266) notes, represents a "premature pluralism."

In this sense I understand this project on the contested site of the family for Chicanas and Chicanos as necessarily guided by an anti-antiessentialist impulse. For if the family "is to be something about which one could write a history—and this is Gilroy's politically pointed goal—it must be something more than the name for a site of multiple displacements and reconstitutions of identity" (Clifford 1997, 267). Establishing a family politic, in ways similar to the formation of a racialized diaspora, allows for persistence of memory, tradition, and collective consciousness in the very process of transformation and hybridity. But since la familia seems so consistently to invoke masculinist identity politics and heterosexual imperatives, I struggle for "something more" than either an essentialist or an antiessentialist vision of family.

Like Gilroy's take on "black" culture, I envision a complex genealogy that hinges on historical disjuncture and cultural difference for at stake is a genealogy of Chicana/o cultural production that is both enduring and potentially transformative. As Foucault (1984, 81) notes, "Genealogy does not pretend to go back in time to restore an unbroken continuity that operates beyond the dispersion of forgotten things"; rather, its task is to "follow the complex course of descent . . . to maintain passing events in their proper dispersion; it is to identify the accidents, the minute deviations— or conversely, the complete reversals—the errors, the false appraisals, and the faulty calculations that gave birth to those things that continue to exist and have value for us." Recognizing the reality and importance of such "continuities" without seeing them as homogeneous, uncontested, or finished is precisely the basis of the anti-antiessentialist project. In this sense we might also tease out the correlation between the family in such terms and Michael Omi's and Howard Winant's illuminating conceptualization of race. For Omi and Winant, "despite its uncertainties and contradictions, the concept of race continues to play a fundamental role in structuring and representing the social world" (1994, 55). As perspectives informing their theorization of "racial formation," the two sociologists maintain that understanding race in such a way—fitting for understanding la familia in terms put forward here—"is to avoid both the utopian framework which sees race as an illusion we can somehow 'get beyond,' and also the essentialist formulation which sees race as something objective and fixed, a biological datum" (55). In turn we might therefore begin to see the various social constitutions of family that do not adhere to heteropatriarchal demands that in turn establish critical attachments that fall outside the boundaries of normative kinship models.

Gilroy's essay "It's a Family Affair: Black Culture and the Trope of Kinship" (1993b) is exemplary for unmasking ideologies of the family as they fuel the heteropatriarchal impulse of black cultural nationalism vis-à-vis racialized community. His essay helps tease out shared historical and ideological practices between Chicano and Black communities in their need and desire to cling to kinship discourse as a means for empowerment. Indeed, Gilroy (1993b, 194) puts his finger on the impulse within Black cultural productions that binds the family with nationalism in the service of patriarchal authority:

> I want to focus on the trope of the family and bio-political kinship and explore the possibility that the growing centrality of this trope within black political discourse points to the emergence of a distinctive and emphatically post-national variety of essentialism. The appeal to family is both the symptom and the signature of this flexible essentialism. The relationship between the ideal, imaginary and pastoral black family and utopian as well as authoritarian representations of blackness is something else that I think we should consider.

The fact that la familia is not a "post-national" phenomenon in the contexts I address marks a possible difference in Chicano and Black cultural and historical situations. Yet in what follows, I will extrapolate from Gilroy's analysis of the family trope as a double-edged sword, a signifier with many meanings that both troubles *and* assists in the struggle for communitarian politics.

Extending and translating the work of Gilroy and his colleagues, my project also situates itself within the trajectory of an emergent field called Chicano/a cultural studies.[9] Chicano/a cultural studies borrows from the aforementioned thinkers by drawing upon their critical insights and theoretical approaches in focusing on Mexican American communities in the United States. Although early Chicano/a scholarship did adopt certain anticipatory methodologies and interpretive strategies, I would argue that the years of 1989 and 1990 mark an important historical moment in which Chicano studies begins seriously to dialogue with cultural studies in its British traditions, black and otherwise.

Renato Rosaldo's *Culture and Truth: The Remaking of Social Analysis* (1989), José David Saldvíar's "The Limits of Cultural Studies" (1990), and Angie Chabram's and Rosa Linda Fregoso's edited special issue of the British journal *Cultural Studies* entitled "Chicana/o Cultural Representations: Reframing Alternative Critical Discourses" (1990) draw upon the work of British cultural studies scholars Raymond Williams, E. P. Thompson, Stuart Hall, Kobena Mercer, and Paul Willis to put cultural studies in conversation with Chicano/a studies. Chabram, who would soon after the special issue write under the name Angie Chabram-Dernersesian, could very well be credited for single-handedly working toward the establishment of an enterprise marked as "Chicana/o cultural studies" in her role as editor for a subsequent issue of *Cultural Studies* entitled "Chicana/o Latina/o Transnational and Transdisciplinary Movements" (1999); an anthology of field-defining essays, *The Chicana/o Cultural Studies Reader* (2006); and *The Chicana/o Cultural Studies Forum: Critical and Ethnographic Practices* (2007), a book consisting of interviews with, and conversational interventions by, scholars mapping the ties between Chicano/a studies and cultural studies. These connections have also come to be relocated under the rubric of "border studies," successfully executed in José David Saldívar's *Border Matters: Remapping American Cultural Studies* (1997). According to Saldívar (1997, 25), "What Chicano/a Cultural Studies offers the loose group of tendencies, issues, and questions in the larger cultural studies orbits in Britain and the United States is the theorization of the U.S.-Mexico borderlands—literal, figurative, material, and militarized—and the deconstruction of the discourse of boundaries." Other integral texts—Arturo J. Aldama's and Naomi Helena Quiñonez's anthology *Decolonial Voices: Chicana and Chicano Cultural Studies in the 21st Century* (2002) and Edén Torres's *Chicana without Apology: The New Chicana Cultural Studies* (2003), for example—have also added to the Chicano/a cultural studies project that works toward dismantling disciplinary and ideological boundaries in order to intervene in the social and political discourses that generate Chicano/a cultural politics. *Next of Kin* therefore endeavors to establish a critical kinship with the aforementioned practitioners of Chicano/a cultural studies, many of whom will be engaged in dialogue and debate.

BONDING ACROSS DIFFERENCE

Admittedly focusing on the work of Chicano men, this book is, however, guided by the critical efforts of Chicana feminists. Highly cognizant that scholarship that emphasizes male subjectivities—even on those which might be called "marginal"—often sidesteps feminist critiques only to situate men, yet again, center stage (see Modleski 1991), my book's approach parts ways with such undertakings by emphasizing masculinity *as a problem*, tracing the damage it does to both women and gay men under the cultural and historical sign "Chicano." Indeed, to carry out this kind of approach necessarily calls for an engagement with works produced by men and the means by which they circumscribe gender and sexuality. Moreover, given the fact that dominant masculinities have typically managed the way the family is constituted and enacted, if women and queers are to retain la familia and other kinship-based bonds as useful organizational categories, the normative codes with which communitarian politics are chiefly saturated demand critical scrutiny. A caveat, however, is in order. In no way does the book wish or intend to collapse gender with sexuality or advocate for a symmetrical understanding of the two categories; rather their often simultaneous mention signals the dual impact of heteropatriarchy as hinging upon heterosexual demands and patriarchal authority. Also discussed is how gender and sexuality require distinction in light of, for example, gay male misogyny.

In *Borderlands/La Frontera: The New Mestiza*, Anzaldúa (1987, 17) interrogates the images of the family that underscore Chicano/Mexicano "culture's 'protection' of women" that keeps "women in rigidly defined roles." Yet her theory of the borderlands, a utopian space encompassing *los atravesados* (the border crossers) (which include, for example, the queer, the half dead, those who cross over), also insists upon reconfigured family ties. "Men," she writes, "even more than women, are fettered to gender roles" (84). Anzaldúa thus locates men as both perpetrators and recipients of gender violence within family institutions. *Next of Kin*'s efforts echo Anzaldúa's call for "a new masculinity" (84), simultaneously entailing a feminist revision of kinship relations around the politics of gender and sexuality and remaining cautious of how patriarchy might be reinscribed even in relations that may be nonheteronormative.

Chapter 1, "Reappraising the Archive," begins by laying down the historical premises that establish Chicano articulations of family, nation, and masculinity. Divided into four sections, the chapter engages with the cultural forms and critical discourses that have provided the foundation on which la familia became adopted as an organizing strategy for communitarian politics. The chapter's first two sections unveil the call for a family-based network in Chicano movement contexts ranging from the manifestos *El Plan Espiritual de Aztlán* and *La Familia de La Raza*, written respectively by members of the Chicano Liberation Youth Conference and José Armas, and Rodolfo "Corky" Gonzales's epic poem "I am Joaquín" to the family discourse emanating from the organizations that have come to define the movement itself. Providing an understanding of why la familia was of fundamental importance to movement intellectuals and writers, these sections critically foreground the emergent nationalist consciousness adopted by Chicanos in relation to the U.S. nation-state. Taking seriously the visual impact of la familia, the third section carefully reads a number of "family portraits"—drawings and paintings, sometimes taking the form of posters, periodical and book covers and illustrations, murals, and postcards—that continue to proliferate into the new millennium. Quite often these images are analogous to literary and textual interpretations of the family in their heteronormative, nuclear visions. While closing on a note that demands a critical view of masculinity as a heteropatriarchal force by unpacking the deployment of machismo and its attachment to la familia for organizing gender roles, the section also registers feminist and queer responses to, and rearticulations of, the meaning of macho.

Addressing the means by which artists embrace visual media—particularly film, video, and television—to delineate strategies crucial for contesting stereotypes and Latino/a invisibility as well as illustrating the high stakes of family representation is the subject of chapter 2, "Shooting the Patriarch." It begins by tracing the development of Chicano/a-produced film and television in conjunction with movement activism. In considering films such as *I Am Joaquín* (Luis Valdez, 1969), *Yo Soy Chicano* (Jesús Salvador Treviño, 1972), *Chicana* (Sylvia Morales, 1979), and the public affairs television series *¡Ahora!* (spearheaded by Treviño and running from 1969 to 1970 on KCET-TV in Los Angeles), it becomes clear that Chicano and Chicana media artists also grappled with family principles for constituting community. The section serves to interrogate the need to shoot the patriarch in Valdez's and Trevino's work while signaling Morales's critical intervention that shoots back at patriarchal governance. Moving from these works to a more recent film that relies upon the bonds of consanguinity, the chapter critically engages with Gregory Nava's *Mi Familia/My Family* (1995). While Nava's film embraces pre-Columbian tropes that surface in numerous movement productions, it diverges from earlier films by favoring a more assimilative than cultural nationalist narrative. My critique of the film is less concerned with the desire to identify as American than with its advocacy of a heteropatriarchal vision of la familia that aims to appease authoritarian ideologies coded as American. Moving beyond the paradigms presented in the aforementioned media works, the following section considers the experimental video work of Harry Gamboa Jr., an artist-activist who participated in movement struggles, namely the high school walkouts to protest educational inequality, in the late 1960s in East Los Angeles. Gamboa's collaborations with the art group Asco and his solo work offer an alternative view of family dynamics by highlighting the limitations of kinship discourse that hinges upon nationalism and patriarchal authority. Videos such as *Baby Kake* (1984) and *L.A. Familia* (1993)—standing in sharp contrast to other Chicano films and videos given their thematic approaches and homegrown production values—importantly resituates community politics for Chicanas and Chicanos in the midst of urban turmoil. The final section turns to more recent media productions—all of which have at root a concern for la familia—in order to assess how heteropatriarchal authority within the Chicano family is both upheld and destabilized in contemporary film and television.

Chapter 3, which rejoins and extends my earlier discussion on the historical formation of a poetic consciousness, examines Chicano rap music and hip hop culture to inquire into the ways la familia is articulated in calls for collective struggle. While there are clear-cut differences between Chicano poetry and Chicano rap, both forms ultimately convey a shared desire for "Chicanismo," that is, "community autonomy, individual self-worth, cultural pride, and political and economic equity" (Gómez-

Quiñones 1990, 189). Fundamentally concerned with Chicano rap as an empowering cultural practice grasped by young, working-class Chicano men, "The Verse of the Godfather" also unveils the way rap is frequently influenced by masculinist and heteronormative protocols. While Chicano rap may challenge state violence around issues of racism and police hostility and unite disenfranchised youths, it often relies upon articulations of community as dominated by men. Indeed, the flirtation with, and outright declaration of gang affiliation, makes clear that "rhymes for *la raza*" have tended to be limited in scope. Not wanting to dismiss the music's radical potential, however, the chapter ends by charting the evolution of "homo-hop" in which many queer Chicano/a and Latino/a rappers participate as well as acknowledging rap's critical quotidian import.

Beginning with a discussion of the role of Chicano gay men in Chicano/a critical and cultural production, chapter 4, "*Carnal* Knowledge," proceeds by illustrating the particular ways male homosexuality has been cast in antifamily terms. Starting with critical readings of texts like Joe Olvera's poem "Gay Ghetto District" and José Armas's 1975 essay "Machismo," the chapter shifts gears to locate the Chicano gay male subject in an unlikely space: the popular culture arena of car customization saturated with the discourse of Chicanismo. In 1981, *Firme Magazine*, comparable to the more famous *Low Rider Magazine*, published an interview with a young Chicano gay man named Victor. Entitled "A Gay Life Style (Only if La Familia Approves)," the interview stands as a remarkable document that both challenges the way Chicano gay men have been rendered "closeted" about their sexuality and maps the complex relations between heterosexual and nonheterosexual men around nationalism and la familia. "*Carnal* Knowledge" concludes by examining an array of Chicano gay male cultural productions, including Al Lujan's video *S&M in the Hood*, the paintings of Eugene Rodríguez, and a poem by the late Chicano gay activist Rodrigo Reyes, to demonstrate how the terms of kinship are expanded by Chicano gay men in the recasting of *carnalismo* (brotherhood) on the stage of desire.

The book's afterword, "Making Queer *Familia*," draws on the influential work of Cherríe Moraga to query the usefulness of kinship and the family for Chicano/a queer contingencies. It shows how Moraga's work does not campaign for a wholesale dismissal of family or nationalism despite their heteropatriarchal attachments. In fact, the reclamation of la familia by Chicano gay men and Chicana lesbians often functions in the service of reimagining new communities while maintaining biological kinship ties. By doing so they enact what anthropologist Kath Weston has called "chosen families."[10] Reading Augie Robles and Valentín Aguirre's 1994 video documentary ¡Viva 16! and Ramón García's poem "Miss Primavera Contest" (1994) in light of the history and cultural contexts they represent, the book ends by communicating the complex ways queers have attempted to forge alternative kinship networks that also incorporate the families into which they are born. Moreover, by extending the family beyond private, domestic space in order to situate it in the public sphere, we see how queers shift the terms of kinship that enable queer models of cultural citizenship. Yet given the complexities and contradictions in such networks, we see how even queer communities—especially those dominated by men—can reproduce the gender inequalities that surfaced in the heteropatriarchal organizations of the movement era. I therefore call for a provisional embrace of queer kinship given how resolving gender discrepancies are never guaranteed in its constitution.

The artists, writers, and thinkers whose work this book engages provide crucial insight for interrogating kinship configurations wedded to masculinity, nationalism, and heteropatriarchy. Working from the fact that what counts as family is hotly contested today in both the arena of Chicano/a-Latino/a studies and in the U.S. public sphere, my examination of diverse cultural productions and practices, a Chicano/a cultural studies project to be sure, takes up the work of Chicana feminists, queer theorists, and cultural studies scholars to specifically unravel these often bound and yet always disputed terms. And just as the book endeavors to show how claims to normative kinship networks that in turn generate limited configurations of la familia circulate within Chicano/a communities, it is also adamant in demonstrating that within these same communities such claims have been disputed by those invested in extending the bonds of belonging.

One   # Reappraising the Archive

> It is impossible to understand the Chicano without understanding the importance of the family.
>
> • • • José Armas, "Chicano Writing: The New Mexico Narrative" (1986)

> The vision of *la familia* continues to be a form of discourse that provides Mexican Americans with identity, support, and comfort in an often hostile environment.
>
> • • • Margarita Gangotena, "The Rhetoric of *La Familia* among Mexican Americans" (1994)

> We must move beyond a celebration of *la familia* to address questions of power and patriarchy.
>
> • • • Vicki L. Ruíz, *From Out of the Shadows: Mexican Women in Twentieth-Century America* (1998)

This chapter undertakes three main tasks. First, it makes a critical inventory of an archive containing manifestos, essays, poems, and artistic images from the late 1960s to the early 1990s that invoke a genealogy of *la familia* in Chicano/a cultural politics. Second, it unravels and rereads the complex discourses that posit family as an exemplary symbolic figure that must ultimately match silhouettes with a politically charged community and extended kinship network identified as *la raza*. Finally, it seeks to understand patriarchy as a system dependent upon paternal governance and heterosexual presumption in relation to Chicano/a community formations as reflected in cultural productions embracing the "militant ethos" known as Chicanismo (I. García 1997).[1]

The upshot is to illustrate how critical discourse on gender and sexuality allows us to critique the ways that Chicano/a cultural nationalism and notions of la familia continue to be codified by dominant articulations of masculinity.

Considering how la familia is never defined in neutral terms, the protean complexities derived from its wide-ranging communitarian import demand the attention of those with vested interest in Chicano/a cultural politics. Indeed, to reanimate la familia in the name of egalitarianism requires an unpacking of its conventional signification. In this chapter I will illustrate the ways in which la familia, as an organizing principle and symbol for cultural empowerment stemming from movement contexts, often rested upon a heteropatriarchal order. Yet because the contexts that give rise to la familia are nothing less than a series of sociohistorical starts and detours, exposing its emergence within a more complex genealogical narrative allows for comprehension of how resistance *within* contributes to its reconfigured political import in light of feminist and queer critique.

SIFTING THROUGH THE ARCHIVE

Begin with the now-classic manifesto *El Plan Espiritual de Aztlán*, known by many as "The Chicano Movement Manifesto" (Pesquera and Segura 1993, 98). *El Plan* was the seminal stratagem for empowerment drawn up at the historic Chicano Youth Liberation Conference of 1969 in Denver, Colorado whose authors included activist Rodolfo "Corky" Gonzales, poet Alurista, and historian and poet Juan Gómez-Quiñones. *El Plan's* rallying cry for political deliverance is crystallized in a four-point plan. The first point, or "Punto Primero," is an urgent call for nationalism, "the common denominator that all members of La Raza can agree upon" (Chicano Liberation Youth Conference 1972, 405). "Punto Segundo" is comprised of seven "Organizational Goals." Goal number six insists that:

> Cultural values of our people strengthen our identity and the moral backbone of the movement. Our culture unites and educates the family of La Raza towards liberation with one heart and one mind. We must insure [*sic*] that our writers, poets, musicians, and artists produce literature and art that is appealing to our people and relates to our revolutionary culture. Our cultural values of life, family, and home will serve as a powerful weapon to defeat the

gringo dollar value system and encourage the process of love and brother-hood. (405)

Furthermore, goal number seven builds upon number six's call for family as community, which would entail a call for a family politics within the realm of social movement:

> Political liberation can only come through an independent action on our part, since the two party system is the same animal with two heads that feeds from the same trough. Where we are a majority we will control; where we are a minority we will represent a pressure group. Nationally, we will represent one party, La Familia de La Raza. (405)

It comes as no surprise that Chicano movement struggles should wish to enlist the family as a point of departure and return. After all, the rampant despair of disenfranchised Chicano/a communities was the motivating force behind the movements of the 1960s and 1970s. On the one hand, the families from which many Chicano student activists emerged were of poor or working-class backgrounds, a fact that jump-started in many an activist the sense of struggle.[2] On the other hand, as Ignacio M. García (1989, 12) explains, young Chicano activists "believed that their own parents and grandparents had been passive and accommodating to discrimination and exploitation." In this view, these activists must render their given families apathetic to in turn recast biological kin as a social collective that took to heart their self-awareness as a political constituency. Within other contexts, one's commitment to the biological family demanded extension into the public sphere to orchestrate kinship networks with one's community in the name of *carnalismo* (brotherhood). In either case la familia necessarily became a constellation of forces inspiring those battles waged for political and economic justice in the name of la raza.

While the Chicano movement cannot be classified as a monolithic entity, requiring instead comprehension as a social force emerging from distinct regions and multiple social justice trajectories, the deployment of the family principle nonetheless figured prominently in various organizational practices and discursive strategies put forth by movement leaders. For example, Reies López Tijerina, one of the movement's earliest leaders chiefly known for mobilizing the movement to restore land grants to pre-Anglo settlement owners, maintains that the family is the fundamental source of nourishment as well as protection from the external damage of the dominant culture. For Tijerina:

> The heart of human dignity is the family. The family is the source of values, virtues, and the love that nurtures harmony and fraternity. Our mothers are the first teachers and then, the nation. Our homes are where the human plants are born. The parents are the gardeners that water these human plants with love water. There is no better school for a child than the home and the family. (Tijerina 2000, 165–66)

Furthermore,

> I came to realize that the family is the root of society. The institution of the family has outlived governments. And, regardless of government ideology, the family remains the same institution. In certain times, government protects the family. In other times, government casts the family aside. In the United States and white European countries, the family has been abandoned. The family has outlived all kinds of governments, in spite of their ideology, including "democracy." In fact, the family has lost ground because "democracy" has robbed the family of its sovereignty. (166)

The gendered contours of Tijerina's critique of "democracy"—shades of which appear in other movement texts that will soon be discussed—are clear when he insists: "The son cannot take the place of the father until he leaves and forms his own family. Even then, the son remains indebted to his father. The home and the family cannot be governed by democratic practices. The father is the head and king of the family; the mother is the heart and queen of the family. Together they make a perfect government" (Tijerina 2001, 166).[3] In a speech delivered in Austin, Texas in 1971, César E. Chávez, the widely recognized labor leader and cofounder of the United Farm Workers (originally named the National Farm Workers Association) made clear the crucial connections between la familia and la raza. Making a plea that we "really begin to look out for our raza," Chávez insists:

> Charity begins at home. For instance, who'd ever have dreamed that one would even consider sending Mama or Papa to a nursing home because they're old? Never! Shameful! Because we have family unity and love as Mexicans. A person who claims love for his raza but does not love his father can't convince me

he loves his people. A woman who can't take in and take care of her mother because she has to work because she wants a color TV or a new car can't tell me she'll be able to love her raza. Because if we have no love for our mother how can we love anyone else?" (C. Chávez 2002, 62)

While Tijerina and Chávez uniquely invoke the biological family to crystallize the need for collective cohesion, it was the Denver-based Crusade for Justice and its key organizer Rodolfo "Corky" Gonzales that would extend the signifying force of la familia from its manifestation in domestic settings into the arena of public mobilization. While I will soon discuss in more detail his effort to create *la familia de la raza* (the family of the people) through speeches and his famous poem, "I am Joaquín," a viewing of Jesús Salvador Treviño's film *La Raza Unida* (1972)—on the first National Convention of La Raza Unida Party, an alternative political party whose leader José Angel Gutiérrez is also one of the movement's major figures—enables one to witness Gonzales's rhetorical desire to conflate la raza with la familia.

Claiming la familia in such politicized ways made sense given the racist terms in which Mexican and Mexican American communities were pathologically rendered. As it were, the Chicano family had been subjected to stereotyping tendencies for decades. For instance, academic inquiry that by and large reflected popular beliefs in the United States often found Mexican American families "dysfunctional" as a result of remaining mired in ignorance and prescribed traditions. Numerous anthropological and sociological studies by scholars of "the Mexican family" in both Mexico and the United States unveiled undesirable renderings that many Chicano and Chicana intellectuals and activists aimed to refute. The writings of William Madsen (1964) and Arthur J. Rubel (1966), Norma Williams (1990, 2) reminds us, "adopted the stereotypical definitions of the majority society in describing Mexican Americans." In the scholarship of Madsen and Rubel, "Wives and daughters were perceived as passive and totally accepting of the husband's or father's authority" and "The man was characterized by his 'machismo,' or dominance over women" (2). This work wielded influential power on studies of Chicano families that succeeded theirs, studies that tended to "generalize about the Mexican American family" (2). Chicano studies emerging at the height of movement activism—studies in which, according to anthropologist Renato

Rosaldo (1986), "the natives began to talk back"—indeed took issue with the assumptions made by these social scientists and their authoritative claims to objectivity.[4]

Movement-era Chicano scholars were intent on wresting the family away from the possession of Western academic studies—especially those that uncritically adopted acculturation and functionalism paradigms. In turn, their hope was to charge la familia with currents fueled by resistance.[5] This act would also entail casting affirmative light on one's own biological family as well as fashioning a sociosymbolic kinship network consisting of the Chicano community at large, that is, the people became the family. Thus the idea of "La Familia de La Raza" proposed in *El Plan* calls for the categories la familia and la raza to complement and service one another. It was widely believed that "new" formations of the family—la familia de la raza—provided the impetus to create social and cultural change. This gesture of "political familism," as sociologist Maxine Baca Zinn defined it in her foundational essay of the same name, sought to promote "a phenomenon in which the continuity of family groups and the adherence to family ideology [would] provide the basis for struggle" (Baca Zinn 1975, 16). And, for Baca Zinn, "family activism" can in effect "challenge women's and men's traditional positions; it changes women's relationship to the family, and it generates conditions for the emergence of women's consciousness" (19).

Baca Zinn ends her essay insisting, "Political familism itself does not transcend sex role subordination" (24). This position is crucial given how gestures of political familism advocated by men inevitably reproduced a Chicano communitarian paradigm in which the heterosexual male, father, and husband were placed at the center of movement discourse. Yet this position was not exclusively proposed and sustained by men. Despite the resistance to this position by many women activist-writers in an emergent print culture of the era (see, for instance, the work of Bernice Rincón [1971], Mirta Vidal [1971], Adaljiza Sosa Riddell [1974], Anna Nieto Gómez [1976], Marta Cotera [1977], and the periodicals *El Grito del Norte* and *Hijas de Cuahtemoc*), some Chicana feminists advocated the conflation of la familia with la raza without challenging male-dominant conceptions of family arrangement.[6] In her landmark essay "The Role of the Chicana within the Student Movement," Sonia A. López (1977, 23) writes that "as early as the Spring of 1969, at the Chicano Youth Conference held in Denver, Colorado, a few vocal Chicana activists raised the issue of the traditional role of the Chicana and how it limited her capabilities and her development." Although it served as a forum for debate, the conference workshop devoted to Chicana issues proposed that such limitations were unimportant given women's assigned role within la familia de la raza. One Chicana observed that, "when the time came for the workshop to report to the full conference, the only thing that the representative had to say was this—'It was the consensus of the group that the Chicana woman does not want to be liberated'" (23–24). To desire liberation meant breaking from what López calls "a socialization process which asserts that men are 'naturally' superior to women," a process that ascertains that the "family structure in the traditional Chicano household is headed by the husband, who exercises authority" while "the role of Chicana abuelitas, mothers, and tías, with few exceptions, has been to bear children, rear them, and be good wives" (23). Consider as well Sandra Ugarte's report from the Chicana Regional Conference held at California State University, Los Angeles on May 8, 1971. Documenting a number of women's opinions on "the relationship to the familia y el movimiento," Ugarte (1997, 154) details that some Chicanas at the conference felt that "the family often had to compete with the movement" and "in the absence of the man from la familia, the woman is to make decisions concerning the family herself." However, the resolutions to such concerns appear under the heading "Achieve New Family Concepts." They state: "the family relationship and involvement with the movement should not be separate" and it is "the man's responsibility to keep the house organized" (154). In this view, political familism was only conceivable in paternalistic-nationalist terms, reverting to the domestic sphere in which women's roles were delegated in particularly narrow ways. Although women's issues were undoubtedly on the minds of many Chicanas given the workshops offered and concerns raised at these conferences, such issues ultimately took a backseat to family normativity. As Beatriz Pesquera and Denise Segura (1993, 99) remind us, "Although Chicanas recognized the need to struggle against male privilege in the Chicano community, they were reluctant to embrace a feminist position that appeared anti-family."[7]

First published in 1971 in mimeograph form and distributed free (and perhaps receiving its title from *El Plan Espiritual de Aztlán*), the manifesto *La Familia de La Raza* by José Armas marked the increased acceptance of the interlocking representations of la familia and la raza.[8] Although movement scholars almost always address the fact that the familia principle was pivotal for Chicanismo, virtually nothing has been written about Armas's manifesto that indeed crystallizes the multilayered meanings behind its title. Armas (1976, 8) explains:

> *La Familia de La Raza* then was supposed to contribute toward our building and organizing efforts. With some limited monies that were pooled from community groups, we published *La Familia de La Raza*. It was well received throughout Aztlán. Within a short period of time, it was used in 15 colleges and universities. It was used for classroom reading. In at least one case, a course was developed around [the] La Familia concept. Graduate counseling groups adopted it . . . The booklet gave birth to the concept of education through the use of publications. . . . We are only now beginning to understand the potential of literature to a developing pueblo.[9]

Armas's *La Familia de La Raza* argued, "the Chicano cultural concept of 'La Familia' contains the basic elements of direction and foundation for a truly human way of life which will allow people to do more than merely survive" (1972, 7). "La Familia" for Armas, however, is not the kinship network one is born into but the one created out of political necessity. This is evident when he states, "The barrio generated the Raza concept of La Familia which engulfed not only the immediate 'blood' family but also the Raza community as a family" (1972, 29, 31).

Furthermore, it makes clear the necessity of connecting political mobilization and consciousness with procreation ("The booklet gave birth") and the establishment of race, nation, and tradition (via a "developing pueblo") through familial unification. Such thought, then, set the groundwork upon which Chicano cultural production would develop. Akin to the insistence of "cultural values" proposed in *El Plan*, Armas saw cultural forms such as literature, music, and art as the means to inform "the pueblo" about Chicano historical genealogy as well as to generate history. Yet in both cases the potential of literature often meant the ordering of a strictly male, potent narrative strategy and maintaining a heterosexual family scenario.

Appropriately, the manifesto conjugates la raza and la familia with familiar, relative terms of nationalist sentiment. They are: machismo, *car-*

nalismo, nation, *compadres*, and land. Each of these factors is necessarily male focused. Even Armas's discussion of land suggests an appeal to "Mother Earth," especially when he states that it is on "La Tierra Sagrada" where "the roots of the Familia drops its seeds and grows, expands and takes nourishment from the tierra and the plant of life, the Familia" (1976, 44). In this context, it is easy to imagine the male penetration of, and ejaculation in, a woman's body, the "natural" process that in turn reproduces the bronze bodies over which adult men ultimately take charge. In his study of Walt Whitman's *Leaves of Grass*, Michael Moon (1991, 25), extrapolating from the historian of sexuality G. J. Barker-Benfield, details nineteenth-century American males' anxieties about "losing" semen through masturbation considering how this "seed" functioned as "the basic form of human 'capital.' " Armas's "family seed"—which ultimately implies the seed of the father—indeed functions in a strikingly similar fashion given its reproductive value.

In his preface to the third edition of *La Familia de La Raza*, reprinted in 1976 as an entire issue of *De Colores: Journal of Emerging Raza Philosophies* (for which he served as managing editor), Armas (1976, 9) argues: "In these days of moral disintegration and spiritual bankruptcy, the traditional values that have kept our community strong carry even more importance." Such values, however, run the risk of sanctioning "normal" as traditional. Though I don't wish to collapse Armas and the political and religious right given how Armas's notion of la familia clearly aims to counter the oppression of the dominant culture, one must note how conservative claims to "traditional values" are also ushered through the family's deployment as a sanctuary from "moral disintegration."[10] In turn, in the process of defining its boundaries, the family must necessarily exclude all who do not adhere to its traditional values (however those might be defined). Indeed, Armas's desire to grasp the family as a cohesive unit depends on traditional values that orchestrate gender politics in particular ways, thus bypassing any inherent contradictions such as inequality between men and women or patriarchal authority that may exist within that otherwise sustaining dynamic. Such matters also lie at the heart of movement struggles for democracy through unity of which Rodolfo "Corky" Gonzales's epic poem "I am Joaquín"—which is also quoted in *La Familia de La Raza*—is representative.

In a comprehensive essay on "The Chicano Movement and the Emergence of a Chicano Poetic Consciousness," Tomás Ybarra-Frausto (1977, 92) notes:

> A prototype of urban activism was The Crusade for Justice formed in Denver, Colorado in 1966. The Crusade organized student walkouts and demonstrations, it supported mass actions against the Vietnam War and mobilized the Denver community against police repression and in support of the community control of *barrio* institutions. Its focus of organization was the concept of "La Familia" and its principal spokesman, Rodolfo "Corky" Gonzales, emerged as a prominent figure within the Chicano Movement.[11]

Commenting on Gonzales's "I am Joaquín," Ybarra-Frausto (1977, 92) claims that "the stirring epic poem . . . remains a high point of the nationalist phase in the contemporary evolutionary process of Chicano poetry." Speaking through the figure of Joaquín, R. Gonzales (1972, 64–69, 100) writes:

> Here I stand before the Court of Justice/Guilty/for all the glory of my Raza/to be sentenced to despair./Here I stand/Poor in money/Arrogant with pride/ Bold with Machismo/Rich in courage and Wealthy in spirit and faith . . . those hordes of Gold starved/Strangers/ . . . overlooked that cleansing fountain of nature and brotherhood/Which is Joaquín./We start to MOVE./La Raza!/ . . . I am the masses of my people and/I refuse to be absorbed./I am Joaquín.

"Bold with Machismo," having bathed in "that cleansing fountain of nature and brotherhood," Joaquín embodies "the masses of my people": "La Raza!" Although he purports to represent the people, Joaquín, perhaps in part because of his proud arrogance, *becomes* the people. As Joaquín (and Gonzales) would have it, his refusal to be absorbed is fueled by the need to absorb la raza, which, in the final analysis, reduces the people to a family of (one) man. It is also important to note that The Crusade for Justice, headed by Gonzales, sponsored the Chicano Youth Liberation Conference from which *El Plan Espiritual de Aztlán* emerged. As noted earlier, Gonzales was one of its primary authors. It makes sense, then, to read "I am Joaquín" as a companion piece to the resolutions made at the

Conference as well as *El Plan,* given that Chicano family politics inform each text.

In their reading of the poem, Angie Chabram-Dernersesian and Rosa Linda Fregoso view Joaquín as a tour-guide-like figure on the quest to uncover buried "Aztlán, the legendary homeland of the Aztecs, claimed by Chicano cultural nationalism as the mythical place of the Chicano nation." After all, they insist

> Chicano identity was framed in Aztlán. And, Aztlán provided a basis for a return to our roots, for a return to an identity before domination and subjugation—a voyage back to pre-Columbian times. In its most extreme cases, Aztlán was said to be located in the deepest layers of consciousness of every Chicano, an identification which thereby posited an essential Chicano subject for cultural identity. (Chabram and Fregoso 1990, 204–5)

In their view, Joaquín exemplifies that "essential Chicano subject for cultural identity"; Joaquín was to help "undo fragmentation and alienation" in the same way "the Chicano student movement was recovering a past by stressing our common culture and oneness" (Fregoso 1990, 204).

My present analysis shifts attention away from Aztlán and brings the argument closer to home, so to speak. In fact, I would suggest that the connection between the trope of the family and Chicano cultural nationalism holds much more symbolic (and material) currency than tracing nationalist roots and routes to the phantasmatic geography of Aztlán. Although "I am Joaquín" is indeed laden with pre-Columbian references and other historical antecedents, the goal in its conjuring was to provide a springboard for Chicano movement mobilization in the (then) present. Fregoso and Chabram underline this fact with a nod to the Chicano student movement, the movement context in which the poem had considerable impact.[12] For the poem to prove effective in its struggle to liberate la raza, all differences had to be collapsed, leaving Joaquín as the proud-standing, representative (father) figure. But that "essential Chicano subject for cultural identity" represented by Joaquín is not merely an essential subject devoid of context nor exclusively reliant on the imaginary homeland Aztlán, but a subject who derives his power from a material base, a family dynamic reconfigured by and through cultural nationalism. It is no coincidence that in the essay "The Mexican American Family," Nathan

Murillo (1971) cites "Joaquín" at length as a text for family empowerment. (And, perhaps ironically, Andre Guerrero begins the epilogue he wrote for the second edition of William Madsen's hotly contested *The Mexican-Americans of South Texas* with twenty-two lines from "Joaquín.")

In fact, the organizing principles of The Crusade for Justice, spearheaded by Corky Gonzales, were largely contoured by kinship discourse. In his discussion of Gonzales and the Crusade, Ignacio M. García (1997, 97) reminds us that

> nationalism meant rediscovering, promoting, and maintaining those cultural characteristics that came from the grassroots level. Chicanos had to preserve the familia as a social entity and not succumb to the decay of urban life. The barrio needed to return to its role as a communal refuge from the sterility of the Anglo-American world. The music and literature needed to reflect positive aspects of the people in order to overcome the sense of inferiority that many Chicanos felt. Gonzales's nationalism sought to turn back time and to slow down the urbanization of the Chicano family, which he saw as leading to broken homes, parents who could not control their children, and rebellious youth who found camaraderie and family in gangs.[13]

The poem "I am Joaquín" indeed speaks to the urbanization processes that divide the Chicano family and community in relation to, for example, colonization in the United States through mass culture and assimilation. In the poem, "Joaquín" and R. Gonzales (1972, 52) declare, "I look at myself/and see part of me/who rejects my father and my mother/and dissolves into the melting pot/to disappear in shame./I sometimes/sell my brother out/and reclaim him/for my own when society gives me/ token leadership/in society's own name." Simultaneously speaking to and against the Mexican American generation who, according to Ignacio García (1997, 74), strove for middle-class status while adopting an "obsessive" American patriotism, Joaquín could in turn inspire Chicano activists to reject American nationalism's influence on the family and accept Chicano nationalism's alternative network of la familia. Yet for as much as a Chicano familia marked a radical departure from Mexican American family values that were predicated on American conformity, they often bond around ideologies pertaining to gender and sexuality (we shall see this issue surface again in the next chapter with respect to Gregory Nava's film *My Family/Mi Familia*).

In *Mexican Ballads, Chicano Poems: History and Influence in Mexican-American Social Poetry,* José E. Limón (1992, 128) reads "I am Joaquín" as a "rebellious self-styled 'epic'" that "makes a strong, if unconscious, claim to replace that which came before it." What came before, Limón argues, were paternal narratives known as *corridos.* In reading "I am Joaquín" as the rebellious son in the would-be genealogical lineage Limón calls the "critical tradition" connecting Mexican ballads with Chicano poems, the poem's rebellious impulse forces "I am Joaquín" to remain that enfant terrible "too ideologically bracketed within a self-centered socially restricted youth culture" (129). Joaquín's inability to grow up is the stymieing factor that keeps it "adolescent in its rebellious attitude toward the father." "I am Joaquín," Limón concludes, "remains a primer for poetic and political adolescents, which we all were in 1969" (129).

Although I admire Limón's savvy reading of Gonzales's poem, I am, on the one hand, compelled to remind him that adolescents, too, become fathers and thus produce their own families and, on the other hand, eager to signal his quick dismissal of the radical potential of youth cultures highlighted by cultural studies work in both the United States and England.[14] Furthermore, to ignore the dissemination of "I am Joaquín"'s ideological seed as a past and present procreator of Chicano nationalism, and Gonzales's appeal to activist youths, as noted by Christine Marín (1977), is to disregard its patriarchal influence on Chicano popular narratives, such as contemporary Chicano rap lyrics, in which nationalism and la familia are couched. Rodolfo "Corky" Gonzales (1973, 425) notes: "Nationalism becomes *la familia.* Nationalism comes first out of the family." As a prominent figure of the Chicano movement, Gonzales, like Joaquín, embraces his responsibility as patriarch and propagator of an emergent political Chicano kinship in his way with words. I am not denying the connection Limón wishes to make between the poem and corridos. However, doing so requires a questionable historical stretch and, ultimately, glosses over the revisionary impact the Chicano movement (for better or worse) has on contemporary expressive forms. Moreover, Limón's argument assumes that all who were adolescents in 1969 have now grown up. Such a move assumes that "we" are all now mature enough to know better. Seen from a viewpoint outside heteronormativity this is hardly true.

Alfred Arteaga (1997, 146) argues that in "I am Joaquín," "Gonzales served as the epic poet or the genius of the cultural nation, one who both related and embodied the spirit of Aztlán." However, the spirit of the family is that which Gonzales and Joaquín both relate and embody. Arteaga points out that Gonzales writes on the back cover of the Bantam Books edition: "The sounds of the movement, the literary and anthropological quest for our roots, the renewal of a fierce pride and tribal unity, are the reasons why *I am Joaquín* had to be shared with all my *hermanos y hermanas,* fathers, mothers, and grandparents" (147). Gonzales and Joaquín reproduce a Chicano nationalist sentiment by way of their need to embody the nation to and for whom they speak. And they define this nation in terms of familial relations (*hermanos, hermanas,* fathers, mothers, grandparents). Their ability to reproduce this sentiment, however, depends on their status as fathers who disseminate not only a verse that addresses "the people," but one in which they *become* "the people" as well.[15]

FAMILIA PORTRAITS

While Chicano/a studies scholars have commented extensively on paternal nationalist currents in Chicano movement-generated literary production, little has been written on the images and their social signification that coincided with the family-nation dyad of movement cultural politics. These images—from their display at marches and protests to their publication in various print media—were in fact inescapable during the 1960s and 1970s and continue to pervade the genealogy of Chicano cultural production. Indeed, such images highlight a visual economy of family empowerment that more often than not requires nuclear arrangements to motivate kinship-based community networks.

For instance, the father figure and his placement at the proscenium of the familia-raza performance takes form in a widely circulated image for the Chicano movement. In a discussion on how "Chicano men and women are drawn together . . . and are closely bound into a family structure that exaggerates unequal gender roles and suppresses sexual nonconformity," Tomás Almaguer (1991, 98) identifies this kinship "solidarity" in "the early Chicano movement poster fittingly entitled 'La Familia.'" He writes, "This poster symbolized the patriarchal, male-centered privileging of the heterosexual, nuclear family in Chicano resistance against white racism" (90, 98). The poster was in fact an adaptation of a charcoal and pencil portrait entitled *La Familia* by Joaquín Chiñas, which has, according to Cesar A. González (1982, 147), "come to be identified with

Raza groups throughout the United States."[16] In his essay "'La Familia' de Joaquín Chiñas," González (147) tells "the story of how this sensitive and powerful picture has become one of the symbols of *El Movimiento.*" Discovered by González in the home of the sculptress Margarite Brundswig Staude who owned the piece, *La Familia* was the creation of Joaquín Chiñas, an artist born in Tehuantepec in the state of Oaxaca, México in 1923. González (1982, 149) writes:

> I believe he lives somewhere in Baja California, is married, and has a family. He has worked as a seaman, gardener, and carpenter. Since 1958 he has had exhibitions in San Diego, at the Pan-American Union in Washington, D.C., and in other galleries. His work is included in the collection of the Phoenix Art Gallery. . . . Not long ago I heard *rumores por ay'* that "La Familia" was being attributed to an artist somewhere in Texas. The fact of the matter is that the *artista* who drew "La Familia" is Joaquín Chiñas, and the year of the *obra* under his signature is '62.

There are three figures in *La Familia* (see figure 1): a man (the husband and father); a woman (the wife and mother); and a boy (the son). The husband and father takes his place at the center of the picture. He is stoic, almost cracking a smile but not quite. He is handsome with a firm jaw, a mustache in place, and deep, serious eyes topped by smoldering eyebrows. The husband and father fixes his gaze on the viewer of the portrait while placing his enveloping right hand on the wife-mother's right shoulder. Not surprisingly, this hand is massive; it symbolically registers the strength necessary to hold a family together. Perhaps fueling the movement currents in which the image circulates, the husband-father seems to be recruiting in Uncle Sam fashion: "I want you for La Familia de la Raza." In many ways it also functions as an ethnic-specific rendition of the Holy Family upon which Christian and Catholic heteropatriarchal values rest.

The wife and mother does not look at us. She looks to the right, dutifully facing her husband and son. Her high cheekbones, pointed nose, and firm mouth exemplify her beauty. Her black, most likely long, hair is covered in a *rebozo.* If she does not gaze at the viewer, perhaps she is heeding Enriqueta Longeaux y Vásquez's advice that

> when a family is involved in a human rights movement, as is the Mexican American family, there is little room for a woman's liberation movement

FIGURE 1 Charcoal and pencil portrait by Joaquín Chiñas, *La Familia.*

alone. There is little room for having a definition of woman's role as such. . . . The woman must help liberate the man and the man must look upon this liberation with the woman at his side—not behind him, following, but alongside him, leading. The family must come up together. (1975, 171–72)[17]

The wife and mother, in other words, does not need to look to us to recruit for "woman's liberation." In fact, she does not appear to need women's liberation given the strength she absorbs from within the patriarchal embrace. Alongside her man, her concerns can be addressed only within the space of la familia. Her liberation is possible only through conjugal unification and motherhood.[18]

And the son? It seems as if he is unsure of where to look. Can he assume the gaze of his father? Has he yet undergone the dissolution of the Chicano Oedipus complex to assume this gaze? Integrated in the bottom right-hand corner of the portrait, the son is faced with a number of responsibilities for la raza and la familia. He must procreate. He must assume his father's role. In fact, I would argue that his resemblance to his father is hardly coincidental; in many ways, he must become his father. He must reject his mother and secure another woman to ensure the reproduction of la familia de la raza. But why does he not look directly at us? For the sake of his mother, is he refusing the pull of the direction of his father's gaze? Or, with his head in motion, albeit feeling some pull of trepidation, will he soon face his viewer for the service of recruiting others into the scene in which he's been placed?[19]

It should come as no surprise that Chiñas's portrait appears on the cover of Armas's original booklet titled *La Familia de La Raza*, as well as in the opening pages of the *De Colores* reprint. Yet before its use as an illustration for Armas's work, Chiñas's *La Familia* makes an appearance on page 2 of the September 1968 *La Raza Yearbook*. The title "La Familia," however, is nowhere to be found. Instead, the title under the portrait reads "La Raza." As Cesar González (1982, 148) notes

> It was from that issue of *La Raza*, I believe, that the *obra* created its own momentum and spread across the U.S. I have seen it reproduced by farmworker groups, legal aid groups, schools, and church organizations, to mention only a few. [Poet] Alurista published photos of other *obras* by Chiñas in the Fall 1977 and Winter 1979 issues of *Maize*. A full-sized mural reproduction of "La Familia" is on a store front in Los Angeles on Maple Avenue between 23rd and 24th Streets—a few blocks from where I was raised, and where my mother and niece still live.

La Familia also shows up on the cover for both the December 6, 1971 issue of *El Grito del Norte* from Española, New Mexico and on page 10 in the first and only issue (dated 1972) of *Somos Aztlán*, from the publications office of United Mexican American Students at the University of Colorado at Boulder. While both publications tag the image "la familia" (without crediting the artist), the plea "La Causa Needs You!" is centered right beneath Chiñas's portrait in *Somos Aztlán*. The text assigned to the image underscores how, in movement discourse, "la familia" was frequently indistinguishable from "la raza" as well as *"la causa."*

Chicano and Chicana artists soon followed suit by creating similar portraits. Take, for example, a pen-and-ink drawing by Arturo Anselmo Román, entitled appropriately enough *La Raza*, which appeared in Carlota Cárdenas de Dwyer's 1975 anthology *Chicano Voices* (see figure 2). In the same vein as Chiñas's *La Familia*, the piece depicts a family comprised

FIGURE 2 Pen and ink drawing by Arturo Anselmo Román, *La Raza*. Reproduced with permission by the artist.

of father-husband, mother-wife, and son; although this time we see a daughter and a dog. Looming large in the background we see pre-Columbian motifs that frame the family. The design strikingly resembles an eagle, which, for me, conjures up the image of the United Farm Workers eagle symbol that has commonly come to represent the Chicano movement. As in the Chiñas piece, the only member of the family to catch the gaze of the viewer is the husband-father; he looks straight at us. He sports a mustache, throws a stern look, and possesses a muscular arm (we can only see one of them). The wife-mother modestly looks down, her left hand grasping her long hair in a *trenza* (braid) that reaches her waist, her right hand grasping the limp hand of her son while staring directly at her daughter. The son, younger than his sister, glances to the right, the same direction the sleeping dog faces.

These two images are far from the only representations of la familia de la raza in early Chicano publications and periodicals. Take, for instance, the cover for the spring 1975 issue of *Aztlán: International Journal of*

Chicano Studies Research. The cover displays a drawing by Judithe Elena Hernández entitled *La Familia*, dated 1975 (see figure 3). The image depicts a woman and a man, paired back to back. She faces left, presumably into the night (she's under the moon) while he faces right into the day (he's under the sun). They are both surrounded by *nopales* (cacti). However, from behind the image of the woman appears a face of a child. The child's gender is not easy to distinguish. Yet the man and woman adopt features we've seen before in the previous images: long black hair, high cheekbones, for her; mustache, deep serious eyes, for him. What is interesting, though, is that they are somewhat mirror images (despite the conventional signifiers of gender difference). Naked, perhaps they are Chicano Adam and Chicana Eve (with Aztlán their Eden?). If this is true, and if Chicana Eve emerged from one of Chicano Adam's ribs, then the similarities are more clearly understood. From one genesis story to another, it would seem that "La Familia" symbolizes the birth of the Chicano nation (and perhaps even of Chicano scholarship). Furthermore, the image by Procopio Palacios on the back cover of the journal—depicting a shirtless, muscular man upholding a flag that reads "Tierra y Libertad" encircled by the inscription "Partido Liberal Mexicano"—contrasts the heterosexual couple with a masculinist politics in the public sphere.[20]

The September 1976 issue of the San Antonio, Texas-based journal *Caracol* also presents to us an image of the family: Roberto Ríos's hand-cut silk screen entitled *La Familia* (see figure 4). Rios's family consists of a father, mother, and three children, all of whom look like boys. Bracketed by two children who strikingly resemble cherubs (sans wings) hovering around saintly figures, the parents enfold a child so closely that all three are in locked embrace—a scene, recalling Chinas's image, etched with shades of Christian faith. Indeed, this family, too, reads quite holy. Announced as a special issue, the March 1977 edition of *Caracol* features a children's coloring book drawn by Gloria Osuña.[21] On the last page of the issue is the image of the nuclear family (which also appears in the coloring book itself) waiting to be colored in (see figure 5). Unlike the other images, each of these figures is facing us with a beaming smile. Present are the mother, father, son, and daughter, with the sun shining brightly behind them. Yet more than just another entry in the gallery of Chicano family representations, this and other images in the coloring book register a distinct familial subscription in relation to *Caracol.* In other words, readers

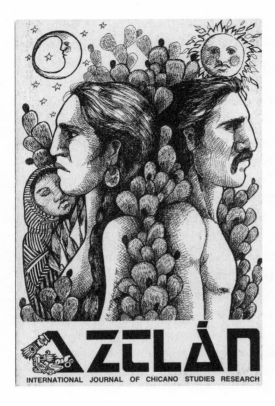

FIGURE 3 Drawing by Judithe Elena Hernández, *La Familia*. Reprinted with permission of The Regents of California from *Aztlán: A Journal of Chicano Studies* 6 (spring 1975), UCLA Chicano Studies Research Center. Not for further reproduction.

presumably have children for whom the special issue was crafted—and thus resemble the family image; or alternatively, readers could pass on the issue to a potential artist who need only color within the lines to produce a reflective family portrait.

The spring 1979 issue of *Maize: Notebooks of Xicano Art and Literature*, a publication of El Centro Cultural de la Raza in San Diego, California, has on its cover an untitled piece by Linda Mary García Pérez. Discernable, however, is an image of what appears to be the ever-present Chicano family (see figure 6). We see a woman to the left and a man to the right, both looking upon the two children who sit between them. The woman seems to be looking at the boy (her son) while the father attends to the girl (his daughter). Above and beneath the image are two avocados.

The previous year, however, the Chicano family image found its way onto the cover of the glossy publication *New West* (see figure 7). What better image to use than Ignacio Gómez's colorful and crisp painting entitled *The Soaring Spirit of Chicano Power*, depicting a couple standing

"LA FAMILIA" HANDCUT SILK SCREEN Roberto Ríos 1971

FIGURE 4
Hand-cut
silkscreen by
Roberto Ríos,
La Familia.
Cover of *Caracol*
(September
1976).

FIGURE 5
Sketch by Gloria
Osuña, Untitled.
Cover of *Caracol*
(March 1977).
Reproduced
with permission
by Roberto
Perezdiaz.

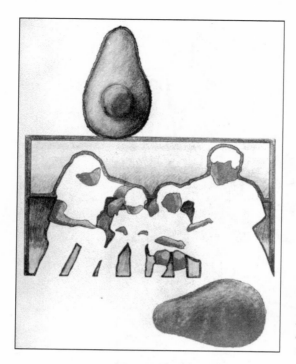

FIGURE 6 Drawing by Linda Mary García Pérez, Untitled. Cover of *Maize: Notebooks of Xicano Art and Literature* (spring 1979).

FIGURE 7 Painting by Ignacio Gómez, *The Soaring Spirit of Chicano Power*. Cover of *New West* (September 11, 1978).

tall with heads held high, for the Beverly Hills-based periodical's September 11, 1978 issue announcing "The Decade of the Chicano" (with the subtitle "California's Emerging Third World Majority")? Like the families in the previous portraits, this couple also has a child. Indeed, the mother cradles her baby (whose gender is difficult to ascertain) who points in the direction its parents are facing. They are undoubtedly looking ahead to what the future holds, poised to take their place as a demographic majority in the California landscape. For the family to emerge, however, it must sustain a decade distinctly marked as "Chicano" as well as the reproductive labor upon which kinship evidently hinges.

The impact of the family principle in visual and print media can also be seen in Chicano muralism of the 1970s. A prime example is *La Familia* (1977) from the Chicano Time Trip series by the East Los Streetscapers, namely Wayne Alaniz Healy and David Rivas Botello (see figure 8). In this mural located in the Lincoln Heights area of Los Angeles, we are presented with the nuclear Chicano family composed of a father, mother, son, and daughter. Here we see them at the center of Chicano history, surrounded by scenarios that depict farmworkers, a parade (for El diéciseis de Septiembre? Cinco de Mayo?), grandparents with their grandson, a football game, musicians, and a mural in process. The quotation at the top of the mural reads: "Our Heritage is the foundation of our destiny. The power of our desires and imagination will determine the future." And yet the future seems possible only though heterosexual coupling and reproduction, hence the focus on la familia.[22]

Upon taking stock of these family images, it is important to ask: Why and how did the insistence on a nuclear Chicano family romance evolve into the "fact" of cultural tradition? How do we distinguish between the family as represented in, for example, fliers for automobile advertisements, mailers for campaigning politicians, and religious-based organizations from the work of the aforementioned artists when they often appear indistinguishable? (See figure 9.) What are the pitfalls of such "traditional" configurations of the family within the social equity project of the Chicano movement? And what makes the image of la familia in Chicano/a art so attractive to Chicanos over thirty years after the appearance of Joaquín Chiñas's *La Familia?* And here I'm thinking of the work of Simón Silva, which seems to be part of the same family tree.

FIGURE 8 Mural located in Lincoln Heights ©1977 by East Los Streetscapers, *La Familia*. From *The Chicano Time Trip Series*. Reproduced with permission by Wayne Healy.

Indeed, the paintings of Simón Silva place great value on highlighting the importance and necessity of heterosexual family networks for Chicano communitarian politics. Silva, who was born in Mexicali, Mexico in 1961 and raised in the small, rural Southern California border town of Holtville, is best known for his portrayals of Mexicano/Chicano migrant workers within a pastoral mise-en-scène. What makes Silva's art instantly recognizable to many is its focus on the family. As one magazine reporter writes: "But what makes a painting a 'Simón Silva' painting? Clearly, it's the emphasis on la familia" (P. Pérez 2000, 50). Silva's paintings are quite popular with working-class and middle-class Chicanos as reproductions in the form of poster prints and greeting cards; indeed, they sell quite well at Chicano cultural specialty stores throughout the Southwest. Silva's paintings have also been used as illustrations for Alma Flor Ada's children's book *Gathering the Sun: An Alphabet in Spanish and English* (1997).

With that said, I will end this section with some more questions in view of Silva's work. What is at stake when Silva's family images are in heavy circulation in a variety of settings? How do particular images

FIGURE 9 Untitled flyer
(2002). Montebello, California.
Artist unknown.

such as Silva's *Familia* establish a family romance that mirrors a nuclear
kinship ideal that, as many would have it, is the stuff of tradition?[23] What
are the dangers of such "traditional" configurations of the family becoming emblazoned on young minds given their frequency in use for bilingual children's books? How do these images command an authority to
represent la familia given their ability to smoothly complement normative kinship networks?[24]

THE DIVORCE OF MR. MACHO AND HIS WIFE

"Machismo" is a term most frequently used within Chicano and Latino
contexts to imply manhood, or masculinity—and it is significant to discuss here given how the term is virtually wedded to studies on gender
and the family.[25] Ray González (1996, xiii) notes in the introductory essay
to his edited volume *Muy Macho: Latino Men Confront Their Manhood*
that "macho" is "the catchword for Latino adult manhood." Though the
adjective "macho" has moved beyond a strict Chicano context to imply

masculinity in general—for example, white men can and want to be macho; and one need only consider the famous line, something of an anthem for many, from the Village People's disco classic "Macho Man": "I want to be/a macho man"—I would argue that to be macho or to evoke machismo harks back to a primitive, racialized brand of masculinity, one that is seemingly more aggressive under western eyes. Omar S. Castañeda (1996, 37) writes: "Machismo is complex and multifaceted and too often, in Anglo-American interpretations, reduced to a self-aggrandizing male bravado that flirts with physical harm to be sexual, like some rutting for the right to pass on genes." Yet for Rodolfo "Corky" Gonzales, "*Machismo* means manhood. To the Mexican man machismo means to have the manly traits of honor and dignity. To have courage to fight. To keep his word and protect his name. To run his house, to control his woman, and to direct his children. This is *machismo*" (Steiner 1970, 386). Indeed, "machismo" is a requisite theme that appears in movement-era discussions of the family, which in turn resulted in the desire for Chicano nationalism. For example, in Armando Rendón's *Chicano Manifesto*, originally published in 1971 (and republished in 1996), he insists

> The society that dominates life in the United States is far removed from that of the Chicano and the Mexican American life style. The essence of machismo, of being macho, is as much a symbolic principle of the Chicano revolt as it is a guideline for the conduct of family life, male-female relationships, and personal self-esteem. To be macho, in fact, is an underlying drive of the gathering identification of Mexican Americans which goes beyond a recognition of common troubles. The Chicano revolt is a manifestation of Mexican Americans exerting their manhood and womanhood against the Anglo society. Macho, in other words, can no longer relate merely to manhood but must relate to nationhood as well. (Rendón 1996, 95)

Unlike Gonzales, Rendón's comprehension of machismo recasts the term from a male-specific trait to one that acts as a mobilizing force for nation formation. Despite Rendón's inclusion of womanhood in the struggle "against the Anglo society," under the pretenses of machismo, womanhood is conceivable only as part of the "symbolic principle" informing machismo as "guideline for the conduct of family life, male-female relationships, and personal self-esteem" (Rendón 1996, 95).

Angie Chabram-Dernersesian comments on Rendón's *Chicano Manifesto* in her article "I Throw Punches for My Race, but I Don't Want to Be a Man" (1992) in which she states:

> Armando Rendón reinforces dominant ideology by identifying "machismo" as the symbolic principle of the Chicano revolt and adopting machismo as the guideline for Chicano family life. Thus, nationalism's preferred male subject is imbued with a masculine, patriarchal ideology that resists the apologetic sympathies ascribed to it by Chicano cultural practitioners seeking to erase male domination from the semantic orbit of machismo. (1992, 83)

Furthermore, Chabram-Dernersesian is on the mark when she argues that "Rendón clarifies that his tendency to view the Chicano revolt as a male-dominated phenomenon can be attributed to his gender status: his being 'macho'" (1992, 83). As I pointed out before in response to Armas's *La Familia de La Raza*, Chicanas are always bound up in male codes of identification, so that even if they are duly included in the family picture (Chiñas) or nation (Rendón), they must appear alongside their man, prove that they are (heterosexual) mothers, and in turn let the men take charge.[26] "Thus he grounds his symbolic treatment of machismo in a specific male body: his, equating macho with Chicano, a term generalized to embrace the nationalist objective: nationhood" (Chabram-Dernersesian 1992, 83). I would also like to suggest, alongside Chabram-Dernersesian's "nationhood," that brotherhood, heterosexual procreation, and patriarchy are elements that inform this insistence on machismo to attain that nationalist objective.

Alma García notes that Chicana feminist positions of the movement era varied on the question of machismo.[27] "Machismo, some Chicana feminists proposed, had been highly exaggerated, especially by white feminists, as it pertained to Chicano men and this constituted an example of white feminists racializing sexism with respect to Chicano men" (A. García 1997, 192). Others, however, while acknowledging this fact, did not hesitate to critique the forces of machismo, particularly in moments of male domination, inflicted upon Chicanas; as Mirta Vidal (1971, 23) writes, it stands as "a serious obstacle to women anxious to play a role in the struggle for Chicano liberation." It is interesting, though, that many Chicana feminists are careful not to discard machismo too quickly. As detailed in Bernice Rincón's influential 1971 essay "La Chicana: Her Role in the Past and Her Search for a New Role in the Future," machismo as an institution entails both positive and negative features. Her list is as follows:

> Positive: 1) Bravery, loyalty; 2) Pride in self as an individual; 3) Responsibility of leadership in the family; 4) Sacredness of the family (La Raza); 5) Human values: Love of fellows: compassion, suffering, liberty for all; 6) Lack of concern for money; 7) Love of music, dancing (joy of life); 8) Love of children; 9) Respect for religion; 10) Respect for elders; 11) Modesty and reserve; 12) Liberal political orientation; 13) Good manners; 14) Willingness to fight when needed.
>
> Negative: 1) Absolute power: a) Exploitation, b) Self centeredness, c) Violence used to maintain power through fear, d) Closed aloofness; 2) Women seen as a subordinate creature created to make man's lot more comfortable and pleasurable; 3) Too much pride; 4) Absolute power-inclination to strong man politics; Hero-worship-dictatorships; 5) There is sharing of the joys of life only as a man sees fit. Woman's place is home; 6) Large families (here the church has also contributed); 7) Too much responsibility placed on the male to maintain his "position"; 8) Drinking, wenching, etc. seen as a sign of manhood; 9) Fighting seen as a proof of masculinity; 10) Too modest and reserved for survival in today's society. (Rincón 1971, 17–18)

Despite Rincón's crucial distinctions between negative and positive displays of machismo, we can see that the positive features still hinge on a necessarily normative la familia/la raza arrangement. My suspicion leads me to believe that retaining the idea of machismo nevertheless leaves open the door for a variety of interpretations that, following Rincón's positive aspects, continually sweep women under the cultural nationalist rug. This rug, woven in the spirit of the family collective, cannot help but furnish a genealogy premised on heterosexual codes of conduct organized around the presence of the father-husband and the mores of paternal male identification. In other words, even if women are to accept machismo in its positive forms—and given that family is part and parcel of those forms—Chicanas are ultimately absorbed by machismo in ways that, too, embody male nationalist desire.

For example, in his discussion of the necessity of machismo, José Armas (1976, 26) insists, along the lines of Rendón, that "dignity and pride exhibits itself today in what is known as 'Machismo'. This machismo is generally attributed to men, but it is also exhibited by the women of La Raza." Although women are invited to adopt machismo to exemplify their dignity and pride, they must do it as mothers, as faithful members of la familia. Armas (1976, 26–28) claims:

> One can see [machismo] easily in Chicana women who are alone with their children. This dignity and pride is manifested by the way the woman carries herself despite humiliation in a welfare line, or defending her children from a racist school principal who still punishes Chicano children from using their native language on school grounds; or fighting to stay alive in a country where it is a sin to be a woman, to be a woman alone, to be a woman alone with children, to be a Chicana woman alone with children. There is a cleansing, refreshing presence which is undeniable in Chicana women.

One would want to ask: How did these "Chicana women" end up alone in the first place? Does "her man" have anything to do with this? Did he seduce her with his macho prowess only to abandon her for other women, say his *gabacha guisás* (white women), as Bernice Zamora puts it in her poem "Notes from a Chicana 'Coed'" (1977)? Indeed, there is a macho (man) lurking in this text. And it is curious that in order for a woman to be a macho, she must first prove herself qualified accordingly through maternal identification. Immediately following the passage just quoted, Armas continues by writing that

> the ultimate manifestation of this machismo which both our women and men have is exhibited in the concern and defense of the family at all costs. Protection and defense of himself and his family at all costs is the test for acceptance and respect in his community. (1976, 28)

For even if a macho woman were to defend her family, she ultimately cannot take the test to prove that she can protect and defend "herself" *and* "her" family at all costs, thus earning acceptance and respect in "her" community. Perhaps if she were to do so, her macho, male-defined status would relegate her to mach*a* status: lesbian, *vendida, malinchista.*[28]

Echoing Chabram-Dernersesian's invocation of the dominant ideology's investment in "machismo," Carmen Tafolla argues in her book *To Split a Human: Mitos, Machos y La Mujer Chicana* (1985) that "machismo" is by far the greatest field day which ethnocentric social scientists have enjoyed. Ignoring their own sexist attitudes, many social scientists accuse Chicano males of being ruthless oppressors and the sole power in Chicano families. The consequences of this attitude, as Marta Cotera has described, are that 'As the role of the man is laden with terribly oppressive characteristics, the woman's role with the family is proportionately described as weak and totally valueless.' The Machismo myth ignores the power which the Chicana has traditionally held in the familial structure, thought by some to be the single most important social unit in Chicano culture. (1985, 40)

Tafolla, insisting that "it is not a contradiction to be a Chicana and a feminist," contends that "few Chicanas want to wear the name tag 'Mrs. Macho Man'" (1985, 44). Responding to the dominant ideology's longing to see Chicano men as machos and Chicanas as conspirators, Tafolla's commentary also applies to those authors of Chicano doctrines who consistently bury women under their dirty laundry. Although Tafolla still remains within the family framework when speaking of Chicanas and their relationship to machismo, her argument on the undesirability of the term "Mrs. Macho Man" is in part a break from an imposed or desirable identification with or as men. In other words, women can embody both roles as mother and father, but they must retain the femininity (and passive and inferior qualities by extension), rather than embrace feminism, which essentially makes them "Chicana women."

On the flipside of the coin, however, lies another Chicano male-defined term used to fix the limits of Chicana gender politics: the "feme-macho." Defined by Chicano movement poet Abelardo Delgado in "An Open Letter to Carolina . . . or Relations between Men and Women"—a response letter or essay that is addressed to a woman named Carolina from whom he has received a letter about the unequal relations between Chicanas and Chicanos—the feme-macho in Delgado's estimation is what women do not want to become, namely liberated to the point of being ostracized by the Chicano community. Insisting that "Chicano women . . . have learned to manipulate tradition and achieve their ends whether it is with their emotions or with their intelligence," women must in turn use this intelligence to prove their worth to the men from whom they demand respect and equality. Delgado tells Carolina:

To break away from that you must earn the respect of those around you whether it be from those most intimately associated with you to those who merely deal with you. You must show them all that your mind is on par or above theirs. You must be careful that you do this with some grace, dignity and humility so that you do not merely win a battle and lose the war. Men might accept your challenges a few times and let it go but if our ego happens to be wounded, then watch out, Carolina, because what follows is cold rejection and a new assigned role of a feme-macho. If you notice what I am saying then you know why women do not see it profitable to approach their liberation on an individual basis as much as we Chicanos do not accept that liberation is the business of one or a few individuals but of all Chicanos. (Delgado 1978, 38)

Like most men who insist that feminism must be regulated (if not outright discarded) given its potential threat to communitarian politics for both Chicanos and Chicanas, Delgado curtails the possibility of self-critique and maps the blame of gendered divisiveness solely onto Chicanas. For Delgado, women are in command of their destiny as free agents who must merely refuse male subjugation. "All it takes is a simple refusal on the part of women to be abused by us men" (35), he insists. Moreover, Delgado is warning Carolina and all Chicanas that if they go too far in declaring their liberation as women, they run the risk of being branded a feme-macho, which, to my mind, is a code word for a lesbian separatist or—even more extreme—a "butch-bitch." As Alma García (1997, 6) notes, Chicana lesbians "precipitated more virulent feminist-baiting"; thus who else, other than the Chicana lesbian, was there to point to when warning against the individualization of liberation over a communal base of struggle predicated on familial principles and heterosexual procreation? In the movement frame of reference, lesbians were individuals who embodied an antifamilia sensibility; they were "individuals" who forfeited their membership to la raza.[29]

The threat of homosexuality I have teased out from Delgado's text is not coincidental. In fact, Delgado carefully navigates around lesbian sexuality and identity prior to coining the term "feme-macho." (I will address what is at stake for Chicano gay men within such terms in chapter 4.) After suggesting that Carolina peruse Octavio Paz's *El Laberinto de la Soledad* to examine how "Chicanos see our women," Delgado includes a sentence that at first glance seems quite curious if not simply out of context. He writes: "For now let it suffice to say that as far as our wives and mothers we make saints of them but remain always in search of a lover with macho characteristics" (1978, 33). Two pages later, Delgado writes that "the question of trust and love (in a Platonic sense) is much more stronger [sic] between a man and a man than between a man and a woman" (35). He continues:

> Thus even the question of husband-wife versus husband-male friend is not as binding. I myself have been puzzled about these relationships and have asked students in my classes to speak about this. I have raised this question with other male friends and female friends to get their reactions and feelings. I conclude that the degree of intimacy reached even in sex is often surpassed by that of compañerismo. I am not sure that it is a phenomenon peculiar only to men. Many men also envy the close relationships that exist between females. Why this is so has been explained to me by those I question. A man and another man find much more in common to relate to each other on a physical and emotional plane. Certainly a woman and another woman can relate as well. (Delgado 1978, 35–36)

There is a level of intimacy established in relationships exclusively between men and between women that exceeds the intimacy achieved by heterosexual relationships, even those cemented by matrimonial vows. Delgado, however, forecloses any possibility of discussing lesbian and gay male relationships because male-male and female-female relationships are cognizantly kept "Platonic" and policed by heterosexual presumption. The macho lover that men are in pursuit of must ultimately be a woman, the same macho woman that José Armas reifies in *La Familia de la Raza.* But when her much-desired macho traits are coupled with feminist politics—henceforth creating the feme-macho—she then becomes unobtainable and therefore irrelevant to the common good of the people.

In *Chicana Lesbians: The Girls Our Mothers Warned Us About,* Ana Castillo (1991) writes against those doctrines of machismo in her essay "La Macha: Toward a Beautiful Whole Self." The title alone plays on the idea of female heterosexual macho identification and uproots it from two directions: gender and sexuality. The use of "mach*a*" feminizes the male masculine impulse of macho while signifying a variety of contested meanings. "*Marimacha*," for example, is Spanish slang for lesbian. "Macha" also implies a butch woman, most likely a butch lesbian. In appropriating macho for a feminist agenda, Castillo is rewriting masculinity for a nonheterosexual context and, as a result, uproots the supremacy of the procreative Chicano family.[30] Lesbians have in fact acutely problematized the codes of masculinity and femininity through butch and femme identities. For example, Yvonne Yarbro-Bejarano's "Crossing the Border with Chabela Vargas: A Chicana Femme's Tribute" (1997) provides a Chicana lesbian rewriting of "masculinity" through an intriguing discussion of butch and femme politics with respect to Mexican ranchera singer Chavela Vargas. (Yarbro-Bejarano intentionally misspells Vargas's first name with a "b" to signify her butch qualities.) In another register, the Los Angeles-based performance group Butchlalis de Panochtitlan (BdP) have insisted on recuperating the term "macho"—albeit by, as they say, "rocking the macho cock-less"—rather than upholding *macha,* from the trajectory of what Judith Halberstam identifies as "female masculinity." Their website declares that members of BdP "are butch dykes/transgender butches/gender queer speaking subjects that are not trying to pass as men; instead, the BdP explores the liminal space of queer boi-dom"—indeed a radical departure from kinship articulations like brotherhood— "and identities and the neighborhoods we claim and are claimed by."

But let us not lose sight (as if that were possible) of male masculinity and what machismo might mean in wider contexts. What is to be done with the terms "macho" and "machismo" with regards to Chicano and Latino men? I am uneasy about retaining the terms even if they are redefined and refashioned. After all, their mainstream and intragroup connotations still wield a hardly desirable authority. In 1976, Micael Tapia, a member of the Gay Latino Alliance in San Francisco and self-identified "Latino-faggot," insisted that "as a Chicano . . . it is imperative to criticize the racist and flagrant misuse of the term *machismo*" since, as he sees it, "*Machismo* is not in itself a cultural ethic for Latinos, but more so a product of imperialism and colonialism" (Tapia 1976, 20). For Tapia, "machismo is an act of overt power over Latinas and less *macho* or effeminate men, but it is power coming from powerlessness" (20).[31] The largely Puerto Rican activist organization the Young Lords realized the pitfalls of machismo when it revised its original "13-Point Program and Platform." In the first version from October 1969, point ten read: "We want equality for women. Machismo must be revolutionary . . . not oppressive." The revised May

1970 version, however, moved the issue up to point five and rejected machismo all together: "We want equality for women. Down with machismo and male chauvinism." The point continues, "Under capitalism, women have been oppressed by both society and our men. The doctrine of machismo has been used by men to take out their frustrations on wives, sisters, mothers, and children. Men must fight along with sisters in the struggle for economic and social equality and must recognize that sisters make up over half of the revolutionary army: sisters and brothers are equals fighting for our people" (Melendez 2003, 234–41).[32] Iris Morales, a member of the Young Lords, insists: "We responded that Machismo could never be revolutionary. That is like saying, 'Let's have revolutionary racism'" (1998, 218). Yet if cultural trajectories make discarding "macho" and "machismo" impossible, we must move beyond their conventional signification to persistently ask: How might masculinity exist in light of feminist and queer critique? In what ways and forms? What precisely do positive aspects of machismo lend to social equality? Do reconfigurations of masculinity in nonheterosexual contexts (say by gay men) necessarily entail a break from heterosexual contexts? If so, in what ways are these reconfigured masculinities useful?

Sociologist Alfredo Mirandé's book *Hombres y Machos: Masculinity and Latino Culture* aims to unveil the "richness and complexity of Latino masculinity . . . to learn more about how Latino men see their roles as fathers, as husbands, and as men and the qualities or attributes that they most respect and admire in men in general and in husbands and fathers" (Mirandé 1997, 6). Mirandé argues for recasting machismo from its status as an oppressive force to one that affirmatively serves the Chicano family. In his essay "Machismo: Rucas, Chingasos, y Chingaderas," Mirandé (1982, 27) defines machismo "as a symbol of the resistance of Chicanos to colonial control." Yet, even this rendering of machismo smoothly precludes the negative forces of sexism and homophobia. While *Hombres y Machos* does indeed raise the issue of homosexuality, the overall project, however, fails to ask how homosexuality problematizes Mirandé's approach to men, an approach that necessarily sees men as fathers and husbands. For this notion of masculinity, within the overriding purview of men as husbands and fathers, reinforces the logic that familia must be chiefly conceived in nuclear terms. Such logic helps Mirandé wrestle Latino machismo away from outsiders who, reliant on stereotypes, render "Mexican culture and Mexican people," and hence family, as "defective" (Mirandé 1997, 6). This returns us to the position that masculinity must always be achieved within a heterosexual and reproductive kinship matrix, a sentiment that underscores most cultural nationalist narratives and mimics the dominant political rhetoric on the family.

Maxine Baca Zinn points out that although machismo may not result in physical violence, it nevertheless establishes prescriptive gender codes. Even if machismo and dominant patterns of masculinity are not one and the same thing, both ultimately affect members of the Chicano family. Among the scholars whom Baca Zinn takes to task is Mirandé who, in his 1979 essay "A Reinterpretation of Male Dominance in the Chicano Family," declares that "there is sufficient evidence to seriously question the traditional male dominant view" (Mirandé 1979, 47; cited in Baca Zinn 1982a, 33).[33] Regardless of "sufficient evidence" that challenges general conclusions about patriarchy as a Chicano family norm, Mirandé's final point suggests that "negative" male domination is pure mythology. This position forecloses all debate on potentially unequal gender relations within la familia. Baca Zinn (1982a, 33–34) notes that although "male dominance may not typify marital decision making in Chicano families, it should not be assumed that it is nonexistent either in families or in other realms of interaction and organization" (see also Ybarra 1982). Alma M. García, commenting on Mirandé's work, claims that "many of these studies of the Chicano family are characterized by a fundamental weakness. Much of this research lacks a critical and systematic analysis of male/female relationships within the family" (García 1990, 23).

Gloria Anzaldúa, while acknowledging the patriarchy embedded in Chicano culture, insists that "[w]e need a new masculinity and the new man needs a movement" (1987, 84). Hence, Anzaldúa asks men to question their privileged positions within family (and movement politics) contexts so as to examine their sense of self-worth, fulfillment, and power. "For men like my father, being 'macho' meant being strong enough to protect and support my mother and us, yet being able to show love. Today's macho has his doubts about his ability to feed and protect his family" (83). Here Anzaldúa recognizes the salvageable aspects of the macho while taking to task the deplorable strands of machismo that are not abstract or mythological. Similarly, Cherríe Moraga suggests that "we ask men to give up being 'men'" (1993b, 174). Here Moraga asks men to challenge their ready access to male authority and privilege. In the strict sense, the need to be a man, and the impact of that need on Chicano cultural nationalist sentiment, has simultaneously codified la familia as a sacred institution in which gender roles are fixed in the name of tradition. Yet in uprooting the ubiquitous presence of the man's man, de-centering the father from Chicano/a familia discourse, and broadening ultimately narrow perceptions of masculinity, la familia may take on a completely different view after all.

Two **Shooting the Patriarch**

> As Hollywood continues to shoot Chicanos, Chicanos will have
> to shoot right back.
>
> • • • Harry Gamboa Jr., "Silver Screening the Barrio" (1978)
>
> We fight back with our families.
>
> • • • Cherríe Moraga, *Loving in the War Years: Lo que nunca pasó por
> sus labios* (1983)

S hooting back, fighting back. When linked and extended, the above
epigraphs, culled from the writings of Cherríe Moraga and Harry
Gamboa Jr., point up the strategies adopted by image makers in
response to the century-long dilemma regarding the politics of Chicano/a
representation in mainstream media circuits: taking aim at Hollywood's
tendencies to marginalize and stereotype has meant fighting back with
and through the family. Indeed, an inventory of the steadily evolving genealogy of Chicano/a media culture—here meaning film, video, and television about Chicanos, written, directed, or produced by Chicanos and
Latinos—reveals the significance of kinship politics in promoting images
that counteract the narrowly conceived visions of, and practices against,
Chicanos in dominant media industry histories.[1] Through a variety of
genres and formats, fueled by divergent ideological commitments, economic resources, and personal ambitions, Chicano and Latino media artists have fashioned competing figurations of *la familia* that simultaneously
"shoot back" at stereotypical portrayals as well as the consignment of Chicanos and Chicanas to the periphery of invisibility. From the public affairs series *¡Ahora!* (1969–70) and Luis Valdez's low-budget documentary

I Am Joaquín (1969) to recent productions debuted on big and small screens such as Gregory Nava's *Selena* (1997), Miguel Arteta's *Star Maps* (1997), Carlos Avila's *Price of Glory* (2000), Patricia Cardoso's *Real Women Have Curves* (2002), *The Brothers García* (2000–2004), and *The George López Show* (2002–2007), these televisual and cinematic projects help constitute an expansive arsenal of Chicano family-based counterimagery on the popular culture battlefield where, in the words of Stuart Hall (1981, 233), "there are always strategic positions to be won and lost."

The divergent political commitments that give rise to media representations of la familia in Chicano/a film, video, and television tell us a great deal about the desire to visually capture the Chicano family as generated by image makers' affiliations and disaffiliations with distinct brands of nationalism. This chapter extends the premise discussed in chapter 1 to take seriously expressive forms that adopt the family as a symbol and kinship as an organizing principle for communal empowerment. Moreover it casts an analytical eye on the ways patriarchal authority is both consistently inscribed and critically assessed within Chicano/a media culture. Divided into four sections, it first begins by mapping an emergent Chicano cinema propelled by movement calls for collective empowerment. Focusing on the work of three pivotal early Chicano/a filmmakers (Luis Valdez, Jesús Salvador Treviño, and Sylvia Morales), the section tracks the deployment and critique of gender politics and kinship discourse vis-à-vis Chicano cultural nationalism. Section 2 critically examines Gregory Nava's 1994 feature *Mi Familia/My Family* that breaks with movement-grounded Chicano cultural nationalism (despite some critics' belief that the film hinges upon it) by rerouting familial empowerment in the context of an "American" national family.[2] The third section considers media activist Harry Gamboa Jr.'s videos, particularly *Baby Kake* (1984) and *L.A. Familia* (1993), and their challenge to both mainstream cinematic productions and independent Chicano/a film, a challenge confronting both film form and ideological content while opening space for dissent in family matters. The chapter concludes with a consideration of recent productions and representations, pondering whether an emergent proliferation of family-centered media has effectively countered the paucity of "positive" Latino imagery while promoting narratives that depart from an adherence to normative kinship practices governed by cinematic Chicano patriarchs.

Part and parcel of seizing cultural production for consciousness raising and mobilization efforts, Chicanas and Chicanos were well aware that film and television were two of the most potent mediums for visualizing movement goals and aims and recruiting farmworker, student, and land rights activists. Additionally, as a reaction to what might be identified as a fetishistic relationship with Hollywood, the television industry, and commercial advertising—that is, the desire for "Latin" bodies on the one hand and yet the dismissal of those bodies in their complex, flesh and blood manifestations on the other—many Chicanos who were moved by the emergent activism of the civil rights and cultural empowerment era saw the need to work as writers, producers, and directors to shoot back at objectionable imagery. In *The Uses of the Media by the Chicano Movement: A Study in Minority Access*, Francisco J. Lewels Jr. (1974, 64) argues that the "need for access to the channels of communication taught the movement's leaders the value of the media . . . in all areas of the civil rights movement." To be sure, there are many angles from which to begin narrating Chicano movement media history. While the account offered here is one painted with brief and broad strokes (I refer my reader to Chon Noriega's *Shot in America* (2000b) for a more comprehensive report), let me nevertheless provide a select roll call to single out key players who helped crystallize Chicano activist participation in the image-making arena (particularly within a California context) and who are pertinent to the chapter at hand. While each lays claim to a unique historical trajectory, as we will see, these filmmakers often wrote about each other, worked together in various capacities, and ultimately contributed to a discernable practice known as Chicano/a cinema.

In 1968, Luis Valdez, a founding member of El Teatro Campesino during the Delano grape strike, put forth *I Am Joaquín*, a documentary film (often regarded as *the first* Chicano film) based on the epic poem by Rodolfo "Corky" Gonzales. Sylvia Morales, a UCLA film student who collaborated with the Ethno-Communications Program, an affirmative action initiative to recruit students of color to UCLA, would emerge as a noteworthy filmmaker who not only challenged the patriarchal cultural nationalism particular to Movement discourse in her work but stood as one of the discouragingly few Chicana directors.[3] Harry Gamboa Jr. and

Jesus Treviño, two activists-*cum*-media artists who participated in momentous movement events (for Gamboa, the 1968 high school "blowouts" for which he was an organizer and, for both Gamboa and Treviño, the August 29, 1970 Chicano Moratorium against the War in Vietnam in East Los Angeles), also played pivotal roles in the practice of Chicano cinema. Whereas Gamboa—along with members of the conceptual art collective Asco—worked outside the realm of traditional filmmaking, producing photographic stills *as* cinema (the No-Movie) and later utilizing less-costly Super-8 and video, Treviño—trained in the federally funded program known as New Communicators Incorporated—emerged as a documentary filmmaker, eventually serving as a writer, director, and producer for public television. In his essay "Silver Screening the Barrio," Gamboa (1977, 7) wrote that the "days of the silent scream" were numbered when "the need to transform this negative stereotypic image"—of "Latinos as either asleep, dead, or too ignorant to know the difference"—"into an effective true-to-life depiction of the Chicano experience was highlighted during the late 1960's when the implications of cultural inaccuracy in the media became of an immediate popular political concern."

To be sure, Valdez's documentary, *I Am Joaquín*, sought to inform Chicanos about their status in history and to ignite their propensity to forge a communal consciousness. Like the poem of the same name, *Joaquín* traces Chicano history from Spain's conquest of Mexico to *el movimiento* of the late 1960s.[4] Clocking in at around twenty minutes, the film is almost entirely composed of shots of still photographs (many displaying murals by José Clemente Orozco, Diego Rivera, and David Siqueiros) and employs voice-of-god narration. *I Am Joaquín* simultaneously features images of famous revolutionary figures in Mexican history (Cuauhtémoc, Miguel Hidalgo, Francisco "Pancho" Villa, Emiliano Zapata, for example) and contemporary Chicanos (especially movement participants), ultimately fusing them to constitute Joaquín, the offspring of five-hundred years of colonization and the empowered, representative subject of the poem and film. According to Eliud Martínez (1980, 507), "the task of Joaquín, the 'I' of the poem who symbolizes the Mexican and Chicano people collectively, is to rescue the past from oblivion, to raise the historical sense, to instill a sense of longing for the whole of Mexican heritage." For certain, this was a chief goal of Chicano movement cultural production, crystallized in Luis Valdez's own body of creative work. As Valdez put it in his now-classic treatise, "La Plebe," the introduction to *Aztlán: An Anthology of Mexican American Literature* that he coedited with Stan Steiner: "In order to regain our corazón, our soul, we must reach deep into our people, into the tenderest memory of their beginning" (1972, xiii–xiv).

In his essay "Chicano Cinema Overview," Jesús Treviño—who aside from his role as a filmmaker was also arguably one of the first Chicano film historians and critics—provides a historical account of the film's emergence:

> On a hot summer evening in 1967, in a crowded sound studio in Los Angeles, California, Luis and Daniel Valdez, founders of El Teatro Campesino, finished recording the music and narration for a 15 minute film which they had produced using the still photographs of George Ballis. Recording live, Daniel Valdez improvised music to Luis' narration for the slide-show-made-film entitled, *I Am Joaquín*. This first filmic effort by Chicanos signaled a new era in Chicano self-determination in film and television. (1984, 40)[5]

According to Treviño, *Joaquín* also marked the birth of Chicano cinematic and televisual expression. As Chon Noriega (1996a, 17) points out, "most filmmakers and critics continue to identify *I Am Joaquín* as the 'first' Chicano film, in the same manner that poets and literature scholars identify Gonzales' 'I Am Joaquín' as the 'first' Chicano poem: both are seen as the first articulations of a political, historical, and poetic consciousness about the 'Chicano Experience.'" While *Joaquín* may not be the first Chicano film chronologically, the cultural capital it commands in the context of Chicano cinematic and media activist history is what ultimately fuels its "primacy."[6]

As I suggested in chapter 1 regarding the poem "I Am Joaquín," being first *also* entails claims to (paternal) authority within a developing cultural tradition.[7] To be sure, the film's generative power rests on the conveyance of a political identity and collective consciousness intimately linked to the movement. The nationalist contours of *Joaquín*—postulated by the annals of Mexican history and a gallery of "great men"—unquestionably overshadow any subsequent films that do not immediately speak to "the people." Furthermore, dethroning *Joaquín*'s status as "first" proves difficult when questions of Chicano film's exhibition, distribution, reception, and signification are raised. In 1998 I taught a class titled "Chicano/Latino Perspectives on Film and Video." During the fifth week of the course, I invited numerous local filmmakers and video artists to class to discuss their craft and their works. One of the presenters, Aurora Sarabia, a Berkeley-based Chicana media artist, began her talk with a personal anecdote that addressed her initial interest in film production.[8] Growing up in a family of farm workers, Sarabia recounted the United Farm Workers' efforts to galvanize the men, women, and children of her community in Stockton, California. Once, she recalled, the UFW brought a film projector and hung a white sheet on a clothesline to act as a screen. The film they showed was none other than *I Am Joaquín*. Sarabia further discussed the emotional and political impact the film had on her and how it provided the impetus for becoming an activist media artist.

I retell Sarabia's story to illustrate how the Valdez and El Teatro Campesino film commands a strong influence on the development of Chicano cinema. There is no denying that there are films that predate *I Am Joaquín*, but their power of influence cannot match *Joaquín*'s or the general ubiquity of the film. What this means, then, is that we must consider the film's power regarding its exhibition, distribution, reception, and signification in relation to Chicano audiences. We must also give full consideration to the ideological propositions of the film vis-à-vis the terms of empowerment it communicates. Arguments for "the first" cannot rely simply on historical chronology but must consider the first time experience with a film like *Joaquín*. In her book *The Bronze Screen: Chicana and Chicano Film Culture*, Rosa Linda Fregoso (1993a, 4) argues that "*I Am Joaquín* represents the historical emphasis of the counterdiscourse of Chicano nationalism to the dehistoricizing tendencies of racist ideology." Linking the film to the antecedent literary text, Fregoso writes: "The poem resonated with the sentiments of powerlessness prevalent among young Chicanos, and located these as stemming from the distortion of Chicano history by the socialization process of institutions such as schools, the church, and the media" (4). Sarabia's testimony reinforces this point, particularly as her developing political and artistic inclinations stem from the film. Elaborating on how *I Am Joaquín* functions as a "quest for an 'authentic' identity" by reconciling "symbolically the crisis brought about by the relation between conqueror and conquered" (namely "the heroes and villains in Mexican and Chicano history"), Fregoso further argues that "Joaquín" serves as "the embodiment of that which survives a past tense of domination and oppression, namely the subject-agent of a present, reproduced culturally in spiritual and artistic forms and practices" (1993a, 5–6).

During her talk Sarabia also raised her objection to the roles of women within the movement in general and in filmmaking in particular since both appeared as strictly male enterprises. Appropriately, Fregoso (1993a, 6) asserts that while "the cultural and the spiritual informs Joaquín's identity . . . the poem also posits its notion of a 'collective' cultural identity that is singularly male-centered." Fregoso continues:

> Multiple identities are subsumed into a collectivity whose narrative voice is enunciated in this historical male subject, Joaquín. The males who inform Chicano cultural identity have names (Cuauhtemoc, Moctezuma, Juan Diego, and so on), but the females are nameless abstractions. Indeed, as opposed to appearing as historical subjects, women are positioned as the metaphors for the emotive side of Chicano collective cultural identity, as "faithful" wives or "suffering" Mexican mothers. (6)

To sustain her critique of the film's masculinist tendencies, Fregoso's argument rests upon the idea that the film "dis-articulates the notion of identity as fusion (mestizaje) and re-articulates its vision of Chicano cultural identity in a pre-Columbian, mythic, and heroic past" (9). For Fregoso, this enacts the creation of an authentic identity; and within these terms, to create an "authentic" identity also entails fashioning a male subject. Clearly, the pantheon of male figures underscores the film's ambition to mold a masculinist "collective cultural identity."[9]

Yet to understand the seminal power of the film and—more pointedly—its nominal subject, Joaquín's role as male progenitor within the context of la familia requires deliberation. Indeed, the poem and the film end with the lines: "I shall endure!/I will endure!" Undoubtedly, these last two lines solidify the normative drive of the film and poem for if "Joaquín" (who represents "the masses of my people") is to endure, heteropatriarchal reproduction (not merely heterosexual reproduction) must be the rule rather than the exception.

When Valdez recites the line from the poem, "They overlooked that cleansing fountain of nature and brotherhood which is Joaquín," the spectator is presented with what appears to be a photograph depicting a father, a mother, a daughter, and a son holding hands. Referencing the Bantam Books edition of *I Am Joaquín/Yo Soy Joaquín* (R. Gonzales 1972), however, would reveal that the photo, credited to noted photographer George Ballis and taken in Delano, California, has been cropped in the film. The photo in its entirety depicts "the family" of the film, but also another boy and a grown man. All six individuals appear to be part of a circle, singing. To my mind, in the book the photo appears more inclusively communal than it does exclusively familial. Although one could argue that even in the book, the additional man and boy fall onto the opposite page, thus making the photo too large to shoot with the movie camera, couldn't the camera have panned the photo to show this more encompassing display of "brotherhood"?

This nuclear family photograph undoubtedly conveyed the sense of brotherhood sustained by a particular ideological kinship network. The two shots that follow this appropriately framed family present a woman with a shawl over her head, bearing a striking resemblance to La Virgen de Guadalupe, and a father holding a baby boy, feeding him a bottle. Indeed, *I Am Joaquín*, with its cultural nationalist agenda also aims to mobilize *la raza* around images of a perceived traditional family. Moreover, the "mother" in this photo is Dolores Huerta, the first vice-president of the United Farm Workers, whose activist career entailed a symbolic break from naturalized conceptions of motherhood.[10] Within *Joaquín*, however, Huerta is diegetically inscribed in a way that eclipses Huerta's role as a feminist activist to instead ascribe to her a traditional maternal identification.

Sylvia Morales's 1979 documentary *Chicana*—using many of the same formalistic elements as Valdez's film and typically understood as a feminist critique of *I Am Joaquín*—also "samples" Mexican murals to generate its historical current, albeit from an angle that is decidedly matriarchal.[11] In her essay "Historic Image/Self Image: Re-Viewing *Chicana*," Elissa J. Rashkin (1997, 106) critically observes that while *Joaquín* preserves the values of the original paintings, "*Chicana* excerpts from the murals in order to revise their interpretations." Morales's film project is precisely about revising the Chicano and Mexicano historical record that, as narrator Carmen Zapata tells us at the start of the film, has largely ignored the centrality of women. Adopting the socialist project of Anna Nieto-

Gómez whose traveling slideshow presentation—"Historic Images of the Chicana"—provided the impetus for *Chicana*, Morales shoots back at the narrow-sighted, patriarchal genealogies mapped by the historians the film calls out (which might very well include Luis Valdez as reflected in the cultural history of *Joaquín*). At the heart of Morales's project lies the principal concern of foregrounding women's experiences rooted in the national history of Mexico that extends into the United States to ulti-mately generate a politicized Chicana subjectivity.

Yet *Chicana* also aims to recast the roles of women in "the present"—a point lost on many critics of the film—evident in the use of live-action shots that bookend the film's historical emphasis on women vis-à-vis its shots of still photographs and murals. As the film begins, Zapata reports on the predicaments of Chicanas within the family matrix and the do-mestic sphere. When she asserts, "As women, our role is to provide an economic and social support system. We free men to work as we prepare the future labor force," we witness a woman wiping the behind of young male child. Another shot captures a woman who washes dishes. "Respect of woman comes late in life," Zapata tells us, as a shot of an elderly woman in a rocking chair—easily read as a grandmother—provides illustration. Necessary as it is to emphasize the financial constraints that shaped the film's production values, the film's form must also be read as strategically linking contemporary Chicanas with those of the past based on their de-valued status both within and outside the home (as in the realm of "pub-lic" history), all the while signaling their crucial role in sustaining the la-bor market.

The live-action shots at the film's conclusion include nameless women who represent everyday "welfare mothers" and "abandoned wives" and three important Chicana movement activists who are introduced by name: Francisca Flores, founder of Comisión Femenil Mexicana and co-founder of the Los Angeles-based Chicana Social Service Center; Alicia Escalante, welfare rights activist and founder of the East Los Angeles Wel-fare Rights Organization; and, as one might suspect, Dolores Huerta. Yet unlike her depiction in Valdez's film, Huerta appears not only "in move-ment" as she addresses a large group of people behind a podium at what appears to be a rally, but also as a speaking subject. That is, in voiceover narration we hear Huerta issue a call to action in the name of social change. In marked contrast to Valdez's film, the women in Morales's *Chicana* are notably cast as self-sufficient actors whose existence refuses domestic containment.

To be sure, these very women are eclipsed by the specific design of *I Am Joaquín*'s kinship network. And while the nameless women at the end of *Chicana* are designated "mothers" and "wives," they are, respectively, on welfare and abandoned; therefore they are not women who (can) rely on the support of men within a nuclear family framework (the absence of men in the film's closing shots fortifies this point). In Morales's film it is not the patriarch who is rendered the solution to women's misfortune but rather better wages and economic support that must exceed the institution of marriage. One might recall the pivotal moment in the film when we hear of Dolores Jiménez y Muro's Mexican Revolution–era plan demanding full rights of citizenship for women, consisting of an independent economic base for women rather than dependence on marriage for a livelihood. However, El Plan de Ayala, the land reform document drafted by Emiliano Zapata during the same era, which sought to grant land rights to Mexican men—and their wives—is upheld. In recounting this historical incident, the narrator chides the move, perhaps given how it resonates with movement aims to liberate women strictly within a familial context.

Like *Joaquín*, Jesus Salvador Treviño's documentary *Yo Soy Chicano* (1972) also resorts to representing woman through conventional, gendered tropes. I deliberately use *woman* here rather than *women* given that Dolores Huerta is the only activist highlighted in the film who is not a man. The film suggests that José Angel Gutiérrez, Reies López Tijerina, and Rodolfo "Corky" Gonzales are the historical descendants of Juan Cortina, Emiliano Zapata, Pancho Villa, and the Flores Magón brothers. Huerta, however, exists outside the historical continuum plotted by *Yo Soy Chicano* given the absence of a nominal foremother with whom she may be identified. According to Fregoso (1993a, 12), "in contrast to the male activists/leaders whose symbolic equivalents are actual historical subjects in the past, Huerta's symbiotic relation is traced to an abstraction, to an abstract identity of land and territory." Thus, rather than tracing Huerta to an actual historical subject, the film metaphorizes her as the most important mother for Chicano nationalism: Mother Earth.[12] We might recall José Armas's discussion of land in the previous chapter, which identified "Mother Earth," or "La Tierra Sagrada," as the location where "the roots of the Familia drops its seeds and grows, expands and takes nourishment from the tierra and the plant of life, the Familia" (1971, 44). As in *I Am Joaquín*, Huerta in *Yo Soy Chicano* is rendered a maternal figure that plays her designated role in providing the means of reproducing la familia de la raza. While Treviño credits Sylvia Morales in his memoir *Eyewitness: A Filmmaker's Memoir of the Chicano Movement* for suggesting the inclusion of Huerta rather than César Chávez in representing the farmworker movement (2001, 251), women are ultimately subsumed under a male-focused genealogy that once again renders Chicanas absent from the historical record.

Much of Treviño's early production—in television, on film, and the constitutive relationship between them (the public affairs series Treviño hosted and served as executive producer, *Acción Chicano*, is where *Yo Soy Chicano* was first featured)—also requires consideration in light of kinship discourse. Prior to *Acción Chicano*, however, Treviño's work as associate producer, writer, and occasional on-air host with another series, *¡Ahora!* (1969–70), secured his role as one of the most influential media activists of the movement era.[13] Funded by the Ford Foundation as part of an initiative at the Los Angeles PBS affiliate KCET-TV, *Ahora!* was a variety show in every sense of the term. While it largely adopted a talk-show format, *¡Ahora!* also showcased musical, literary, and dramatic performances and updated viewers on news and events such as planned protests. Airing live on weeknights at 7:00 p.m. for 175 episodes, *¡Ahora!* defined and disseminated an evolving discourse of Chicano expressive and activist culture, serving as a catalyst for mobilizing the then-emergent Chicano movement within the city of its production.

Like the convergence of print technologies and capitalism that advanced the construction of "imagined communities" and set the stage for modern nation formations (Anderson, 1983), *¡Ahora!* could be seen as representative of how, at the conjuncture of accessible televisual technologies and the emergence of advanced capitalism, a formative imagined Chicano community would in turn make demands for national liberation. Although constrained in manifold ways, particularly with regard to what station managers would air, television series and special programs established an essential arena for Chicano-created representations and the circulation of political ideologies. The success of *¡Ahora!* was a result of the ties of familiarity Treviño cultivated with the Chicano community at large (despite initial doubt about *¡Ahora!*'s commitment to the community). It is fitting, then, that the short-lived yet highly influential series transmitted the family principle that was part and parcel of the movement's evolution.[14]

Harry Gamboa Jr. (1977, 7) notes, "Since the walkouts of the 60's to the drive-ins of the 70's, Jesús Salvador Treviño has been an active proponent and participant in establishing . . . accurate mass media models. Through his film and television productions, he has been able to add considerable volume to the voice of the Chicano." Echoing Gamboa, Chon Noriega situates Treviño within the cultural activist collective that adhered to the goals of the movement as reflected by *¡Ahora!*. "Taken as a whole," he argues, "Treviño's programming on *¡Ahora!* can be seen as congruent with 'El Plan Espiritual de Aztlán' and its demand for cultural expressions that would 'strengthen our identity and the moral backbone of the movement'" (Noriega 1996a, 10). As I showed in the previous chapter, la familia–based ideology was the crux of "El Plan." To be sure, "while the direct political action that created these series followed a masculine code derived in large part from the Mexican and Cuban revolutions and the Black Power movement, the resultant shows and their social function— as with Chicano cultural production in general—were self-consciously modeled on the family" (Noriega 2000, 137).

In his discerning analysis of *¡Ahora!* and Treviño's writings, Noriega (2000b, 137) identifies "a gendered distinction between masculine activism and family-oriented cultural production." In Treviño's writings, "the object of activism is described as a universal 'man' who stands to be either influenced by media stereotypes or informed by film artistry." At the same time, "the role of Chicano filmmakers" is defined "as a didactic one rooted in the Chicano family" (Noriega 2000, 137) and counterposed against the trappings of Hollywood. Treviño asserts:

> Too many Chicanos are seduced by all the attractions that Hollywood, television, filmmaking have to offer and they can compromise on certain things. To put it bluntly, they'll sell out on certain things in order to be able to make a film or TV show. As a result of this tendency, they are viewed by the establishment just like anybody else. He or she can be bought. To me that is not what liberation movements are about. When you talk about independence, about stand-

ing up for justice, you're talking about your mother, your sisters and brothers, your family, your people. It's not something you mess with, it's something you respect as you would respect yourself. (Treviño, c. 1974, 5)

For Noriega (2000, 137), the "father is placed outside Treviño's description of the family, as is the 'you' associated with the filmmaker, suggesting an equivalence between the two as they 'stand up' for the Chicano family *cum* community." With *¡Ahora!*, "the avuncular host was quickly replaced by Treviño and Rita Sáenz, whose youth and heterosexual pairing symbolized the new generation within the Chicano community" (137). It should come as no surprise, then, that *¡Ahora!* and other early Chicano media productions adopted "the family as a model through which to educate, entertain, and engage the [Chicano] community" (137), making them analogous to the printed visual iconography discussed in the previous chapter that illustrates the heterocouple as the crux of Chicano cultural politics. The movie poster for *Raices de Sangre*, the 1976 film Trevino wrote and directed, reveals the film's male and female protagonists positioned as a movement-motivated couple in the struggle. With their fists raised high, the pair constitutes a kinship that aids in securing the reproductive future of Chicano liberation.

But while media workers of this era forged a Chicano nationalist consciousness through their filmic and televisual productions, their stance toward the Hollywood and television industries cannot be reduced to a "margin-versus-center" dynamic. In the case of both Treviño and Valdez, although their relationships to dominant media institutions were nothing short of tense given the regulatory codes with which they were forced to comply, it was these very institutions that enabled the work they would eventually produce from the 1980s on. In fact, Luis Valdez and Jesús Salvador Treviño have since become prominent directors in, respectively, Hollywood and network and cable television.[15] Thus not all Chicano visual media is necessarily peripheral, automatically existing as oppositional to the mainstream. Indeed, productions informed by cultural nationalism (especially those codified by heteromasculinist principles) sometimes square with official brands of state-sponsored multiculturalism. While Chicano media makers may adhere to cultural nationalist plans of action (such as "El Plan," for example) to direct "the people" toward common goals, they are also forced to maneuver within—and often times conform to—mainstream institutions (i.e., Hollywood) and dominant ideologies in the United States if they desire access to technology, funding, mass distribution, and a wider array of spectators. A fitting example is the case of writer-director Gregory Nava and his film *My Family/Mi Familia* (1995). Although Nava's film does not heed the call of Chicanismo like Valdez's and Treviño's early productions, given its investment in imaging la familia, Nava's film takes the cue from his forerunners regarding the import of fighting back with the family. Yet, as we shall see, Nava's investment in the family—as evident not only in the film but also in the film's narrative image—is more concerned with establishing a common bond with a top-down "American family" than with a cultural nationalist articulation of kinship from below.

MI FAMILIA VALUES

Born and raised in San Diego, California, and a self-defined third-generation native Californian of Mexican-Basque heritage, Gregory Nava has become one of the most prolific and well-known Chicano filmmakers in recent years. Having signed an exclusive two-year production deal in 1999 with New Line Cinema to develop Latino-oriented films, Nava's position in a film industry that by-and-large ignores racial and ethnic minorities is nothing short of crucial.[16] A graduate of UCLA's film school with a degree in directing, Nava was widely recognized for directing and cowriting his moving 1983 independent dramatic feature *El Norte*, a collaborative effort with his wife Anna Thomas who served as producer and cowriter. Shot on a budget of eight hundred thousand dollars, *El Norte* tracks the trials and tribulations of a Guatemalan brother and sister who migrate to the United States, Los Angeles to be exact, to escape their violence-torn motherland. The film subsequently received an Academy Award nomination for Best Original Screenplay.[17] Nava went on to direct notable films like *Selena* (1997), a life-story of slain Tejana singer Selena Quintanilla; *Why Do Fools Fall In Love?* (1998), a portrait of African American soul singer Frankie Lymon, commissioned by Warner Bros. studios; *The American Tapestry* (2000), a documentary of the U.S. immigrant experience from various ethnic perspectives; and, of course, *Mi Familia/My Family*.[18]

On May 3, 1995 (two days before Cinco de Mayo), New Line Cinema released *Mi Familia/My Family* in commercial movie theaters throughout major, largely Latino-populated cities across the United States. Director Nava and producer Thomas cowrote the screenplay. While it did not break box office records, the film became a landmark in Latino cinema in the United States in a relatively short period of time with continued success on home video.[19] Renowned movie critic Roger Ebert praised the film, comparing it to Francis Ford Coppola's *The Godfather* since both are "generational epics" (fittingly, Coppola also served as one of *Mi Familia/ My Family*'s executive producers); yet at its core, the film unmistakably reads as an immigrant success story. The film tracks the genealogy of la familia Sánchez, a Mexican-*cum*-Mexican-American family spanning three generations over a sixty-year period of time, focusing particularly on three decades. Unraveling in linear-historical fashion, the film begins in the 1920s and builds up to the present, the 1980s. Along with these two decades, the film broaches the 1950s. As the film narrative unfolds, we follow José Sánchez (played by Jacob Vargas and Eduardo López Rojas) who migrates from a small village in Michoacán to the United States, specifically to "Nuestra Señora La Reina de Los Angeles"; it takes him over a year to get there by foot. Once settled in Los Angeles, he must cross the bridge that divides the brown Eastside from the white Westside to work as a gardener. In Beverly Hills, he meets his wife-to-be, María (played by Jennifer López and Jenny Gago), a domestic worker. After they marry, the Sánchezes have six children, each of whom is unique in character and ambition. They are, from oldest to youngest: Paco (played by Anthony González, Michael González, Benito Martínez, and Edward James Olmos), a writer; Irene (played by Cassandra Campos, Susanna Campos, María Canals, and Lupe Ontiveros), a corpulent restaurateur; Toni (played by Constance Marie), a hotly pursued sister who becomes a nun; Chucho (played by Esai Morales), a rebellious pachuco; Memo (played by Greg Albert and Enrique Castillo), a scholarship boy turned "sell-out"; and Jimmy (played by Jonathan Hernández and Jimmy Smits), the baby of the family and a lost soul whose life is nothing less than an emotional roller coaster. In accord with his role as family scribe, Paco also narrates the film. While some characters are more developed than others—with Jimmy granted more screen time than any of his siblings—the film tracks the trials and tribulations of each family member. The action perpetually revolves around the Sánchez home in East Los Angeles.

Unquestionably "Chicano" based on film content, *Mi Familia/My Family* does break from many of the familiar codes deployed in the early

Chicano cinematic productions. This, of course, is evident with regard to formalistic presentation and production values. The film, however, does embrace the pre-Columbian nostalgia evident in *I Am Joaquín* and *Chicana*. In an interview with Dennis West, Nava reveals that the film has "a strong pre-Columbian mythic structure" (West 1995, 27). Along with motifs and spiritual properties such as the corn patch (*la milpa*) and the owl (*el buho*), the film also conjures up Tezcatlipoca, "the omnipotent god of rulers, sorcerers, and warriors," whose name signifies "the smoking mirror" (Miller and Taube 1993, 167). Tezcatlipoca is "mirrored in the stories of the four brothers" (West 1995, 27). Furthermore,

> the Ometeotl, the creator couple, are mirrored in José and María. So you have a tremendously strong and deep pre-Columbian spirituality that comes from the film, a concept of Olin [an Aztec concept/motif of cyclical movement— DW], the movement around the center, that it is in what you do in life that you find your spirituality. The house represents that concept in a sense because it's centered yet it's always moving and changing colors, and they keep adding on to it. And of course the corn field which is regenerational and cyclical. All of these things are very powerful and form a mythic structure to the film.[20]
> (1995, 27)

Yet *Mi Familia/My Family* confirms that harkening back to a precolonial past does not necessarily translate into a platform for Chicanismo. Indeed, any hypothesis that pre-Columbian history must always serve as a palimpsest for Chicano cultural nationalism is disproved by Nava's desire to underscore a patriarchal family history that resonates with dominant, masculinist renditions of a so-called "American" family. While Nava indeed draws upon this mythical history, it is not channeled as a means for Chicano empowerment against contemporary Western subordination. Not only does the "pre-Columbian mythic structure" within Nava's film primarily remain at a connotative level (with its metaphors planted throughout the film, most of which are lost on spectators who lack the knowledge of this history, notwithstanding the occasional nod made by Paco), but this structure revealingly surfaces as a means for unlinking the anticolonial politics of indigenismo that were part and parcel of Chicanismo. Moreover, the insistence on mythical justification often serves to absolve negligent agents of the state. For example, with regards to Chucho's death, Paco communicates his mother's refusal to subscribe to the widely held belief that the police murdered Chucho. After all, she "knew that he was meant to die at the river. Chucho's life had been on borrowed time, but you cannot cheat fate forever. The spirit of the river had returned to claim what was rightfully his." So while the film could be said to highlight the historical fact of police brutality against Chicanos in Los Angeles, it also plays devil's advocate by mapping the blame of Chucho's death on a mythically anchored notion of fate. This, I believe, is representative of how the film on the one hand desires to stake politically charged claims but ultimately with the other hand erases them so as to put forth a palatable product beyond its Latino/a base. Such is the precise function of the kinship discourse that motivates the public identity the film's director assigns it.

The premise of *Mi Familia/My Family*, as Nava puts it in an interview, was "taking back the very thing the media's always trying to take from us—our culture and family." Hard to dispute, one need not think only of the interminably tenuous relations between Latinos and the media but also the political scene of which the immigrant-phobic Proposition 187 of the 1996 California elections is representative. At the moment when "family values" were being touted by conservative politicians and their faithful followers, the figure of the "illegal alien"—typically represented as a single male Mexican—posed a threat to a nuclear family structure that was wholesome, complete, and normal.[21] The numerous commercials television networks ran during the elections depicting hordes of "illegals" storming the border also highlight the way media images and politics have collectively contributed to the vilification of a despised and feared population.[22]

U.S. nationalism, with its intimate attachments to patriotism and xenophobia, has a remarkable way of collapsing into a single group racialized, economically disenfranchised peoples whose histories relate to the establishment of its border. All Latinos, then, would reductively be seen as incapable of matching the "family values" of the white, middle-class American citizenry. Critiquing this assumption is at the heart of Nava's project; the pulse is easy to pick up on. From the capture and deportation of María Sánchez during the Great Depression—in which "Americans" from all sectors "lined up to back the deportation of Mexicans" (Acuña 1988, 202; see also Balderrama and Rodríguez 2006)—to a conversation between two white women in which one declares, upon seeing the other's pregnant Latina maid ("They're always getting pregnant. As soon as you get one trained, teach her some English, she can answer the phone and boom: she's pregnant!"), the film offers a biting critique of citizenship and kinship conveyed in Anglo-American history and popular ideology, hence the film's need to "shoot back" with the family.[23] During the scene of María's deportation, narrator Paco offers some important historical insights on these issues. "It was the time of the Great Depression. I guess some politicians got it into their heads that the Mexicanos were responsible for the whole thing. I mean they were taking up a lot of jobs, jobs that were needed for what they called 'Americans'. . . . It didn't matter if you were a citizen like my mother. If you looked Mexicano, you were picked up and shipped out." His words resonate well with recent U.S. immigration legislation. However, I would like to note some problems the film produces in wrestling with the forces of the dominant culture of the United States only to in turn ally la familia with a nation-based patriarchal American family.

Nava claims "the film is about redemption. In our community, we find meaning in our lives and in our families, despite the injustices, the oppression and the poverty. We're a life-affirming culture, and that's a great message for everybody" (quoted in Nieves and Algarín 1997, 223). In speaking to the disparity of Latino media representation in general, Nava asserts:

> I do think more new kinds of images and films need to be made, I really do. I hope that, as society develops and more films like *My Family* get made, they will continue to be successful and we will be able to see more images up on the screen . . . that are not stereotypic but that are positive, that place us in the society and with our communities, put family in the center of culture, which it is. Images that allow us to retain our culture—one which is thousands of years old, with very deep roots, and which has something very beautiful to contribute to the nation. (West 1995, 27)

It is clear that Nava's reference to "the nation" is not the Chicano nation (least of all Aztlán) but rather "America."[24] Yet imperative as it is to include Chicanos and Latinos within the history of the United States, given their undeniable historical presence and formative contributions, it seems to me that Nava relies upon a romanticized idea of the United States as a nation that might willingly encompass Chicanos and Latinos as citizen-subjects—despite an occasional hurdle or two—who principally exist to bestow diversity upon the nation. While Nava may be signaling the importance of Chicano and Latino acculturation within "American culture," I do not wish to suggest that this position must be argued down; rather, what I take issue with is the way that Nava's familia values become closely aligned with normatively sanctioned American family values.

Nava argues, "TV and films depict Latinos as mostly dysfunctional and family-less" (Nieves and Algarín 1997, 222). Thus, "For the first time in a film, *Mi Familia* puts family in the center, as it is in our culture," claims Nava (221). One wonders, however, if Chicano and Latino families that do not match the one he represents must be written off as "dysfunctional." How exactly does one distinguish between positive and negative family images? What gets to count as family/*familia* values? Although I want to celebrate *Mi Familia/My Family*'s frequent resistance to dominant claims for reactionary family values as a means by which to confront various strands of violence and oppression, Nava's film in many ways functions as an offering to patriarchal America that we, too, are like "your" family. Thus, while Nava presents to us a poignant critique of anti-Latino sentiment in the United States, he simultaneously takes away the critique and replaces it with a utopian vision of national, multicultural unity. Of course, this may be part and parcel of Nava's Faustian pact with Hollywood for the film to receive wide distribution.

Indeed, Wahneema Lubiano (1997, 140) distinguishes certain Hollywood films as performances—"a form of 'drag' assumed to construct masculinity"—staged on behalf of "a straight, politically and economically powerful white male gaze" (see also Herman Gray [2004] who makes a similar argument regarding the politics of television). This makes sense if we contextualize *Mi Familia/My Family* within the film industry enterprise. In speaking about "positive images" and Black representation in Hollywood, Manthia Diawara (1993, 12) suggests, "symbolic representation and positive images serve the function of plotting Black people in White space and White power, keeping the real contours of the Black community outside Hollywood." While I do not want to insist that Chicanos must necessarily work outside of Hollywood in order to produce more authentic or true-to-life Chicano and Latino images, it is common knowledge that minority filmmakers—when working within "White spaces" and in contact with "White power"—are always forced to negotiate with the terms established by the film industry. In other words, "symbolic representation" and "positive images" never exist outside the regulatory borders of mainstream permissibility and marketability. With a recent contract with New Line Cinema, Nava is expected to "develop a series of Latino oriented films that are targeted to Latinos but designed to have a crossover appeal" ("Nava's New Line Deal" 1999, 5). Given the racial and gendered composition of Hollywood industry executives, it should not seem unusual that a white heteropatriarchal gaze—undoubtedly charged by an attendant unconscious ideology—invariably polices productions such as *Mi Familia/My Family* in order to ensure the goal of wide-reaching appeal. And the gaze spoken of here is not simply that of the occasional spectator of the film in the movie theater or the living room but of the studio heads and media distributors, as well, whose gaze aids in the "gatekeeping" service of institutional regulation. As African American filmmaker Spike Lee puts it, "The gatekeepers—these are the people that decide what goes on television, what movies are made, what gets heard on the radio, what's getting written in the magazines—I can tell you those are all exclusively white males. These are the guys making the choices for all of Western Civilization. There are seven or eight guys, and they decide, boom, this is what we're gonna do" (Goldstein 2000, 49). So while the family functions as a means of purportedly "shooting back" at stereotypes, the family trope is also one that has become sanctioned as recognizable by both "the guys making the choices" as well as the film's potential spectators who presumably require something "familiar." In his article for *The Chronicle of Higher Education* titled "'American Family': Mi Casa Es Su Casa," Chon Noriega (2002a) reviewed Nava's then-new television drama series directed for PBS, the appropriately titled *American Family* (discussed further below). According to Noriega (2002a, B15), "the fixation on family—or gangs that serve as surrogate families—has been a dominant trope of Latino filmmakers trying to enter the mainstream since the 1990s. In those instances, family is used as the fulcrum for leveraging universal appeal from a minority cultural setting."

Impossible as it is to deny the ideological forces contouring the production of Hollywood films, the parallel phenomenon of films generating ideological forces within the social milieu in which they circulate demands consideration. For example, Virginia Wright Wexman argues in her book *Creating the Couple: Love, Marriage, and Hollywood Performance* (1993) that Hollywood productions have historically wielded a great amount of power in fixing the codes of conjugality in America. Thus, Nava's film must be understood in relation to the family ideologies emerging from an established continuum between Hollywood and American social and political institutions. In their review of the film, Santiago Nieves and Frank Algarín (1997, 222) rightly point out that, in Nava's depiction of three generations of the Sánchez family, the sense of a "sappier, passive perception of family" might have been prevented "if the director had not chosen to exclude in any real way (perhaps it was too threatening for a broader audience) the Pachuco riots of the Zoot-suit era and the whole struggle Mexicanos waged against American imperialism." While it strives to do justice to the representation of Chicano and Latino families, Nava's *Mi Familia/My Family* is governed by the necessity of "crossover" appeal for a "broader audience"; ignoring the movement all together is one way to ensure a smooth crossover by either downplaying or eliding the historical tensions between Chicanos and subordinating cultural institutions in order to quickly achieve solidarity in a market-driven multicultural moment. It might seem ironic that *Mi Familia/My Family* is devoid of any Chicano movement traces given that the film's mise-en-scène is East Los Angeles (one of the movement's key locations). Yet, in cultural imaginations from all sides of the spectrum, East Los Angeles often functions as a site of colorful cultural production and folk life to the point where pastoral renditions eclipse its simultaneous socially complex and economically impoverished conditions. There are indeed moments in the film that may be read as challenges to dominant family narratives, but in Nava's own words, the film's ambition is to show that "we're" not all that different from "you." Even though Nava comprehends *Mi Familia/My Family* "as a film to entertain people, not teach them" (West 1995, 26), one cannot ignore its cultural pedagogical performance within an American mainstream misinformed about barrio life.[25] And while the film overlooks the movement and its particular masculinist manifestations of the la familia–organizing principle, *Mi Familia/My Family* nonetheless evokes the stereotype that Chicano and Latino families are inherently ruled by patriarchy, which is, we're told, a positive thing. To be sure, most mainstream-sanctioned film and television that center on the family often orbit around the domineering father figure who presumably stands at the center of Chicano and Latino culture. The desire to shoot back at stereotypes in many instances results in their being supplanted in refurbished form.

In seeking to capture the American mainstream family, the film must furthermore rest upon heteronormative demands. Though some critics and spectators have questioned the sexual identity of Paco, the narrator of the film played by Edward James Olmos (after all, they note, he is a writer and remains single), arguing about whether or not Paco is gay is a merely speculative and, more to the point, futile effort, given the clues we are offered.[26] On the contrary, Nava's *Mi Familia/My Family* could in no way allow an openly queer character to enter into the family scene as it remains closed to sexualities not premised on heterocoupling. Even Toni, the daughter who becomes a nun, leaves her order when she falls in love with and marries David, a white former priest played by Scott Bakula. Aiming to undo the perceptions of a spectator for whom Chicano families are otherwise dysfunctional, the film conceives a family that is a procreative and progenerative culture. One might recall María Sánchez's lecture to her children when Toni—in the role of a Latin American human rights activist—arranges the marriage between her brother Jimmy and a Salvadoran refugee Isabel (played by Elpidia Carrillo) to grant her political asylum: "Marriage is something you don't spit on." Moreover, the film's "narrative image" (Heath 1981, 121)—that is, how the film is represented through stills, advertising, and so forth—also reinforces the conjugal proclivities of *Mi Familia/My Family.* The promotional poster and the DVD and video cassette box covers are exemplary of this sentiment with their display of the wedding scene (over which three faces of the film's most famous male actors—Morales, Smits, and Olmos—loom large), the key moment establishing an appropriate family (see figure 10). Our heterosexual family, Nava suggests, imitates that of the straight, white majority "American" citizenry.

For some spectators, the film clearly establishes a masculinist impulse within the terms circumscribed by Hollywood in its desire to bond with Anglo-American patriarchy. Carmen Huaco-Nuzum (1998, 142) insists that the film "circumvents the efforts of some Chicana/o, Latina/o writers, artists, cultural critics, and film theorists to break down established and dominant representations of Chicano, Latino patriarchy." For Huaco-Nuzum, the film "is centered on male discourse that emphasizes and reinforces male positions of power within the structure of culture, nation, and the dynamic within the Mexican-American family" (146). Noting how

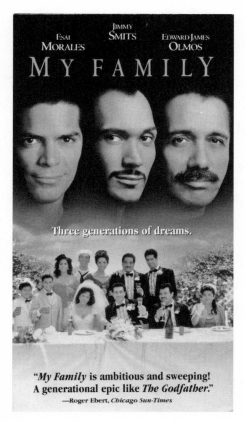

JIMMY SMITS
ESAI MORALES   EDWARD JAMES OLMOS

MY FAMILY

Three generations of dreams.

"*My Family* is ambitious and sweeping! A generational epic like *The Godfather.*"
—Roger Ebert, *Chicago Sun-Times*

the film privileges male characters over female characters, she observes that women are "made responsible for the socialization of the male" (148) within the family, a point similarly conveyed in Sylvia Morales's *Chicana*. On the whole, women are ensconced within the heterosexual family matrix, performing the gendered roles expected of them as women. To be sure, the genealogy the film plots is unabashedly male, thus allowing minimal diegetic space for women. Elaborating on the film's use of corn, a motif pervasive in *Mi Familia/My Family*, Huaco-Nuzum insists that

> Corn represents the place of male privilege in the family. In times of crisis, men seek out the growing stalks of corn, which represent sanctuary and re-membrance, to validate their cultural heritage. Particularly for the patriarch, Juan, corn represents tradition, cultural roots, and a Mexican past largely

forgotten by most of his sons, except for Jimmy and the promise that Carlitos represents. (147)

While Huaco-Nuzum's point about the film's use of corn, which symbolizes a romaniticized past and "the indigenous bucolic life Juan once led" (147), is compelling, more convincing is her identification of a Sánchez family lineage in which Juan, Jimmy, and Carlitos stand as its chief members. Indeed, Juan's other sons are seemingly excommunicated from this genealogy. Like his older brother Chucho—shot dead by the Los Angeles Police Department—Jimmy carries on an antagonistic relationship with the law. But unlike Chucho who is perpetually at odds with his father, Jimmy sustains a father-son bond with Juan. It seems, therefore, as if Chucho dies not only as a result of being prone to crime but also given his defiant stance toward his father. For one might recall the scene where Chucho knocks his father down to the floor after a heated dispute that is, fittingly, the last time Juan sees his son before his death. Recall as well how Chucho's first conflict with the fittingly named Butch (played by Michael De Lorenzo), his rival whom he later stabs to death (thus yielding a police warrant for his arrest), takes place outside of his sister Irene's wedding reception. Chucho's defiant persona must be recognized as impossible to assimilate within the all-important marital scenario traditionally crystallizing family formation.

The theme of "good son/bad son," then, precisely informs the film's pivot on procreation and the sustenance of a male-centered genealogy. Chucho must literally be shot since he functions as a potential risk to the patriarch who enables the family narrative in the first place. Moreover, Jimmy not only grants his father respect, which Chucho does not, but Jimmy goes on to provide the patriarch with a grandson who represents the perseverance of the Sánchez family (see figure 11). As Huaco-Nuzum (1998, 150) argues, "Jimmy and Carlitos represent the promise of the new generation upon whom the culture rests, promising to perpetuate the theme of remembrance, cultural identity, and, unfortunately, the validation of patriarchy." In sum, one can conclude—as Huaco-Nuzum emphatically does—that the "story of family and social conflict needs to continue to be told with more gender equity and without a Hollywood gloss that detracts from the power of the message, character representation, and visual aesthetic" (149–50). Let us turn to a media artist whose work is

not bound by such formal and ideological constraints in visualizing Chicano family politics and yet emerged from the Chicano movement of late 1960s East Los Angeles.

THE POLITICS OF DYSFUNCTION

In spite of the exclusionary practices of Hollywood, the advent of the so-called "video revolution" provided Chicana and Chicano independent media artists with access to image making as never before. In "Video: The Access Medium," Tetsuo Kogawa differentiates between the distinct histories and practices of film and video yet ultimately suggests that "video becomes cinema" when its contents are packaged in a fashion similar to film, that is, "given its hermetic nature, the packaged video offers a mere window onto performative events, one that is technologically reified as monitor and projector" (1996, 52). In Chicana documentary filmmaker Lourdes Portillo's terms, however, access takes on a whole different meaning as her concerns move beyond the theoretical concerns of the film-versus-video debates.[27] For Portillo, video as an access*ible* medium signals the affordability and aesthetic alternatives offered to the media maker that allow for the production of images that may not have otherwise been produced, especially on film. Portillo explains:

> In video production we see a nascent spark of what Chicana production will be in a few years. As a result of video's portability and low cost, the director's struggle to impose authority at all levels of production is minimized. And it is precisely that immediacy that frees the videographer to bring about a work of greater intimacy and truthfulness. It is in video and not in film that imagination is being exercised with greater rigor. And it is in video where the conditions for a new stage of development exist for the Chicana director in the 1990s. (Portillo 1995, 282)

Portillo's commentary points specifically to the possibilities for an emergent and proliferating field of Chicana visual representation given video's status as an *accessible* medium. Media activist Ray Santisteban (1999, 126) concurs when he argues that "the democratizing effect of access to small format [video] cameras and their low-cost, post-production counterparts, home computers, will, I believe, yield a great many of the next generation of Chicano and Latino media producers." Although I don't want to sidestep Portillo's gender-specific rendering of the radical potential of video imaging (especially given how Chicana *films* are few and far between), I do believe that video for both Chicana and Chicano artists allows for what she understands as a sense of "greater intimacy and truthfulness," especially when it comes to representing more heterogeneous images of the family.

Take, for instance, Harry Gamboa Jr.'s low-budget experimental video work that enables spaces for alternative visual fashioning unseen in Hollywood-financed productions as well as on celluloid itself when issues of kinship take center screen. In the mid-1980s, Gamboa began "to produce a series of 'conceptual dramas' or experimental *telenovelas* that deconstructed both stereotypical and traditional notions about the Latino family" (Noriega 1996b, 215). While Gamboa's videos have yet to receive considerable critical attention, cultural critic Coco Fusco (1990, 314) has importantly observed that Gamboa's videos "explore the alienating underside of conventional social relations, which are usually seen as linchpins of Latino community stability."[28] For example, *No Supper*, Fusco observes, is

> theatrically staged, presenting the archetypical nuclear family's decay in decelerated slapstick style. His mother, father, and son, absorbed in unsuccessful food preparation and consumption, are framed by deadpan commentary by a sardonic announcer who makes the work seem like a parodic cross between family sitcom and "Twilight Zone"-like tales of supernatural disaster. (314)

Indeed, Gamboa's explicit critique of the notion of food in *No Supper* as the unifying force that brings the Chicano or Mexican family together also parodies the notion that family culture is always found at the dining room table, a notion replayed time and again in numerous Chicano film productions. To be sure, the family representations in Gamboa's videos, as I will explain below, are a far cry from the family scenes depicted by filmmakers previously discussed.

Contesting cultural stereotypes—both of the dominant and interethnic variety—was at the heart of the Chicano avant-garde performance group Asco, which—along with Patssi Valdez, Gronk, and Willie Herrón—Gamboa formed in the early 1970s. Participants in the East Los Angeles school "blow outs," Asco members drew their artistic inspiration from the Chicano activist impulse of the late 1960s and early 1970s. Gamboa brought the group together after activist Francisca Flores requested that he take artistic charge of *Regeneración*, the community-based publication she published and edited. Their artistic contributions to *Regeneración* generated much controversy given the powerful yet unconventional, mostly Chicana-centered images that graced the pages of the journal. The controversy made sense given how, unlike other Chicano/a artists of their generation and thereafter (including the aforementioned filmmakers Luis Valdez and Gregory Nava), the artists comprising the Asco collective refused to channel Mayan and Aztec history to ground contemporary Chicano identity, instead contesting narrow brands of cultural nationalist discourse—what Gamboa calls "traditionalist sentiment" (1998, 77)—while simultaneously critiquing the ways in which Chicanos and Chicanas were caught in the traffic of United States mass media and the popular culture of their respective era. The members of Asco were therefore impelled to explore and negotiate their roles as artists, actors, and activists in the figurative shadow that Hollywood symbolically casts over East Los Angeles.[29] Fittingly, Gamboa has likened Asco to a kinship network on more than one occasion: "almost like an incestuous family" (Burnham 1986, 53) and "a nonnuclear family" (Gamboa 1998, 80). In her essay "Quandaries of the Incest Taboo," Judith Butler (2000b) has argued for rethinking the prohibition on incest as a critique of normative kinship. Indeed, Gamboa's categorization of Asco as both "incestuous" and "nonnuclear" points up the way the group aimed to subvert social norms in its contestation of conventional genders and sexualities. Moreover Asco performances never failed to trouble gender roles and sexual identities through, for example, the use of makeup and glam-inspired fashions, thus provoking some onlookers to denounce them as, among other things, "putos" (Gamboa 1998, 41).[30]

Ironically, Asco's first effort to produce a cinematic product was the infamous "No-Movie," a means of "projecting the real by rejecting the reel" (Gamboa 1998, 27). When asked in a 1976 interview "What is a No-Movie?," Gronk answers:

> I use the three point dot system for preparation of a No-Movie. First: no film. Second: thinking within an 8 1/2" × 10" format. Third: postal distribution. The No-Movie is a concept that involves the aforementioned system. (Gamboa 1998, 27)

In short, No-Movies were photographic stills masquerading as movie stills. Recorded on 35 mm slides, Asco would send these "film stills" to magazines and newspapers, dubbing them as actual films. The publications would in turn publish the photos promoting them as such. The No-Movie offered a way to produce Chicano cinema without financial burdens or Hollywood dependency. As C. Ondine Chavoya (1998, 5) points out, the No-Movie simultaneously critiqued the "evasion of the Hollywood studio system, denouncing the absence of Chicano access to and participation in the mass media" and "the utopian nationalism of the Chicano art movement" (see also Chavoya 2000a and 2000b; Noriega 1998; and James 2005).[31] Continuing with the previously cited interview:

Chismearte: At what point did you reject the celluloid format of cinema?

Gronk: When I realized Chicano filmmakers were making the same movie over and over again.

Gamboa: When I discovered for myself that a multimillion dollar project could be accomplished for less than 10 dollars and have more than 300 copies in circulation around the world. (Gamboa 1998, 28).

While No-Movies are certainly some of the most unique avant-garde Chicano films (n)ever made, Gamboa's videography has led him one step closer to (although still far removed from) conventional filmmaking.[32] His video work emerged in 1983 with *Imperfecto* as his first production. Following *Imperfecto* during the same year was *Insultan. Blanx, Vaporz*, and *Baby Kake* debuted in 1984.[33] Every one of these productions—collaborative efforts with numerous artists and Gamboa's siblings who would constitute the "second phase" of Asco—was created for the public access channel Falcon Cable Television in the Los Angeles suburb of Alhambra, California. In his essay "Past Imperfecto," Gamboa explains that their creation was far from easy:

The cameras, VCR's, lights, cables, edit controllers, and necessary peripheral hardware were frequently malfunctioning or checked out to several of the many public access producers. The equipment was eventually rendered useless as the entire system was allowed to fail due to breakdowns without repair. The few videos which I was able to produce during that year were each shot and edited within a 48 hour period that was often dictated by restrictive scheduling practices of the TV cable company. The conditions which affected production also included ongoing poverty, poetry, and painful impropriety. (1998, 93)

Gamboa's videos that "reflect the alienation, dysfunction and hatred which can be found beneath the veneer of romantic/manic relationships" (93) nevertheless commanded an impressive circulation record in the Los Angeles area. Despite the "raw stylistic technique of straight cut edits, poor lighting, and rough camera motion . . . all the video works which were produced for public access were each cablecast a minimum of ten times" (93). These videos, produced throughout the 1980s and 1990s, also represent an important moment in Chicano/a media culture in which shooting the patriarch precisely means taking aim at paternal authority.

One such video pertinent to the subject of the family is 1984's *Baby Kake*. Almost six minutes in length, the video begins with a shot of

Humberto Sandoval (complete with mustache and beard) as Baby. He chugs a bottle of Gerber's cranberry juice as the title of the video is displayed at the bottom of the screen. Mom, played by Barbara Carrasco, runs her hand over her forehead and through her hair, speaking the first lines: "I can't stand this!" She continues: "I remember when my life was in full control. I had money, cars, houses, businesses, men. Everything was wonderful. But then the baby came. If only he would have died during delivery. But no! He had to be a healthy one hundred and fifty-pound bouncing thing. If only I had a simple way out of this domestic trap."[34] As Mom speaks, the camera captures her stoic face before panning Baby's food-stained bib and a disheveled kitchen table. After Baby piercingly screams, "Mama! I need more!" Mom retorts: "Shut up! If only you'd choke on your [corn] flakes!" When Baby quiets down, Mom insists that he "eat [his] crumbs while [she] waits for [his] daddy."

Out of thin air appears a drag queen played by Ruben Zamora, dressed in aristocratic garb, portraying a character akin to a fairy godmother (or rather, a fairly good mother in contrast to Mom), something of an angel who cares for men—here, Baby and Dad—after they leave the world of the living. Throughout the video, "she" is the "real" woman who sardonically comments on Mom's deteriorating state of mind. Zamora's character declares, "Always waiting. Waiting for money, waiting for men, waiting for life to go smoothly." Mom, puzzled as to who Zamora's character is, asks if she is Marie Antoinette. "Here's my ID," claims "Marie" as she flashes a pair of orange-flavored Hostess cupcakes. To be sure, her identity is nothing short of the "sweet" mother Mom could never be.

Mom, however, informs Baby that his "father is coming home for his monthly visit." "We want him to go for full custody, don't we?" asks Mom. "Papa?" he asks. Baby then yells, "I hate Daddy. He never buys me any toys!" Enter Dad, played by Gronk: "Dad's home! How's my lovely family?" In her review of Nava's *Mi Familia/My Family* Carmen Huaco-Nuzum (1998, 147) notes, "home functions as a metaphor for the culture and is the anchor of familial stability, reinforcing religious, cultural, moral, and patriarchal identity." It is clear that *Baby Kake* counters the traditional mise-en-scène of household stability by undermining traditional gender roles and exposing the stakes of betrayal and dismay frequently downplayed in Chicano family films. This isn't to say, recalling Nava earlier in the chapter, that "to put family in the center of culture" necessarily entails the desire to create "something very beautiful to contribute to the nation"; rather, to put family in the center of culture allows for an interrogation of the romanticizing tendencies that promote an exclusionary or sanitized national consciousness of family politics.

Baby Kake closes with Baby choking on his food. Mom rejoices: "At last I'm Free!" Dad, too, is happy: "No more alimony, no more once a month pay." Marie Antoinette as the fairy godmother reprimands the two, asking, "Is this what modern parenting is all about?" Before Dad sneaks out the front door, Mom stops him in his tracks (infantilizing the estranged husband and father by asserting "Not so fast, little boy") and stabs him in the chest with a pair of sewing scissors. Marie sighs, "Now I have two men to depend on my love and affection." Mom, however, retorts, "I don't want anyone to depend on me, or me to depend on anyone. At last I'm free, at last I'm happy." Mom smiles into the camera as the screen fades to black. While *Baby Kake* is undeniably comedic and campy, it pointedly uproots the social norms ascribed to women in conventional representations of the Chicano family by highlighting Mom's freedom from codependent relationships. Moreover, by killing off Dad (which Baby threatens to do prior to his choking incident), Mom short-circuits the privileges granted to the father who once took for granted his ability to "come and go" and to elide any responsibility for Baby, therefore delegating it to Mom.

In a similar vein, Gamboa's thirty-seven-minute video *L.A. Familia* (1993) disturbs the normative Chicano family romance presented in Nava's *Mi Familia/My Family* even though it predates the film.[35] Breaking with Nava's monologic notion of la familia, Gamboa situates family in the context of post-industrial Los Angeles to reveal how poverty, marital commitment (or lack thereof), drugs, generational strife, misogyny, homelessness, and the prison system alters Chicano kinship units in the would-be City of Angels. Following the typical "slapstick style" of Gamboa's earlier video work, *L.A. Familia* borrows from yet mixes documentary filmmaking practices in its adoption of styles such as cinéma vérité while employing the formal device of talking heads. The video "examines the meltdown of a Chicano nuclear family amid the environment of an abandoned, visually distorted, and anonymously populated contemporary Los Angeles" (Gamboa 1998, 125, 127). In doing so, it reveals the interactions between Dad (played by Asco collaborator Humberto Sandoval), Mom (played by Gamboa's wife Barbara Carrasco), and Son

(played by the director's son Diego Gamboa), all of whom portray social outcasts struggling to come to grips with their placement within the
family in particular and society at large. Though the backdrop of *L.A.
Familia* almost exclusively takes place in downtown Los Angeles, the
opening shot is a bird's-eye view of Los Angeles from the Hollywood
Hills, a shot that frames the family who will descend from the heights of
kinship and come crashing down on the city pavement as the action unfolds. The camera then pans to the left, capturing a dispute in media res
between Mom and Son (who, as in *Baby Kake*, are categorized as non-
nurturing and unwanted respectively). As the narrative progresses, the
heated verbal exchange continues:

Mom: I've tried everything to keep you in line. Nothing seems to work.
Son: Yes it does.
Mom: I've tried to be nice . . . I've tried that "tough love" shit but that doesn't
       work. Nothing works.
Son: Money works.
Mom: Money spoils.
Son: I think we're gonna have to break up.

Mom and Son are evicted from their home and anxiously ponder their
next move. Broke and with nowhere to go, they blame each other for their
misfortunes. Beyond the obvious lack of mutual respect and the insults
they casually hurl, Mom and Son continue to dialog with each other—
and *L.A. Familia*'s spectator(s)—with regard to their desperate situation.
The sound of a departing airplane intensifies their verbal exchange and
appropriately creates a diegetic space overwrought with white noise. Dad
soon enters the picture, emerging "from L.A. County Jail after an earth-
quake has rattled the computers into releasing him from imprisonment a
year earlier than expected" (Gamboa 1998, 127). We first see Dad in boxer
shorts and leather shoes. Eventually, he manages to secure some "nice
threads": a shirt, slacks, and tie, presumably taken from a dead man's
body discovered on an Los Angeles street. Dad immediately declares his
desire to find his wife and son (see figure 12).

What soon follows is a series of chance encounters between the three
family members. Although the dialog is coated with humor and sarcasm,
the issues broached are dead serious. The hatred, dismay, and frustration

FIGURE 12 Pictured (from left): Diego Gamboa (Son) and Barbara Carrasco (Mom). *L.A. Familia* © 1993, Harry Gamboa Jr.

that permeate this family drama signal a parting of ways from that previously seen on Chicano film, television, or video. As Gamboa explains:

> *L.A. Familia* chronicles the half-lives of the family members as they respectively experience isolation, alienation, arguments, aborted reunions, dysfunctional confessions, and an ongoing sense that everything is crashing inward. (Gamboa 1998, 127)

Shot within a "sporadic twenty-four-month shooting schedule," *L.A. Familia* figuratively documents the temporal shifts each character undergoes within that time span. According to Gamboa:

> Dad undergoes various transformations as he appears as a hardened ex-convict, a schizophrenically confused street person, a repentant father, and an urban outcast. Mom is presented in a cyclical pattern of being strong-willed, emotionally paralyzed, reprimandingly moralistic, and existentially erased. Son literally grows up, but there is a sadness that is permanently attached to his acquired survival skills for life on ground zero. (127)

L.A. Familia highlights numerous pressing issues affecting contemporary Chicano families. The fact that the action explicitly takes place in Los Angeles's urban landscape is hardly coincidental. Hot on the heels of the

Rodney King verdict and the subsequent uprising, a time at which Latinos were curiously absent or curiously represented in televisual media, Gamboa (1998, 125) importantly casts Chicanos in what he identifies as "a picture-imperfect urbanscape of dead ends, skewed horizons, and artificial social turf." *L.A. Familia* further raises the stakes in its illustration of the ways in which this urbanscape impacts the (de)formation of the Chicano family. Gamboa's video, to draw from the geographer Edward J. Soja, initiates a "spatial deconstruction by resituating the meaning of space in history and historical materialism" (1989, 73).

Also suggestive is *L.A. Familia*'s mise-en-scène: *downtown* Los Angeles. In *Thirdspace: Journeys to Los Angeles and Other Real-and-Imagined Places*, Edward J. Soja writes:

> Downtown Los Angeles . . . is almost pure spectacle, of business and commerce, of extreme wealth and poverty, of clashing cultures and rigidly contained ethnicities. . . . Young householders are virtually non-existent. In their place are the homeless, who are coming close to being half the central city's resident population despite vigorous attempts at gentrification and dispersal. (1996, 297)

Whereas Gregory Nava's familia is situated a mere six miles away in the "poor but rich with culture" setting of East Los Angeles (a position his film frequently evokes), Gamboa's downtown Los Angeles familia must contend with the inequities that are part and parcel of their geographical placement.[36] Poverty and homelessness, factors that bear upon familial disenfranchisement, are the forces that jump-start Gamboa's video.

> The concept and reality of the average American family is extinct. Parents and children are diffused entities that have no model of "home" when there is no "house." The living room is in a vacated alley, the kitchen is spread along an endless stretch of asphalt, and the master bedroom is any public space with concrete pillows. White picket fences are reinforced with razor wire. Opportunity never knocks when there isn't a door to slam shut at the end of the day. The slice of the pie is rotting in the gutter. (Gamboa 1988, 125)

Although Nava's film pointedly broaches issues such as police violence, the impact of the prison system on young Chicano men, gang violence, anti-immigrant legislation, and the race and class divisions within *greater* Los Angeles, it ultimately fails to sustain a critique of these forces, absolving state-sanctioned violence bearing upon Chicano communities so that these problems can be solved within the patriarchal family. This is why *Mi Familia/My Family*'s closure is decisively and deceptively smooth, glossing over the tribulations of the past in favor of romanticizing the triumphs of the present, namely through its comforting formula of la familia values.

L.A. Familia does not result in this redemptive social dynamic given the means by which its family clashes with conventional kinship politics. At the risk of depicting la familia as "dysfunctional," Gamboa's irony-laced video situates family discourse within the purview of social and economic inequality. But while *L.A. Familia* takes pleasure in uprooting idealized *Mi Familia* values, it does not end by writing off the family. Toward the end of the video, Mom, Dad, and Son reconnect by what we're told is pure coincidence. Dad immediately notes that Son is holding a video camera; Dad proudly points out that he's become a Chicano filmmaker (and takes pride in how Chicano he looks, thus naming him Cuauhtémoc, undoubtedly after the Aztec icon of the same name). Son is initially seen shooting the traffic on an Los Angeles overpass, then he turns his camera on Dad. Mom soon joins the family scene. Perhaps as a result of his distress over being shot by Son, Dad pulls out a gun and threatens to shoot back with a different weapon. Dad then proceeds to chase Son and Mom down Los Angeles streets only to come to his senses, insisting that he didn't mean to shoot. Dad pleads: "Let's be a happy Chicano family in L.A." Rather than read Dad's request as petitioning for a normative Chicano kinship network (as if this were possible after thirty minutes of confessing how much they hate each other), the family's (dubiously guaranteed) reunification ultimately rests upon a collective navigation of the social structures of violence and despair that underscore their Los Angeles street-based living situation. In bringing the family together, Gamboa parodies Chicano cultural politics in which the problems confronted by Chicanos (particularly in Los Angeles) are always resolvable within the nuclear family. Moreover, family unity does not depend upon Dad's ability to save them; in fact he remains an untrustworthy character to the very end, and his would-be patriarchal authority is critically shot by Gamboa well after Son's camera has been shut off.

The "resolution" Gamboa offers is certainly not one of pure visual pleasure. Frustrating to watch and imbued with disturbing dialogue, the tape's formal elements complement its message that a radical notion of familia cannot be about all pleasure and no pain. Thus Gamboa's *L.A. Familia* adopts and embraces what might be called a politics of dysfunction in its potential movement toward familial mobilization. Family egalitarianism, the tape suggests, must reassess the meaning of biological kinship ties and excavate internal and external strife. (And for the spectator who cannot identify with the movement's and Nava's idealized families, he or she could see Gamboa's family as an alternative in the face of displacement.) In sum, Gamboa's Los Angeles-as-home video acutely illustrates how the cultural capital of the family often falls prey to the rising tide of racial and economic subordination that makes "fabricating the 'brown peril'" (Davis 2000, 67–76) a necessary component of the global economy.

NEW MILLENNIAL EPISODES

In the fall of 1999 serious concern surfaced regarding neglect on the part of the four major television networks—ABC, CBS, NBC, and Fox—in representing Latinos "in the industry both in front of and behind the camera" (F. Sánchez 1999, 46). Influential organizations such as LULAC (League of United Latin American Citizens), the National Council of La Raza, MALDEF (Mexican American Legal Defense Fund), and the National Hispanic Media Coalition bonded together to form the National Latino Media Council in response to the ongoing neglect of Latinos on network television. For two weeks, from September 12–25, the Council called for a boycott of TV, or a "brownout," during which time Latinos were encouraged to rent videos and read books that did what the networks did not: offer affirmative portrayals of Latinos.[37] The boycott was successful in that it made national headlines as many faithfully heeded the call for protest while the networks minimally listened.[38]

Following the brownout, a few major film studios and television networks advanced a handful of Latino productions. Among them were a film and a cable television drama: Carlos Avila's feature film *Price of Glory*, released in early 2000 by New Line Cinema, and *Resurrection Blvd.*, a dramatic series for the Showtime Cable Network and Viacom Productions, created and produced by Mexican American and Italian television writer Dennis E. Leoni, for which Jesús Treviño was invited to direct the pilot. Treviño would go on to direct numerous episodes, and he eventually became executive coproducer until his departure from the show before the third and final season in 2002. With the dubious honor of being the entertainment industry's first major Latino-themed series to be produced, written, and directed by Latinos, under Treviño's influence many Chicano/a media makers had a hand in crafting episodes of *Resurrection Blvd*, including Sylvia Morales who occasionally sat in the director's seat.

Bottom-line family dramas, *Price of Glory* and *Resurrection Blvd.* also pay homage to another popular theme particular to Chicanos and Latinos: boxing. And while these two productions served in many ways as a breath of fresh air, they also conjured up a well-worn narrative vehicle that many saw as stereotype dependent. But this thematic deployment should come as no surprise given that a great deal of Latino representation is anchored in the boxing ring.[39] Indeed, there are not only the historical and cultural dimensions that reveal the actual participation of Latinos in the sport (lest we forget that one of Chicano nationalism's founding fathers, Corky Gonzales, was also a boxer) but its qualification as a likely cultural premise that film and television industries are inclined to finance. And when boxing and family narratives are coupled, one cannot help but think that the "common" American spectator may be reassured of their *familiarity* with Latinos.

For many critics *Resurrection Blvd.* succeeded in breaking with stereotypical Latino media images, but it was also rightly subject to critical scrutiny given the terms in which it was presented. As anthropologist Arlene Dávila (2001, B16) points out in her review of the program, "the show is one more American fable—along the lines of *The Cosby Show* and *Home Improvement*—in which a patriarch keeps family members in line, urging them to follow their hearts and seek out their dreams, and dispensing in the process the well-known American dream of upward mobility—except that it all happens in Latino L.A." In his insightful and compellingly argued essay "Media Advocates, Latino Citizens and Niche Cable: The Limits of 'No Limits' TV," Scott Wible adopts a cultural policy studies approach to read *Resurrection Blvd.* from the trajectory of liberal governance whereby media reform depends upon a responsible Latino public to fulfill their role as "citizen-consumers." While Wible importantly notes how the series was often touted as a show about an average American family as a means for creating a "universal humanism," he hurriedly equates *Resurrection Blvd.* and *American Family*—Gregory Nava's PBS series that also followed on the heels of the brownout—because of their "family-centered focus . . . that looks familiar to the white, upper-middle class television audience to which television executives feel comfortable pitching their shows" (Wible 2004, 54). While his argument may at first take correspond with my reading of Nava's work, my commitment to textual analysis forces me to part ways with Wible. To be sure, Wible is able to make this claim—and another maintaining that "the television screen fails to depict the heterogeneity of Latino imaginations, lives, and cultures" (55)—because his essay fails to read any episodic content of each series, which would in turn allow him to mark their distinctions.[40] Conversely, Michelle A. Holling (2006) insists that in its promotion of the figure of "el simpático boxer," *Resurrection Blvd.* can be seen as offering images of Chicano masculinity that contrast with hard and fast "macho Latino" images given their contextualization within "a rhetoric of *la familia.*"

Yet while the patriarchal figure of Roberto (played by Tony Plana) does wield power in the Santiago household, it is not executed without resistance or—to employ the language of boxing—defeat. Similar to Gamboa's Los Angeles familia, the Santiagos are incessantly feuding (most often with Roberto) in their continuous struggle, ironically perhaps, to keep the family intact. Though boxing remained the central theme, the series raised key issues such as police harassment, drugs, racism, sexuality, the Vietnam War, gang violence, interracial romance, teen pregnancy, gay identity, and gender inequality in the domestic sphere. This is what made *Resurrection Blvd.* compelling as compared to Gregory Nava's *American Family.*[41] Predictably titled, the series premiered in January 2002 and ran for two seasons until July 2004, casting Edward James Olmos in the role of the unshakably conservative patriarch Jess González. In many ways the father figure in *American Family* would mirror the one in *Price of Glory*, a film that pivots on a patriarch whose dream of becoming a prized boxer is sabotaged after a money-hungry promoter mismatches him in exchange for sixty thousand dollars. To compensate for his short-lived success, he forces his three sons to step into the ring and assume his former role. In a fashion hauntingly reminiscent of Nava's *Selena*, *Price of Glory* begins by painting a portrait of a father whose domineering behavior could be called nothing short of abusive. However, at its closure the film ultimately rescues the patriarch from criticism by anointing him as a well-meaning savior.

The unifying thread that ties *American Family* to *Price of Glory* is the shocking ability to humanize patriarchy. Speaking about the film, actor Jimmy Smits (who plays father Arturo Ortega) draws parallels with his on-screen role and his own father. Smits claims, "The Ortega family has higher ideals, it wants the kids to be better, to do only what is best for them. . . . My father was a major disciplinarian. 'You *will* go to school. You *will* stay in your room three hours to do your homework. You *will* make yourself better.' Hey, that's as American as apple pie" (Beitiks 2000, C6). Like the rhetoric circulating around *Mi Familia/My Family*, Smits's appeal to "Americans," suggesting that Latino patriarchs have much in common with their white brethren (not to mention that patriarchy is virtually indistinguishable from "higher ideals"), and Nava's categorization of the González clan as an American family resolutely cling to a patriarchal structure that is not only counterintuitive in the effort to shoot back at stereotypes but bankrupt in light of the complex kinship representations with which Latino spectators are undoubtedly familiar in quotidian family affairs.

Moreover, in its depiction of Tommy, the gay nephew and son played by Douglas Spain, *Resurrection Blvd.* remarkably throws into question the heteropatriarchal norms of productions like *American Family* and *Price of Glory* wherein lies the impossibility of Chicano gay male representation. In the 2002 episode "Pararse," directed by Sylvia Morales, Tommy returns to Los Angeles from Boston (where he attends college) for his mother's birthday. While Tommy's "coming out" was the subject of a previous episode ("Saliendo," directed by Tony Plana), "Pararse" (Spanish for stand up) reveals Tommy's break up with his boyfriend Jeff and his resulting desire to return home. Tommy tells his mother Bibi (played by Elizabeth Pena) that he wants to be "back around [his] familia, back where [he] grew up." Bibi dubiously supports the idea due in large part to the rift between Tommy and his father Paco (played by Esai Morales) who is unwilling to accept that his son is gay. The episode of course leads to the obligatory confrontation between Tommy and Paco at the family picnic in the park thrown in honor of Bibi (which is not to ignore the essential moments when Tommy calls out family members on their homophobia, particularly their heterosexual male anxiety). During the altercation, Paco charges Tommy with trying to live "the American dream" with his "blond haired, blue-eyed" boyfriend. Paco shouts back, revealing to his father that Jeff left him (perhaps signaling the inevitable failure of the American dream?). Tommy storms off, only to happen upon three random Latinos in the park, one of which refers to a *pinche maricón* (a fucking faggot)— but not per se in reference to Tommy—as he passes by. Tommy meets the challenge of their phobic discourse and literally fights back. Paco enters the fight in his son's defense.

While Michelle A. Holling's point that Tommy's "overt displays of masculinity based on aggression" enables him to "reassert his position within *familia*" is well taken, reading Tommy's decision to fight as a challenge to homophobia rather than simply an attempt prove his manhood for familial inclusion would grant his character more agency than Holling's position would allow (Holling 2006, 106).[42] Furthermore, Morales's directorial intervention requires consideration for the episode does not end with the fight in the park (that is, the masculinist public sphere) but in a kitchen (a private space conventionally deemed feminine) where Paco and Tommy reunite as father and son in the course of cooking a meal. Recalling Morales's *Chicana* enables reflection on the filmmaker's assertive challenge to the gendered contours of the domestic sphere, a challenge that persists in all of her most recent work. And while Morales did not write the script for "Pararse," the pivotal role she plays as director compels me to signal her critical contributions in her recurring role as one of the shamefully few Chicana filmmakers who continues to shoot back at heteropatriarchal authority placed at the center of so much Chicano film and television. With the feminist lens used for *Chicana* as a means of shooting back, Morales arguably facilitates an interrogation of the gender politics of private and public space that in turn establishes queer-affirmative possibility within both la familia and Chicano/a media culture in a new millennial episode.

Three

The Verse of the Godfather

The time is now to let the world know that Chicano and Latino
Rap exist. The doors have been blown wide open with such tal-
ent as Baby Bash, SPM, Lil Rob, Cypress Hill, Fat Joe, Big Pun
(RIP), and many others. It would not exist without the forefa-
thers of Chicano and Latino Rap: Frost, Mellow Man Ace, A
Lighter Shade of Brown, and Proper Dos.

• • • Jesse G., "It's Time" (2004)

They rally round tha family, with a pocket full of shells.

• • • Rage Against the Machine, "Bulls on Parade" (1996)

This song's dedicated to my family/That's been there for me/
I know if it wasn't for you/There would be no me.

• • • Lil Bandit, "Dedication to My Family" (2005)

The editorial by Jesse G. that opens the inaugural July 2004 issue of *Chicano Rap Magazine* makes a crucial, if not ironic, observation: almost four years into the twenty-first century Chicano and Latino rap remain, on the whole, largely invisible (for which the
magazine intends to serve as a corrective) despite the existence of those
"forefathers" who have produced a new generation of Chicano and Latino hip-hop talent. That Jesse G. refers to these predecessors who made
their indelible mark in the early 1990s as "forefathers" is fitting given how
kinship discourse permeates the Chicano rap and hip-hop landscape,
foregrounding the father—ranging in appearance from "the forefather" to

"the godfather"—and his irrefutably formative influence. While aiming to chart the historical, material, and social significance of Chicano rap music, an effort in solidarity with Jesse G.'s demand that "the world know that Chicano and Latino rap exist," this chapter seeks to address the politics of masculinity and working-class identity in relation to the family and cultural nationalism as mobilizing forces within a contemporary popular culture frame.

Rap, as defined precisely by Tricia Rose (1994, 2), "is a form of rhymed storytelling accompanied by highly rhythmic, electronically based music." Rap (or the art of "MCing") is but one link in the signifying chain of hip-hop culture that has also included, since its inception, graffiti, urban aesthetics, break dancing, DJ technologies, and, particularly in a Chicano context, tattooing (sometimes derived from graffiti, as exemplified by Los Angeles–based Chicano tattoo artist Mr. Cartoon).[1] Rap and hip-hop culture require critical consideration and investigation given the global cultural capital they command as well as their effectiveness as a vehicle for reflecting social and historical phenomena. Highlighting strands of Chicano rap and hip-hop rhetorically and politically, stemming from the genealogy of poetic consciousness emerging from the 1960s and 1970s that advocated *la raza* and *la familia* as twin keys for liberation, reveals how popular cultural forms like rap may serve as a means to empowerment when channeled within everyday life contexts.

As in the previous chapters, my investigation of cultural formations entails a critical unveiling of the problematic tenets that underscore the too-frequently assumed egalitarianism of tacit categorical—that is, Chicano and familial—alliance. As I take seriously Shirley Anne Williams's claim that "intellectuals have been slow to analyze and critique rap's content," often refusing "to call that content, where appropriate, pathological, anti-social, and anti-community" (1992, 168), and as I remain cautious of lapsing into hasty criticism, the questions that guide this chapter include: How is la familia a major trope in Chicano rap? Who gets to count, and why, as "family" in Chicano rap discourse? Why must parents, gay men, and women frequently fall outside certain renditions of the family? In what ways do "nonnormative" (i.e., queer) rap narratives shift the content of hip-hop's supposed prescriptive patriarchal and heteronormative form? What repercussions surface in rendering gangs as family (or, to recast Rage Against the Machine's critique of imperialism, rallying around the family with a pocket full of shells) in Chicano rap narratives as well as within the communities where Chicano rap circulates and emerges? And yet how do articulations of kinship and nationalism "from below," namely by working-class Chicano/a youth, enact a sentiment of resistance through family-based discourses that speak forcefully against racial, political, and economic injustice? Conversely, how might these articulations potentially enforce or take for granted state power and institutional conventions regarding gender and sexual politics?

The two previous chapters delved into the meaning of la familia at the height of the 1960s and 1970s Chicano movement not only to narrate its past function for organizational efforts and as a strategy of representation but also to locate its significance in contemporary cultural practices whose manifold valences are akin to those decades earlier. In making sense of the "rhymes for la raza" along these lines, the work carried out under the rubric of Black popular culture studies proves comparatively and theoretically instructive. The work of African American studies scholars Tricia Rose, Paul Gilroy, Joan Morgan, Wahneema Lubiano, and Robin D. G. Kelley, among others, provides exemplary models for exploring urban popular cultures—particularly rap and hip-hop—from social movement history trajectories. This chapter extrapolates from some of this work, especially those writings that focus on kinship discourse's profound impact on gender relations in black culture and politics, since it often translates usefully for Chicano family affairs.

For example, Paul Gilroy's influential essay "It's a Family Affair: Black Culture and the Trope of Kinship" (1993b) examines a number of Black rap narratives that promote the family as a site of political mobilization. In these narratives he uncovers a sentiment that deems the family coterminous with masculinist cultural nationalism in the service of patriarchal authority, as well as an imperative initiative to understand the significance of the family for collective empowerment. To best show how this sentiment operates, he offers his readers a number of tracks and asks them to listen closely to the lyrics of, for example, KRS-1 of Boogie Down Productions, who touts "I'm black which makes me part of the African family," alongside those of Ed O.G., which, Gilroy notes, make a "small gesture" worth celebrating: a moment of negation from reifying strict biological kinship ties. According to Gilroy (1993b, 203), KRS-1's claim reinforces the point that "family has come to stand for community, for race and for nation," resulting in "a short-cut to solidarity." Ed O.G.'s invocation of kin, however, challenges the community imagined by KRS-1 as his gesture departs from "the biological payback involved in family life," thus countering the conventional understanding of "the family" as necessarily given as well as the recurrent privileging of male offspring over female ("he is not saying be a father to your son—he is saying be a father to your child.") (206).

To be sure, embracing a family principle as a modality of unity and community must remain held in tension. Or, put another way, a healthy dose of suspicion is required when the family serves as the metaphor par excellence for community as well as race—or raza—consciousness, particularly when continuous returns to it become the chief solution to male destitution. Gilroy argues:

> This discourse of race as community, as family, has been born again in contemporary attempts to interpret the crisis of black politics and social life as a crisis of black masculinity alone. The family is not just the site of cultural reproduction; it is also identified as the mechanism for reproducing the cultural dysfunction that disables the race as a whole. The race is nothing more than an accumulation of families. The crisis of black masculinity can therefore be fixed. It is to be repaired by intervening in the family to compensate and rebuild the race by instituting appropriate forms of masculinity and male authority. Even hip-hop culture—the dissonant soundtrack of racial dissidence—has become complicit with this analysis. (1993b, 204)

Taking Gilroy's cue, I will examine the moments of Chicano hip-hop culture in which the solidification of the racial family becomes synonymous with national empowerment. These moments, as we shall see, allow us to identify and unpack an emergent struggle for cultural hegemony through Chicano popular forms. But since rap indeed serves as an important medium for claiming identity and constituting community, a critical interrogation of la familia and the tendency of kinship discourse to stabilize gender relations and affirm the supposition of heterosexuality cannot be diminished if Chicano popular forms are to wield democratic potential.

Before addressing specific rap tracks within the terms I've outlined above, I want to provide some key historical, cultural, and theoretical contexts for understanding Chicano rap and hip-hop. Begin, then, with the fact that Latino participation within hip-hop culture in general is not a new phenomenon (as is too often assumed). In fact, Latinos played leading roles since hip-hop's inception. The East Coast street scene, for instance, at the tail end of the 1970s on through the 1980s and 1990s has almost always been, as Juan Flores (2000) and Raquel Z. Rivera (2003) remind us, Puerto Rican *and* black—never *strictly* black—as mainstream media (from MTV to hip-hop books published by major presses) have many believing.[2] However, Latino movers and shakers like Rubie D. (Rubén García) and Charlie Chase (Carlos Mandes) of the Cold Crush Brothers, Crazy Legs (Richard Colón), KMX Assault (Jenaro Díaz), Prince Whipper Whip (James Whipper) of the Fantastic 5, the Devastating Tito (Tito Jones), and Master OC (Oscar Rodríguez Jr.) of the Fearless Four always seem to drop out of histories of hip-hop culture, thus contributing to what José Albino (1999) has termed "selective amnesia" regarding rap's roots.[3]

Conversely, Chicanos played and continue to play a fundamental role in rap and hip-hop's production, exhibition, signification, and reception on the West Coast, although such truths are never readily evident. From the late 1980s, famed Los Angeles African American rappers like Ice-T (Tracey Marrow) and the late Eazy-E (Eric Wright), formerly of N.W.A. (Niggaz With Attitude), assisted Chicano rappers in gaining public notoriety. (In 1981, Ice-T helped Kid Frost (Arturo Molina) get signed to the Electrobeat label, which released two of his first three records; after an important stint at Virgin Records, Eazy-E signed Frost to his label Ruthless, a subsidiary of Relativity Records.) Producers and DJs Tony G. (Tony Gonzales) and Julio G. (Julio Gonzales), whose names circulate widely in hip-hop circles, are often credited as influencing and single-handedly facilitating the careers of numerous Latino and African American artists, including N.W.A. In the early 1990s, Chicano disc jockeys Eric and Nick Vidal—alternatively known as The Baka Boyz—drew vast audiences for their morning show on Los Angeles hip-hop station Power 106 (although rather curiously at that time, Power 106 rarely programmed Chicano rap, the exception being a one-night-a-week show—Friday Night Flavas—on which it was occasionally featured).

The station, however, currently boasts a Sunday night show—Pocos Pero Locos—that does exclusively showcase Latino rap. For the new millennium, then, one might forecast a turning tide given the publicity of Chicano rap in key media spaces. Another example: *The Source: The Magazine of Hip-Hop Music, Culture, and Politics*, the longest standing, and arguably the most influential, hip-hop periodical, acknowledged its awareness of Chicanos and Latinos in and around the scene as evidenced in a section entitled "Latino Uprising" in its February 1999 issue. *The Source* appropriately couched the feature within the terms of Chicano and Latino activism, mapping a resurgence of "brown power" in politics, music, film, and activism.[4] On June 11, 2000, the *Los Angeles Times* printed Fred Alvarez's "The Latino Rap Scene: Chicanos' Time for Rhythm and Rhyme." Locating an emergent Chicano hip-hop culture in the greater Los Angeles area, Alvarez offers an insightful look at the production, distribution, and circulation of Chicano rap, as well as the controversies and calls for celebration provoked by diverse interpretive communities.

Since its inception, however, Chicano hip-hop history has been documented and critically examined by a number of journalists, advocates, and scholars. For instance, "Brown Pride" (brownpride.com), a web site established by three Chicano engineering students at California State University at Fullerton, provides visitors with news on recent releases and performances by Chicano rap artists, as well as news on, and historical accounts of, these artists. Chicano rap and hip-hop are given serious consideration in pioneering books on the history of Chicano and Latino music; take, for example, Steve Loza's *Barrio Rhythm: Mexican American Music in Los Angeles* (1993), David Reyes's and Tom Waldman's *Land of a Thousand Dances: Chicano Rock 'n' Roll from Southern California* (1998), and Ed Morales's *The Latin Beat: The Rhythms and Roots of Latin Music, from Bossa Nova to Salsa and Beyond* (2003). Articles in scholarly journals by Ted Swedenburg ("Homies in the 'Hood: Rap's Commodification of Insubordination" [1992]), Gregory Stephens ("Interracial Dialogue in Rap Music: Call-and-Response in a Multicultural Style" [1992]), and Josh Kun ("What Is an MC If He Can't Rap to Banda? Making Music in Nuevo L.A." [2004]) insightfully position Chicano rap as reflecting and responding to contemporary social concerns. Filmmakers have also sought to record the Chicano hip-hop phenomenon of which the documentaries *Heroes of Latin Hip Hop* (Joe Ritter and Fred Sherman, 2002) and *Pass the Mic!* (Richard Montes, 2002) are representative. Furthermore, Puerto Rican music journalist Ronin Ro's polemical *Gangsta: Merchandising the Rhymes of Violence* (1996) begins with a revealing and informative cluster of chapters on the cross-section of money, gang life, and urban violence in relation to Chicano rap. Ro's flagrantly sensationalist account of Chicano and Latino hip-hop nevertheless interestingly blends journalism and ethnography, documenting up-close encounters with rappers like Frost, ALT (Al Trivette), Slow Pain, Mellow Man Ace (Ulpiano Sergio Reyes), and A Lighter Shade of Brown.[5] Finally, Chicano academics like Rosa Linda Fregoso, Rafael Pérez-Torres, Pancho McFarland, Curtis Márez, and José David Saldívar—whose work I will momentarily discuss—gauge in assorted ways rap as a Chicano-adopted cultural form with which to contend.

Alternatively, many casually shun or violently dismiss the pertinence of Chicano rap, undoubtedly perpetuating its relegation to peripheral status. This range of responses are exemplified by Latino journalist Rubén Martínez's reductive classification of it as "a curious phenomenon" (1992, 12), hip-hop fans of varying backgrounds shunning it based on its lack of authenticity, and racist Chicanos questioning its authenticity as a mode of Chicano expression, such as the one who once confronted DJ Chilly Bean and Yoatl from Aztlán Underground, demanding that they "take that fucking nigger shit off the fucking turntables" (Kelly 1993a, 267). To be sure, such responses help nourish the all-too-customary belief that the expressive form is strictly for, by, and about African Americans.[6] As S. Craig Watkins (2005, 150) has recently argued, "Efforts to mobilize a political base in hip hop typically start with the false premise that the movement is essentially black."

The point of writing about Chicano rap has everything to do with its proliferation and import as an expressive vehicle that drives home the relevance of popular culture against the grain. Although Chicano rap is hardly as "popular" to the white or black public eye, perhaps because there is no Chicano equivalent to Ice Cube, Snoop Dogg, 50 Cent, Eminem, or the late Tupac Shakur, its catalogue expands as it is produced and received primarily by Chicano youths, most notably in California.[7] Since the early 1990s, Chicano rap has maintained a steady—and commands a growing—audience of consumers and listeners, not to mention the fact that a multitude of new performers continue to appear on the scene, progressively turning out and distributing their music despite limited financial resources, technological and studio accessibility, and mainstream acceptance. In fact, the garage is often cited as the key location where "underground" rap comes into fruition.[8] Indeed, as much as pioneer performers such as (Kid) Frost, ALT, Tha Mexakinz, Juvenile Style, Funkdoobiest, Cypress Hill, and A Lighter Shade of Brown, as well as more recent names like Lil Rob (Robert Flores), Jae-P (Juan Pablo Huerta), 2Mex, and Akwid, have come to define the field, their audiences are not always simply consumers but rather they, too, have adopted the role of cultural producer by cobbling together the basic resources to make their own tapes and CDs without requiring backing by a major label, thus contributing to Chicano rap's expanse. Browsing a stand selling music at many swap meets (also known as flea markets) in California, particularly in predominantly working-class Latino communities, affords one the chance to glimpse or purchase recordings by lesser-known artists who go unnoticed by, on the one hand, those who search for music only in large chain music stores and, on the other hand, many writing about rap music and hip-hop culture. Aside from the more popular artists who have received a fair amount of recognition, numerous acts, including those just mentioned, require examination in greater detail.[9] With the advent of the internet, Chicano rap—including that on small-time record labels—has increasingly become more obtainable. Even the virtual music stores housed at Amazon.com and BarnesandNoble.com carry CDs that may be difficult to find elsewhere. Furthermore, one need only type "Chicano" in the search box on the immensely popular on-line auction block eBay to discover scores of Chicano rap CDs. One also cannot forget how rap in general circulates in the public sphere, performed anywhere from spoken-word events to buses and subway trains in Los Angeles, Oakland, Chicago, and New York—cities where I have witnessed its presentation in such venues—and that these artists might perhaps never record their work. In its early years, rap festivals sprung up all around California to promote awareness of Chicano and Latino politics and to raise money on behalf of Peace in the Barrio or the Zapatista movement in Chiapas, for example. Most of the acts that participated in these events were—and went—unsigned.

It also bears mention that although I and others categorize them un-der the banner "Chicano rap," a good number of these artists differ with regard to, for example, ethnic identity, geographical location, political ideology, group membership, and community alliances. (Appropriate to the context at hand, Raquel Rivera [2003, 104] has noted how both East and West Coast rappers—Jack from Psycho Realm and Fat Joe respec-tively—have deployed "*latinidad*-based notions of family.")[10] Acts that are sometimes identified as "Chicano"—as witnessed in spaces like *Chicano Rap Magazine*—command a membership that is more than just Mexi-can American. For example, Funkdoobiest's membership consists of both a Puerto Rican and a Chicano, whereas the Cypress Hill trio lays claims to Cuban American, Cuban-Mexican, and Italian American backgrounds. Akwid and Jae-P, predominantly Spanish-rapping performers sponsored by the Spanish language media conglomerate Univision, are mainly rec-ognized (both by self-nomination and marketing) as Latino even though they are of Mexican descent. Perhaps because such acts command a large Chicano audience, especially in Los Angeles where they're based, their work is likely to be situated within the trajectory of Chicanismo, espe-cially given their occasional adoption of certain cultural politics and po-etics that resonate with those more easily classifiable as Chicano. For example, Jae-P's "Latinos Unidos" (2004) resonates with Proper Dos's "Mexican Power" (1992), which also mentions the word "Chicano" in the song, while his song, "Pa Mi Raza" (2006) (and the eponymously titled CD) clearly reverberates with Kid Frost's "La Raza" (1990) a decade and a half earlier as both aim to infuse a sense of cultural pride in their listen-ers, a key element of the Chicano cultural pride project. Fittingly, on the Univision Music Group's website, Jae-P is identified as the "New Poet of the Urban Regional Movement."[11] So while one can indeed trace its ge-nealogical ties and map its discursive linkages, Chicano rap cannot be reduced to a monolithic entity nor is its existence contingent upon the usage of the term "Chicano." "Chicano rap" does, however, persist as an identity, if you will, whose sociohistorical particularities and political im-pulses are demanded both by performers and fans given the way Chica-nos in particular habitually drop out of the category "Latin/o," especially in East Coast contexts.

Given the unique historical and social circumstances that give rise to the emergence of Chicano popular culture, the study of Chicano rap cannot strictly focus on what is popular in the "mainstream" but must consider practices and productions that resist or fall outside the realm of mass-produced and mass-accepted popular culture. Adhering to this mode of inquiry calls for an awareness of working-class locations in which marginal, popular forms are produced, performed, and received.[12] Indeed, grasping the evolution and dissemination of Chicano rap necessarily entails understanding the social phenomena that motivate and influence popular culture's content and form. Stuart Hall, after Antonio Gramsci, has noted the strategic significance of "the national-popular," or the ways in which "cultural hegemony is made, lost, and struggled over" (S. Hall 1996, 469). "The national-popular" is instructive for locating the emergence and function of Chicano popular forms like rap music. As Hall argues,

> The role of the 'popular' in popular culture is to fix the authenticity of popular forms, rooting them in the experiences of popular communities from which they draw their strength, allowing us to see them as expressive of a particular subordinate social life that resists its being constantly made over as low and outside. (469)

The "national-popular" formulation sheds light on our understanding of cultural nationalist sentiment in rap discourse stemming from racialized, working-class locations, a sentiment informing Chicano rap's resistance to dominant cultural formations and the struggle for hegemony. Importantly, it situates cultural discourses within the communities they circulate in and necessarily considers the sociopolitical forces that inform their ideological currents.

Yet as Hall and his collaborators demonstrate in the pivotal study, *Resistance Through Rituals: Youth Subcultures in Post-war Britain* (Hall and Jefferson 1976), the struggle for cultural hegemony is always riddled with complexities and contradictions as resistance to dominant cultural formations does not equal a complete break from them. Rather than obtaining immunity from their impact and influence, this struggle must always be positioned within the space of negotiation as, for example, globalization, hierarchal gender relations, urban violence, and racial inequality are the forces through which they are filtered. Stuart Hall (1996, 468) writes that cultural hegemony "is never about pure victory or pure domination (that's not what the term means); it is never a zero-sum cultural game;

it is always about shifting the balance of power in the relations of culture; it is always about changing the dispositions and the configurations of cultural power, not getting out of it." To understand Chicano rap and hip-hop culture within these terms enables comprehension of their oppositional impulses (exemplified—and ascertainable by title alone—in a scholarly essay like Pancho McFarland's "'Here Is Something You Can't Understand . . .': Chicano Rap and the Critique of Globalization" [2002] and in what I will detail as the assenting power of cultural nationalism), but also recognizes their "being embedded." As such, "counternarratives" generated by popular cultural formations may potentially rescript non-egalitarian relations. Hall focuses our attention on this dynamic, locating it within the realm of identity politics, when he writes:

> Thus, to put it crudely, certain ways in which black men continue to live out their counter-identities as black masculinities and replay those fantasies of black masculinities in the theatres of popular culture are, when viewed from along other axes of difference, the very masculine identities that are oppressive to women, that claim visibility for their hardness only at the expense of the vulnerability of black women and the feminization of gay black men. The way in which a transgressive politics in one domain is constantly sutured and stabilized by reactionary or unexamined politics in another is only to be explained by this continuous cross-dislocation of one identity by another, one structure by another. (S. Hall 1996, 469)

In this chapter I attempt to grasp the tensions within the struggle for cultural hegemony in Chicano rap discourse, showing how resistance on the one hand does not necessitate erasing dominance on the other. But yet this does not diminish the crucial questions of culture that indelibly shape Chicano sociopolitical concerns.

MAPPING NATION CLAIMS

Scholars have acknowledged or gestured toward understanding the significant influence of cultural nationalism and working-class consciousness in Chicano rap. In her influential book *The Bronze Screen: Chicana and Chicano Film Culture*, Rosa Linda Fregoso (1993a, xviii) briefly employs Frost's "These Stories Have to Be Told," from *East Side Story*, to talk about mixed-race identity and how European ancestry or having one parent who is white disturbs the phylogenetic claims of Chicano nationalist sentiment. That she includes a discussion of this track makes sense given that Edward James Olmos's *American Me* (1992) and Taylor Hackford's *Bound by Honor/Blood In, Blood Out* (1993), two "gangxploitation" films she discusses, signal the predicament of Anglo-Chicano-mixed male characters. One may also speak to the intertextual dimensions of Chicano rap and film. The first track of *East Side Story*, "The Man," is a lyrical montage, set to a beat, of lines spoken by El Pachuco, played by Edward James Olmos, in Luis Valdez's 1981 film *Zoot Suit*, a film on which Fregoso has written extensively. Clearly, Chicano rap draws its influence from, or at least overlaps with, Chicano film, especially regarding their shared strands of cultural nationalist masculinity.

Although mentioning Frost's "earlier romanticized and misogynist rap persona in his debut *Hispanic Causing Panic*" and representing the frequently criminalized Chicano youths of Los Angeles, José David Saldívar (citing the exact same passage as Fregoso in his *Border Matters: Remapping American Cultural Studies*) yet glosses over its significance in particular and the overall literary and lyrical importance of Frost's work in general. Rather, Saldívar locates Frost's music on *la frontera:* that is, lumping it "with punk, conjunto, polka, technobanda" to espouse a politics of hybridity characteristic of music that exemplifies "border culture" (Saldívar 1997, 126–27).[13] I hardly want to deny the mixture of various regional and cultural sounds present in Frost's music as they certainly speak to the potential of coalition building through music as well as adding a necessary dimension to Gilroy's and Saldívar's arguments. However, I want to draw attention to how Saldívar does not ascertain the ideological implications behind Frost's historically specific Chicano poetic consciousness. Borrowing from the essay "Against Easy Listening: Audiotopic Readings and Transnational Soundings" (1997) by Josh Kun, Saldívar invokes hybridity to save the day from discussing the complex (and unpopular?) politics of Chicano cultural nationalism—although quickly mentioning the occasional "uncritical hymns of Chicano protonationalism"—that are part and parcel of Frost's music. Kun, arguing against Gilroy's "relying on strictly textual critiques" of both black nationalist rap and Kid Frost's "La Raza," claims "If we go beyond the level of the text and lyric with Kid Frost and listen to the music he raps over, a much different and much more enabling critique results in which music manages to connect the East Los Angeles Borderlands with the black diaspora via both 1990s rap and 1960s jazz" (Kun 1997, 293). This move, which at first take seems clever, proves ultimately ahistorical in that it overlooks the presence of the Chicano nationalist poetics that inform the song, not to mention that it assumes "*we* can go beyond the level of the text and lyric" (emphasis mine) when it is the text that excludes many of us whom the song purports to address. Conversely, postcolonial literary studies scholar Neil Lazarus (1999, 205) has warned against prioritizing the import of music form over that of lyrical content. In his analysis of Paul Simon's commercially successful *Graceland*, Lazarus signals the "discrepancy between the self-conscious 'One-Worldism' of the music and the unselfconscious 'First-Worldism' of the lyrics."

In a similar vein, Deborah Wong's "'I Want the Microphone': Mass Mediation and Agency in Asian-American Popular Music," makes a crucial observation about Asian American rap that resonates with the point I'm making about the culturally specific mode of address in Chicano rap. In her essay Wong (1994, 165) notes how "the oppositional voice of African-American rap not only passes powerfully through [Filipino rapper] La Quian . . . but is transformed in the process into something consciously Asian American, directed to a consciously Asian-American audience." Saldívar and Kun, unlike Wong, overlook the fact that Frost's music is indeed consciously Chicano, directed to a consciously Chicano audience (although who counts as Chicana remains in question).[14] It is true that the hybridity of Frost's musical form may be oppositional, but it cannot account for, or take precedence over, the masculinist nationalism explicit in his lyrical content (after all, nationalism and hybridity are never mutually exclusive categories).[15] With this in mind it is hard to bypass the text and lyric or sidestep issues of Chicano nationalism and communitarian consciousness. To be sure, the production of distinctly Chicano rap music is never "specifically Chicano." For instance, Steve Yano, a Japanese American who was raised in East Los Angeles, is the founder of Skanless Studios in La Puente, California and the Skanless record label to which the influential Chicano rap act Proper Dos belong. The compilation CD *Rap Declares War* (1992), a collection of songs by Proper Dos, War, A Lighter Shade of Brown, Hispanic MCs, Kid Frost, 2Pac, Ice-T, Mellow Man Ace, Too Short, and the Beastie Boys (among others) that pay tribute to the Chicano-influenced African American group War by way of sampling and collaboration, was also released on Skanless. However, the political current of many Chicano rappers continues to embody a sense of Chicano-ness that appeals to culturally specific identities framed by, for better or worse, nationalist thinking. Yet this strand of nationalist thinking is not the only strand to speak of. The mobilization of cultural nationalism by subordinated populations is often premised on the element of uplift and empowerment, a fact that cannot be casually dismissed.

For Pancho McFarland, "Cypress Hill has been active in critiquing Chicana/o nationalism that overemphasizes Chicana/o solidarity at the expense of a broader working-class and youth solidarity" (2002, 306). He cites Cypress Hill's contentious debate with (Kid) Frost over the continuous references to la raza and brown pride in his raps that, as McFarland puts it, ignores "other youth who might benefit from hip-hop solidarity" (306). In a footnote, McFarland equates nationalism with "parochialism," maintaining that, as such, it "limits even our ability to fully understand Chicana/o experiences because without an analysis of globalization and the location of Chicanas/os in the new world order vis-à-vis groups throughout the world we are unable to accurately assess the ideologies, structures, and policies that negatively impact Chicanas/os" (2002, 313). Were McFarland to understand it—as I will detail later in this chapter—as a subjugated knowledge that may be deployed against the state, as well as a mode of consciousness that may entail, for example, a stance against market capitalism, he might not so easily conflate cultural nationalism with what reads more like cultural essentialism. Indeed, such a reductive understanding of cultural nationalism cannot help but foreclose an analysis of why nationalism within Chicano hip-hop and other cultural forms are key—socially, politically, and historically—in the first place. Moreover, while McFarland is right that a sense of solidarity may be eclipsed by cultural nationalism, the pressure points of homophobia and misogyny that often fuel cultural nationalism are pointed out with such brevity that there can be no mention of how Cypress Hill in particular has been complicit in their perpetuation.[16]

In "Brown: The Politics of Working-Class Chicano Style," Curtis Márez puts his finger on the impulse of working-class consciousness informing the work of artists such as Kid Frost, ALT, JV, A Lighter Shade of Brown, The Funky Aztecs, and Aztlán Underground. Yet like Saldívar, he ultimately reifies certain aspects of the Chicano rap phenomenon without carefully examining its discursive claims and the layered modalities of its reception (regardless of his claim that "Most of these rappers are regular performers on the national lowrider show circuit"). Diverging from Saldívar's quick dismissal of Chicano cultural nationalism, Márez cites Yoatl Orozco from Aztlán Underground who says he doesn't "believe in the whole national cultural mode of thinking" that then, as Márez insists, does not "locate the nation in the blood reality of 'la raza'" but rather "in a set of sites (Chicano Moratorium, Chicano Human Rights Council, etc.) that, by virtue of the Treaty of Guadalupe Hidalgo, have been designated 'Aztlán' by brown activists" (1996, 129). Even though Aztlán Underground may indeed call Aztlán "a nation under the Treaty of Guadalupe Hidalgo," thus connecting Chicanismo to "the contingent effect of negotiated representations and not a primordial, pregiven category" (1996, 129), this says nothing about the tendencies of a clearly nationalist discourse (their name alone betrays Yoatl's point about being bound to a "national cultural mode of thinking") whose essentialist attachments have historically eclipsed or made it difficult to engage issues such as gender and sexuality. Márez (1996, 128) cites Mandalit Del Barco's report that "today's Chicano activists say they've learned from the mistakes of their predecessors and have embraced the ideas and strategies of feminists, gays and lesbians, [and] African American activists," yet he does not confirm whether Chicano rappers are part of this activist camp and how exactly their work speaks to this point.

Furthermore, although Aztlán Underground's or Márez's Chicano nation may not be contingent upon "primordial, pregiven" categories, this does not mean it is exempt from invoking inextricably bound ("blood reality") issues such as la familia or sweeping issues of gay and lesbian sexuality under the nationalist carpet. In fact, in the interview from which Márez pulls this quote, the next question asked of Yoatl is: "Could you talk about the concepts of carnalismo and la familia?" Yoatl answers:

It's been used a lot by gangs, the whole concept of carnale [sic], but chicanismo embodies carnalismo, the brotherhood, right? These guys right here are my brothers, I love them, they're my brothers—and the whole concept of uniting, that's like a big family—the Chicano people. Self-determination for the whole family. The family is real important growing up as a Chicano, the family values, really tied into chicanismo as a whole. Once again the ego is playing a role where we will divide our family and step on our brothers and sisters. Also in the indigenous people the family is important, so it's part of our make-up. (Kelly 1993a, 266)

Had Yoatl said only what Márez cites, perhaps one could argue that his thought, and, by extension, the music of Aztlán Underground, was devoid of the "essentialisms" (what Márez perceives as "primordial," "pregiven," and "blood reality" attachments) that have typically defined Chicano cultural nationalism. Moreover, Márez's intention of loosening the tight nationalist hold in Chicano rap proves difficult given its enduring investment in "la raza."

THIS IS FOR LA RAZA?

Gilroy (1991, 115) has noted how "Hispanic hip hoppers in Los Angeles" have "borrowed . . . the soul and hip hop styles of Afro-America, as well as techniques like mixing, scratching, and sampling, as part of their invention of a new mode of cultural production and self-identification." While this is true, I would argue the "borrowing" is more of a two-way exchange, especially if we add clothes and car customizing, as well as other cultural markers most often noticed in California. Lorraine Ali importantly observes:

> Chicano gang culture is another aspect of Latino culture that has become chic in the 1990s. *Lowrider* is among the fastest-growing magazines in the nation and is even published in Japan. Lowrider-style cars, seen in videos by Ice Cube and Kriss Kross, are all the rage even outside of L.A. In fact, MTV recently raffled off Dr. Dre's Chevy Impala—so it's likely some goofy kid in Idaho will be pumping hydraulics in a Wal-Mart parking lot. (1993, 72)

David Reyes and Tom Waldman (1998, 161) similarly remark, "some of the better-known black rappers from L.A. used lowriders in their videos which exposed this long-time fad to teens all across the country and overseas." Rather than debate who owns what and what belongs to whom, if we were to consider musical acts such as the predominantly African American composed group War, whose music is very "Latin inspired" and also popular with Chicanos, we would discover this "borrowing" is in fact more of a cross-cultural exchange, a point crucial to mention given how it is still lost on a range of commentators. John Storm Roberts, author of the influential book *The Latin Tinge: The Impact of Latin Ameri-*

can Music on the United States, questions the Latino authenticity of Los Angeles rappers like Kid Frost, Proper Dos, and Hi-C featuring Tony A., insisting that their respective songs "La Raza," "Mexican Power," and "Froggy Style" are, "despite its Spanglish, basically imitative of black rappers," "straight African-American in style and accent," and possessing "a great bass line but [there is] nothing particularly Latino about it" (Roberts 1999, 234–35). Yet what is "real" Latino rap? Although Roberts is clearly invested in maintaining the purity of culture, music historian Tony Sabournin recognizes that "None of these styles exists in isolation anymore. Many of these trends are a natural by-product of the socialization between blacks and Hispanics. Black influence has been present in much of the music, just as black artists have co-opted rhythmic elements from our sound" (Holston 1993, 130).[17] Although his point is well taken, one must ask if these styles ever did exist in isolation. For how could one forget the significance of "oldies" (now part of a music genre called "Old School" and heavily sampled in Chicano rap) among Chicanos, music performed primarily by African American artists from the 1950s onward, broaching Motown and classic soul songs. Even influential African American performer Brenton Wood (who also collaborates with Chicano rapper M.C. Blvd.), quoted on the back cover of the CD *Brown Eyed Soul: The Sound of East L.A., Volume Three*, insists these tunes constitute "a way of life—music that is passed from generation to generation like a family heirloom. If there is one word to describe Mexican culture, I would say it's *loyalty*. The Latino community is like one big family. I've had the good fortune of being adopted into this familia by loyal fans and friends. *¡Viva La Raza!*"

Along with the interethnic borrowing that exists between Chicano and black cultural producers, Chicano and black rap similarly sample from the cultural nationalist discourses emerging from their respective historical contexts. In a footnote, Gilroy (1991, 115) writes: "Kid Frost's absorbing release 'La Raza' borrows the assertive techniques of black nationalist rap, setting them to work in the construction of a Mexican-American equivalent." This is true, especially in light of the point Gilroy raises about the conflation of race and family, but it also poses a set of problems as to who counts as that family of "La Raza" and why, especially when we listen to this track sequentially with "Raza Unite" from *East Side Story* (1992) and two tracks off his third LP released in 1995 entitled *Smile Now, Die Later*, "La Familia" and "La Raza Part II."

First, an introduction is in order. Kid Frost—frequently called the pro-tégé of influential African American rapper and actor Ice-T—was born Arturo Molina Jr. on May 31, 1964 in Los Angeles, California. Although he was raised on military bases in Guam and Germany, his home base has always been the streets of East Los Angeles. Frost's hip-hop career began in the early 1980s, joining the ranks of the hip-hop outfit Uncle Jam's Army (UJA) and performing as the opening act for rap groups like Run-DMC who were beginning to make their mark on the scene. In 1984 he cut his first records, "Rough Cut" with Ice-T and "Commando Rock" with C-Jam, followed by 1985's "Terminator." Mistakenly oft-cited as his first single, "La Raza" was first released as a single in 1990 and appeared on his first LP for Virgin Records, *Hispanic Causing Panic*, during the same year. Both single and album, though, are indisputably foundational moments of Chicano rap music given how they put Chicano discourse on the airwaves, music charts, and the hip-hop map.[18]

Kid Frost and "La Raza" also revived the tropes of Chicanismo emerging from the cultural discourse of the 1960s and 1970s Chicano move-ment and situated them in a contemporary, popular frame. And just as Corky Gonzales is recurrently credited as one of Chicano social poetry's forefathers given the pervasive impact of "I am Joaquín" (stemming from the family-based nationalism of the Crusade for Justice), which had a similar wide-spread circulation both in and outside academic circles, Kid Frost, in related terms, would soon be rendered the godfather of Chicano rap in view of the fact that his promotion of la raza in "La Raza" similarly catapulted Chicano consciousness by way of kinship association.[19] Frost's nomination as "godfather" makes even more sense given his role as a forefather and predecessor in Chicano and Latino hip-hop culture and the continued prominence of his image.[20] The genealogical convergence of rap and poetic forms that unite Gonzales and Frost help us understand both the poetic articulation of cultural nationalism in these forms and the deployment of kinship discourse in the creation of community empower-ment narratives.

Aside from the formalistic differences between poetry and rap mu-sic (technological differences, for example), the ideological, cultural, and historical contexts from which they develop closely align these two re-lated expressive forms. Indeed, when comparing Chicano rap and poetry, one can clearly see a "family resemblance." In "Chicanismo: A Rhetorical Analysis of Themes and Images of Selected Poetry from the Chicano Movement," Michael Victor Sedano (1980) observes that movimiento poetry can be recognized by, for example, its identificatory grounding of archetypal figures such as the farmworker, the pachuco, the Indian, and specific topographies (either the barrio or Aztlán). The themes and images Sedano identifies in Chicano poetry are the very content of Chicano hip-hop culture. For example, Kid Frost's work mirrors an ethic of cultural, community values advocated in *El Plan Espiritual de Aztlán* while the overlapping desire for self-designation in "I am Joaquín" and "La Raza" is striking given how Joaquín declares "I am the eagle and serpent of/Aztec civilization" (R. Gonzales 1972, 16) while Kid Frost says, in "La Raza," "It's in my blood to be an Aztec warrior." Finally, Chicano rap and Chicano movement poetry must be read as resistance narratives, especially given how both emerge from youth culture and social movement trajectories.[21]

The family-*cum*-nation in Chicano rap especially solidifies the genealogical linkage to movimiento politics. Both Raegan Kelly and Mandalit del Barco rightly contextualize Chicano rap within Chicano movement (literary) history. In "Hip Hop Chicano: A Separate but Parallel Story," Kelly (1993b, 73) begins the section of her essay entitled "It's a Tribe Thing" with a quote from Carlos Muñoz Jr.'s book *Youth, Identity, Power: The Chicano Movement* (1989) that reads: "I am a revolutionary . . . because creating life amid death is a revolutionary act. Just as building nationalism in an era of imperialism is a life-giving act . . . We are an awakening people, an emerging nation, a new breed." This quote is in fact from Corky Gonzales who, as Kelly rightly notes, "brought people from every corner of the varrio together in the name of self-determination and La Raza" (73) under the auspices of the Chicano Youth Liberation Conference in 1969. Likewise, Mandalit del Barco, in "Rap's Latino Sabor," argues:

> In the same way the old-school Latinos identified with Boriqua nationalism, Frost followed a tradition of Chicano identification with the myths and symbols of ancient Meso-American cultures for national self-determination. In the sixties and seventies, during the height of the Chicano movimiento, when César Chávez was organizing farm workers for better wages and living conditions, when the Brown Berets were fighting oppression, racism, and war, poets like José Montoya, Alberto Alurista, J.L. Navarro, and Raul Salinas gave voice to Chicano revolution, pride, and identity. (del Barco 1996, 72)

Del Barco goes on to cite five lines from Montoya's "El Louie," linking it to Frost's song "Spaced Out" from *East Side Story* in which the listener is invited to "enter into the mind of a Chicano storyteller," clearly a lyrical and literary "descendant of Salinas's barrio poem 'A Trip through the Mind Jail'" (73), and his 1980 book of poetry with the same title, I might add. Del Barco is right on the mark in citing these particular poems by Montoya and Salinas. Since del Barco mentions the names J. L. Navarro and (Alberto Urista) Alurista, I would also add "To a Dead Lowrider" (1972) by Navarro; "Nuestra Casa Denver '69" and "Pachuco Paz" from *Nationchild Plumaroja* (1972) by Alurista; as well as Tino Villanueva's "Pachuco Remembered" (1972) as key moments in the genealogy of Chicano poetic consciousness from which Frost's music, in particular, and Chicano rap music, in general, emerge.[22]

Conversantly, the pachuco plays a significant role for Chicano rappers and Chicano poets given how he stands as a symbol of cultural nationalist opposition to the state. Commenting on Chicano movement-era poetry by Montoya, Salinas, and Villanueva, critic Rafael Grajeda—building on the arguments made by Frantz Fanon on the emergence and development of a national culture—argues that, "the pachuco experience of the past then becomes not only a 'set piece' in the hands of the writer, not only the source of 'interesting,' exciting, quaint and escapist literature, but instead is 'brought up to date', made appropriate to the needs of the liberation movement" (Grajeda 1980, 55). Yet while the pachuco may embody Chicano nationalist desires for resistance and empowerment, he also "personifies the myth of Chicano manliness" (Fregoso 1993b, 271).[23] As Angie Chabram-Dernersesian (1992, 82) has observed, the Chicano cultural subject has been typically defined by a "myriad of male identities: el pachuco, el vato loco, el cholo, the Aztec, the militant Chicano, the existential Chicano, the political Chicano, the precocious Chicano, the Jungian Chicano-o-o-o," and the "mostly authoritarian fathers" are identifiable by first name alone: Antonio, Joaquín, Adan, Miguel, Juan, and Louie. Chicano hip-hop lines up the same archetypal figures (especially the pachuco and the gangster) and also highlights seminal rappers identifiable by "first name" alone; among them: Frost, Blvd., Conejo, Lil Rob, SPM, Sir Dyno, and Slow Pain.[24] Ultimately, the rapper-poet "creates and defines an audience and converts that audience to the identity the poet defines" (Sedano 1980, 178). Like Corky Gonzales's Joaquín, the identity created and defined within Frost's "La Raza"—and embodied by Frost himself—is ultimately framed by heteronormative masculinity.

A legendary anthem for Chicanos indeed, "La Raza" represented for many a shift in comprehending rap and hip-hop as solely black cultural productions and reinforced the positions taken by Nancy Guevara (1987), Juan Flores (1988), and Mandalit del Barco (1996) about Chicano and Latino empowerment via these particular urban expressive forms.[25] The "absorption" of this song was phenomenal, as Los Angeles radio stations, booming sound systems in many cars and trucks, and music video programming (MTV, Friday Night Videos, and Video One) frequently played the song and video (directed by Andrew Doucette) in 1990. In the liner notes to the CD compilation *Latin Lingo: Hip-Hop from La Raza* (1995), Gabriel Alvarez equally observes: "'La Raza' is simply the Mexican hip-hop theme song. Whether it be a Cinco de Mayo celebration or a quinceañera, Kid Frost's 1990 nationalistic declaration plays loudly." I remember the sense of pride the song ignited for many Chicanos, young and old; after all, this song was for them: La Raza. Or was it?

Who is "La Raza"? And who can claim "La Raza" as theirs? In the advertisement for the album *Hispanic Causing Panic*, we are told: "No sabes lo que esta pasando/Que pasa/De todas manera no es para ti/Porque es para la raza." The ad also shows only Frost, *sin la raza*. The song "La Raza" repeats this sentiment with its lyrics which, translated from the Spanish above, go like this: "Some of you don't know what's happening/¿Qué Pasa?/It's not for you anyway/Cuz this is for La Raza!" Yet the song is not only addressed to La Raza—that is, an extended brown family; it is also addressed to "some of you" who don't know what's happening. And even though the song is not for "them," it is used as a vehicle to confront "them" for not "getting it." Are "they" white people in particular, or generally those who aren't Chicanos? Recall Frost's reference to "us" at the beginning of the song: "vatos/cholos/you call us what you will." We know it's in his "blood to be an Aztec warrior" and he's "Chicano" and "brown and proud," yet those who are as well may not find it as easy to put in a bid for inclusion into his nation of "La Raza." Just when we think it is that non-Chicano he's rapping to ("The foreign tongue I'm speaking is known as caló"), he makes it clear that maybe it is a "Chicano," who's not really a Chicano in his estimation, to whom he's speaking: "¿Y sabes que loco?/yo soy un malo/¿tú no sabes nada?/your brain is hollow/been hit in the head too many times with a palo" ("You know what, crazy?/I'm a bad dude/Don't you know anything?"). In the process, this "you" is emasculated and, basically, fucked in every sense of the word: *he's* a "pee-wee" who "can't get none never"; when he tries to act cool, he's told "you're so cool I'm gonna call you a culo" (asshole); and he's so pathetic, his own "varrio [neighborhood] doesn't even back you up/they just look at your ass/and call you a poo-butt." While this guy is reduced to an (uncontrollable) asshole, emasculated, and "fucked," he is nonetheless important enough to be the subject of address.

As I understand it, his manhood doesn't measure up enough to be considered part of "La Raza." This *"vavoso"* (slobbering idiot) isn't "hard" enough. And where does this leave Chicanas? Can they enter the raza scene? After Kid Frost equates his homeboys with "La Raza," it doesn't seem likely. In the article "Kid Frost: A 'Hispanic' Spreading Panic!" Fernando Savage (1990a, 38) cites Frost as claiming: "Ever since the movie *Colors*, everyone thinks the Blacks started gang banging, they don't realize we Chicanos have been gang banging since the forties." Savage responds: "Something all of us Chicanos should be real proud of, La Raza snuffing Raza." Although an explanation of the predicament of Chicano gangs could take volumes, Savage is on the mark when he charges Kid Frost with pitting "La Raza" against raza.[26]

PUTTING FAMILY FIRST OR BOY'S NOISE AND GANGSTER LEANINGS

In Frost's reduction of la raza to an exclusively self-defined familia, or as Gilroy puts it, merely one instance of the many versions of family in the racial "accumulation of families," unity is the product of preferential selection since it embraces the brown bodies that, in his estimation, count. I don't wish to gloss over the complex reasons why gangs have united under the banner of family, and how Frost recognizes this when he claims: "There are thousands and thousands of little gangsters who took the song to heart" and "gangs are a subject that's plagued the streets of L.A. for a long, long time. Reality is hard and most people don't want to hear it" (Savage 1990b, 10). Frost, though, implies that only straight Chicano men experience hard reality. So what about the "hard realities" of other raza? Frost's song creates a divide between *his raza* and those who are *not really raza.*

In a different yet not unrelated vein, "La Raza" could be said to mirror "I am Joaquín" in that the song establishes that all-seeing, masculinist autobiographical "I" claiming to represent la raza, a common move in Chicano rap. Although Frost has claimed that he "didn't know [he] was going to become a Hispanic spokesman" (Savage 1990b, 10) and "I'm only a role model to my kids" (A. Ruíz 1996, 28), he has also remarked that he "considers [himself] a voice for Hispanics, a voice for La Raza, a voice for the young Chicano minority that's out there living in the streets" (del Barco 1996, 72). I am inclined to believe the latter claim given how the narrative voice of "La Raza" inevitably assumes an "I" that speaks for the collective "La Raza," just as the "I" in "I am Joaquín" embodies the Chicano community. As Alfonso Ruíz (1996, 28) writes, although Frost, "like a lot of rappers these days, goes to great lengths to say he's no role model, no voice for his people . . . that may be hard to do" considering he has "hits like . . . 'La Raza' under his belt."[27]

Similarly, the Santa Ana–based Chicano Brotherhood adopts the technique of employing the representative speaker of the nation, who also embodies the nation.[28] Although Chicano Brotherhood was originally composed of four members (whose first tape "Cruising Bristol" [1991] was a local success), founding member Wino (Manuel Moreno) retained the name even after the other three men left the crew. Chicano Brotherhood has since released two compelling cassette singles with Moreno solely at the helm: "G.T.A./That's What It's Like" (1994) and "The Finished Product/Way of Life" (1995). The publicity photo for Chicano Brotherhood (see figure 13), however, shows Wino dressed in almost all black, in a squatting position, with one hand over the other; he is facing the camera and viewer and presumably stares us down behind his "maddoggers." The paradox, however, lies in the fact that to the left of Wino the vertical lettering announces "Chicano Brotherhood." By looking at this image alone, are we to assume this one man alone is Chicano Brotherhood? The text on the back of the photo answers in the affirmative: "They call me Wino, a.k.a. The Brown Boracho. Chicano Brotherhood is comprised of myself and no one else. However Chicano Brotherhood represents not one man, but a union of crazy Aztecs fighting the system." As Frost speaks for la raza and Joaquín represents the masses of his people, Wino's notion of Chicano Brotherhood is ultimately predicated on the experience of the individual. Furthermore, Wino informs us: "I like to rap the songs as if I'm talking to a homeboy."[29] This points to the gendered dynamics of poetic performances that function as homosocial acts in which men perform for

Chicano Brotherhood™

FIGURE 13
Promotional
photograph
for Chicano
Brotherhood.

other men. The contradictions evident in Wino's discourse also extend to the point of denying his association with "brown pride." He insists: "I don't waste my time talking about brown pride, though I am all for the raza and the brown movement." But whether or not he wishes to talk about "brown pride," it virtually becomes an inescapable endeavor given the fact that Chicano Brotherhood's name alone, not to mention the subject matter of his raps, stages a performance that is explicitly marked "Chicano," thus making an unmistakable contribution to the "brown pride" meta-narrative infusing the Chicano hip-hop scene. Indeed, his "Brotherhood" recalls the rhetoric espoused by the likes of José Armas.

Yet let us again return to Frost. In "Raza Unite" from *East Side Story* (1992), Frost addresses the violence Savage claims he (Frost) promotes in "La Raza." The lyrics speak to the pervasive fact of gang violence affecting countless Chicano youths. And the fact that he claims "the barrio Aztlán" in this track signals his refusal to identify with a particular neighborhood or street in favor of the Chicano nation. Within this nationalist topography, he warns, we must "stop letting the blood spill man." This instance, for me, is rather powerful, a moment in which family or blood must be kept together so as to prevent "fratricidal" gang-related murders.

As Gilroy (1992, 331) notes about African Americans calling themselves "brothers and sisters," this articulation of extended or chosen kinship ties "carries the ambiguity of a democratic tradition of struggle." Brotherhood may indeed prove to be an important familial trope in the service of halting gang violence, and one cannot lose sight of this. And yet we cannot overlook or dismiss the violence affecting young Chicanas in and around gangs, a point emphasized in Allison Anders's film *Mi Vida Loca/My Crazy Life* (1994), and thus calling into question the presumption of "fratricide" in light of homicidal acts that cut across gender lines.[30]

The trope of the male-centered family materializes in the 1995 *Smile Now, Die Later* in which Frost (who has now formally dropped the Kid—a disavowal of Oedipal ties perhaps?) hones in on the family "proper."[31] Set to replayed samples of El Chicano's "(Se Fue Mi) Cha Chita" and Sly and the Family Stone's "Family Affair," Frost raps "La Familia," which is supposedly about creating kinship ties based on last names since "we're all in the same gang." He continues:

> Kid Frost back and I'm down/and my familia's anyone whose skin is brown/ rancheros in their trucks or the grape vans/taggers in the alley with a bag full of spray cans/here come the jura/gotta bail out/and even them coconut cops/ but they sell out/The cholos, the cholas who went soft/It's the mean mafioso Gangsta Frost/Commin' atcha don't try to slam me/Cuz Mexicans always got a big ass family/The cuetes, the valas/The Chevy Impalas/The gang bang cycle's what the media calls us/So if you're brown/You're down/So stay proud/And remember no busters allowed/Cuz the Mexican peoples is a big ass gang/ Yeah/It's a family thing. ("La Familia" 1995)

Frost also informs us his barrio is "East Los/Aztlán." That, however, shouldn't matter since, paraphrasing Eric B. and Rakim's famous declaration, "It ain't where you're from/It's where you're at." That is, Chicano identification based on one's place of origin is secondary to politico-familial allegiance. If this were true, Frost could be said to be opening up admission into "La Raza," welcoming new members into a collective he now calls "La Familia." But while he accepts the coconut cops, the rancheros, the "gone-soft" cholos and cholas, taggers, and, last but not least, "anyone whose skin is brown," one wonders just who are the "busters" who aren't allowed. Also, at the same time Frost includes a grab-bag selection of familia members; la familia, like la raza, seems to collapse into a "gang"-centered family: "The gang-bang cycle's what the media calls us." La familia, then, is based on blood ties yet excludes the unwanted despite claiming to embrace all "whose skin is brown." Again, I don't think "busters" or "culos" are simply white people. However, they do stand as a threat to the Chicano family circle.

"La Raza Part II" (1995) returns to la raza as an organizing principle. The track begins with a voice over from Taylor Hackford's film, *Bound by Honor/Blood In, Blood Out,* which states: "You got no fucking idea what la raza means do you? It's about our people out there, working, surviving with pride and dignity. That's raza." Again, who exactly is this "you" being addressed (and why does Frost assume the "you" listens to his music)? Frost kicks off his rap by claiming that many things have changed since 1990; he has a lot more homeboys and *gente* (people) behind him. While the tune revives many of the brown pride tropes raised in earlier tracks, he informs us "a brown fist represents Frost in the house," "It's all about the red, white, and green," and the "lump in [his] throat" is there because he "just can't swallow [his] brown pride." The connections to "I am Joaquín" are more obvious here, especially when Frost's first-person "I" does all the speaking and the rhetorical foundation of this "I" sets in motion a staunch male-centered narrative contoured by cultural nationalism: "Here I go again/And I'm bound to win/ Because I'm proud of the color of my skin/You see I'm kinda like [Oscar] de la Hoya/I'm filled with the spirit of an Aztec warrior."[32] With Mexico as "the motherland" from where he draws his familial bond, the "solution" he comes up with "is brown revolution/So pump your fist to this/And wear your Mexican flag/ And be proud that your khakis sag."

In this equation, brown revolution, then, is for those whose mother is Mexico, who wear sagging khakis and Mexican flags. But what about those who wear the flag yet not the khakis or who don't call Mexico mother? Again, the question arises: who is la raza? While I understand he wants to embrace those who are, simply put, affiliated with "gangs" in some form or fashion, the collapsing of la familia and la raza to tout his paternalistic notions of inclusion and exclusion raises red flags—

alongside those that are red, white, and green—regarding his political commitments. Frost alleges in an interview,

> You gotta realize that I come from the streets of East Los Angeles, California, where the gangs and stuff don't just band together for the name of a street or a barrio, but it's more of a familia. It's a family thing. And if you're down with the family, then you're protected. That's your family. It's not your mom and your dad, it's your homeboys. (del Barco 1996, 73)[33]

To cap it off, "La Raza II," which loops El Chicano's "Look of Love," ends with the line "This is for the raza." Five years later and not much has changed. To claim la raza and la familia, in Frost's estimation, one must be male, preferably with gangster leanings.

If it weren't for the gang-as-family trope so evident in his work (something Corky Gonzales would surely not approve of despite Frost's wake-up call to "Moms and Dads [who] need to get out and see that kids just ain't connecting with them" [A. Ruíz 1996, 28]), I would suggest that Frost is operating in the same vein as movement-era scholars Octavio Romano-V. and Nick Vaca in that they, too, contest Anglo images of the Chicano family. In Frost's own words: "In that movie *Colors*, they made us look stupid as fuck; unorganized, no stability. You're talking about organized street gangs that have been around since the 1940s, established in East L.A. way before the Crips and the Bloods in the 70s. Don't tell me our organization and families are loose-knit." (Ali 1993, 72). Frost's godfather image (see figure 14) must also be linked to the influence of gangster culture on the hip-hop scene (in "La Raza" Frost likens himself to Al Capone) as well as the street culture with which he aligns himself.[34] Frost, however, never fails to insist that he does not promote gang *violence*. In fact, he maintains that his music discourages it:

> I'm not glorifying or glamorizing the gang life and going out and telling these gangsters to go out there and gang bang and kill each other. In fact, what we're doing is totally the opposite, man. We're working with the Coalition to End Barrio Warfare, we work with the movement for La Raza, which is about uplifting the minds of young Hispanics, to take them to another level. (del Barco 1996, 73)

The explicit contradictions in Frost's logic call our attention to who really belongs (in his estimation) to la familia de la raza. Because his narratives

FIGURE 14 Promotional photograph for Kid Frost. Reproduced with permission by Rocky Schenck.

rely upon fixed codes of masculinity (even if he steers clear of nuclear kinship formations)—urging his listener to remain hard, so to speak, and persist in creating familia not with one's mother and father but one's homeboys—Frost cannot but help conjure up a methodology that sanctions a gang arrangement. That is, although he may not condone the violence of gangs, he implicitly supports the gendered factionalism that sustains their existence within the contours of his Chicano family or nation.

Ultimately, Frost's construction of a family-based nationalism rests on the threat of emasculation to the point that his sentiment mirrors the patriarchy that is part and parcel of the dominant culture. Thus, the authority he wishes to contest through the political solidarity of la familia is in fact transposed by an authority dictated through the (god)father's law. In such terms familial nationalism sustains a patriarchal hegemony that also thrives upon gang formation, given its reification within the dominant media and the legal system. I do not want to suggest that Chicano rappers endorse the state violence that regulates and disciplines economically disenfranchised ethnic communities. As noted, their defiant stances against racism and criminalization, for example, are necessary strands of political thinking and emergent mobilization. Yet to maintain an exclusionary platform contoured by a regulated gender politics and group (read gang) membership is to minimize claims for community solidarity.

The "gangsta rap" genre, in which numerous recent Chicano rappers situate their work, often espouses a misogynist sentiment issued by all-male acts whose membership, demarcated along gender lines and sexual hierarchy, mirrors and embodies the all-male membership of street and prison gangs.[35] Moreover, many Chicano rappers who adopt the "gangsta" stance are not mere "studio gangsters" (that is, record company–constructed gangsters). Some of the first rap acts to declare their allegiances to actual street gangs include Brownside, who announces itself "stra8 off the streets of East L.A.," and Los Angeles Chicano rapper Conejo, who unabashedly declares his gang associations on his 1999 CD *City of Angels.* Publications such as *Latin Rap Magazine* have broached the issue of gang affiliation and the tensions existing between rap artists and audiences based on claims to geography (e.g., Southern California versus Northern California).[36]

In *Nuthin' but a "G" Thang: The Culture and Commerce of Gangsta Rap*, Eithne Quinn (2005) has teased out the kinship discourse that underscores black gangsta rap, clearly articulated with regards to Death Row Records' "label-as-family" trope. Yet some scholars believe that family and gangsta narratives might be disentangled and distinguished from one another. Compellingly suggesting that a black family- or black nation-affirmative song like Tupac Shakur's "Keep Ya Head Up" is "more disturbing than gangsta rap . . . precisely because it is so easily accommodated, so easily routinized in ways that reproduce the status quo," Wahneema Lubiano (1998, 247) argues that family values campaigns staged by rappers are not always in synch with procreative kinship networks advocated by dominant society. However, the family in gangsta rap discourse in many instances refers to all-male collectives. It is important, then, not to insist that family values discourse is more insidious than gangsta rap given their frequent codependency. Consider The G-Fellas, headed by rapper Slow Pain, who, in an ad for their CD in *Low Rider Magazine*, pose in gang-familia, mafioso style. The photo of three men is surrounded by a frame as if it were a family portrait. That Chicano rappers borrow from the Italian mafioso image highlighted in films such as *The Godfather*, *Scarface*, and *GoodFellas* is also hardly surprising given how family for the mafioso is one of life's most valuable assets but not as important as the value of monetary exchange and the provisions of (male) omnipotence.[37]

Yet consider, in another register, the rapper and singer MC Blvd., an ITP Records recording artist based in Los Angeles, who has been called a "reality rapper . . . on a mission of reality" (Rodríguez 1993, 62). Blvd. speaks to the plight of gangs while the overriding message of his music, he has said, is "to have a good time and accept each other as brothers" (62). On the covers of his CD and cassette *I Remember You Homie*, the rules of thumb to which Blvd. adheres, and that figuratively and literally frame his image, are placed in the four corners of the sleeve: Respect, Honor, Loyalty, and Family.[38] With this is mind, consider the track "We-R-Family," off his LP *I Remember You Homie* (1994), which samples Sister Sledge's dance classic "We Are Family" as well as Laid Back's "White Horse." The song begins with the urgent plea to "love your family" since they are, as Blvd. puts it, the "number one priority." This family, as it is made fairly obvious, is biologically tied; but not for long. Soon the focus on family shifts to engage the "brother on brother" violence mentioned above. When Blvd. hears about a "brother" killing another "brother," he tells his "carnal" whom he's addressing in the song that "it hurts more than a mother." Enter the mother, who embodies the pain and suffering of the community as well as has her hands full representing Mexico (or Aztlán).[39] Blvd.'s solution is to establish raza unity: "Viva la familia/And La Raza de hoy/Come together brown people/Understand me homeboy/Somos *familia*." Here we see familia and raza operating on parallel lines of political impetus for uniting "brown people." Blvd.'s intended audience is obviously male, specifically homeboys. In the final analysis, the message is that we are family, we are raza. Yet the exchange of information is strictly between men, and the male-only familia or raza is the modus operandi for self-empowerment.[40] If the exchange of information is not explicitly an exchange between brown men, then, as Frost has shown us, it is one in which white men are implicated or invited to listen in (no matter what their position) as well. As Paulla Ebron (1991, 27) puts it in her discussion of the music of 2 Live Crew and Public Enemy: their music is more often than not "Black men bonding with white men over gender and over the control of women [that] enables Black men to collude in practices which devalue women."

Similarly, Wahneema Lubiano draws our attention to identical matters found in the film *Deep Cover* (1992). In "Don't Talk with Your Eyes Closed: Caught in the Hollywood Gun Sights," Lubiano (1997, 140) cleverly unveils "the way black nationalism most thoroughly coalesces into a conventional master narrative . . . by means of its centering of the family romance." The force behind black nationalism in her terms consists of the following:

> Within the terms of black nationalism, the black dreamed-of, autonomous subject is inevitably male, heterosexual, and in training to be a powerful patriarch—only in and on "black" terms, terms that are both separate from and continuous with those of the hegemonic culture. (1997, 139)

Citing an essay on the Anita Hill and Clarence Thomas case in which she discusses the recuperation of black nationalism in such a manner (Lubiano 1992a), Lubiano also finds value in "some deployments of [black nationalism that] have allowed those of us engaged in black cultural studies to consider as a corrective to other racist concepts." For these deployments, she is "appreciative" (Lubiano 1997, 139). Working in tandem with Gilroy, Lubiano's position—which could easily be dismissed on the basis of essentialism or nationalism—is in fact a position that resists sidestepping historical specificity; it considers African Americans as social subjects defined by and through discourses of power.

Despite the critical interrogations I'm calling for, we must not fail to locate value in similar deployments for Chicanos, especially for disenfranchised Chicano and Chicana youths moved by the rhymes and rhythms for la raza. In the collection *Black Popular Culture* edited by Gina Dent (1992), following the presentation of Paul Gilroy's "It's a Family Affair: Black Culture and the Trope of Kinship" (1993b), readers are presented with transcribed discussions that took place at the conference of the same name. Fittingly, Lubiano remarks on Gilroy's paper. Her response:

> It's probably ironic, but not surprising, that your critique of black nationalist tropes of the family might do the work that feminist critiques seem not to have been able to do. And when I say feminist, I mean black and non-black, lesbian and straight. The reason I find it ironic is that, given the way the trope

works, there's a particular part of the family that always saves another particular part of the family. I'm still ready to warm my hands at the fire of anybody's critique of the family . . . [African American women writers'] critique of the family trope gets called anti-black, but maybe yours will be more successful. (Lubiano 1992b, 331)

Intriguing is Gilroy's quick response to Lubiano: that his paper does not wish to rule out "family" as provoking instances of resistance. Although he claims in his paper that "the familialization of politics is still a problem" (Gilroy 1993b, 207), he doesn't want to simply discard the family as an organizing principle:

I just want to be clear about what I said and what I didn't say. For me, there is a promise in that notion of family which maybe—we can struggle over it—in this new democratic politics we're trying to construct, we can make over. But it has to be somehow disorganically figured. . . . I'm saying that I would like us to try and be more imaginative about it or, at the very least, to think before we invoke it. (Gilroy 1992, 331)

As my analysis works to interrogate the authority of the biological family for Chicanos and Chicanas, decentering the chauvinism of masculinist and heterosexual kinship figurations, I also want to follow Gilroy's complicating remarks. It is true that family is not our only option for community formation, nor should it be. However, it remains an important index of possibilities for unity, and thus we should not be too quick to subtract the value of kinship discourse from the constitution of Chicano communitarian politics.

Chicano rap is saturated with familia references on numerous levels. The label on which Norwalk's Most Wanted, ES Clique, Brown Pride, Lil Rob, N'Land Clique, The Brown Intentions, and The Young Pachucos appear is aptly titled Familia Records, based in the southern California city of Artesia. In 1998 the rap collective Darkroom Familia from Northern California released *Penitentiary Chances*, a short video written and directed by José and Ed Quiroz and an accompanying CD soundtrack on Dogday Records. I'm inclined to think that the use of the term "familia" is in direct reference to the prison gang La Nuestra Familia, and perhaps this is the intention of some rappers and collectives.[41] However, given that both Northern and Southern California rappers refer to "la familia," the term more often than not functions as a metaphor for carnalismo.[42] For there is also the Denver-based Unforgotten Records outfit, Unforgotten Familia, and the California collective, Underground 805 Family. One factor links these disparate acts, though: they more often than not command an exclusively male membership.

STATES OF SUBORDINATION

While their role within it has largely gone unrecognized due to the depressingly few recordings that have surfaced, Chicana performers have nonetheless contributed to and interrupted the male dominance of the Chicano hip-hop scene. Chicana MC JV's *Nayba'Hood Queen* (1994) marks a key moment in Chicano rap history in which a woman disproved the suspicion that the scene was one strictly reserved for the participation of men. With titles like "Girlz Do It Better" and "Stompin' on the Concrete (Like I Own the Street)," JV's voice unapologetically lays claims to female sexuality while touting the "brown and proud" rhetoric of her male counterparts. Curtis Márez (1996, 126) persuasively argues that JV "reappropriates the power of the Virgen de Guadalupe—commonly called the 'Reina de México y Emperatriz de América'—so as to construct a working-class Chicana 'gangsta' persona." And yet, in the case of JV, one must ask how much control she had in crafting her own image given the way her "lyrical persona" often relies upon the backing of these counterparts. Indeed, "I Need a Man's Touch," one of the tracks on *Nayba'Hood Queen*, could be taken to mean that this touch must be one that the godfather himself needs to provide since Frost helped write and produce several of her tracks including "G-String," "Dog U Out," and "Slow Down" for a label, Thump Records, which prior to her CD privileged male MCs.[43]

In a footnote to her aforementioned essay, Mandalit del Barco (1996) identifies two "underground" Chicana rappers who, "on the feminist tip," have moved beyond merely expressing their sexuality and directly challenged "macho MCs": Laura Segura from Salinas, California and Alexandra Quiroz, also known as "Teardrop, the Brown Queen," who has worked with A Lighter Shade of Brown, notably on their single "Latin Active." Del Barco cites the lyrics of untitled songs by both rappers that forcefully confront the Cuban American rapper Mellow Man Ace whose track "Mentirosa" was simply a diatribe against a gold-digging, sex-crazed tramp. These lyrics are certainly worth citing here. First, Segura: "Eres un

Latino/Yeah, you're all the same/Quit playin' that game of macho/'cause I'll send you home in shame/So let me tell you, straight up/Time to school you with a lesson/A woman's not a game, much less a toy that you be messin'." Second, Teardrop: "So the girls think you're cute/Hmmm/No me importa/But you had to go chase girls and play me for a tonta/So who's this girl named Lola?/Yeah, the one who said hola/Everytime she looks at you/Detienes por la cola/I heard she asked you out and of course, you said sí/Fueron a cenar and you forgot about me/You're a mentiroso, A big time baboso/Don't dare play me out/Porque eres un chismoso" (del Barco 1996, 93–94). Such pointed comebacks should not be surprising given the position in which Chicanas have been placed in the raps of their so-called Chicano and Latino brothers. When Chicanas do surface in Chicano male rhymes, they are sketched along the lines of the woman addressed in Mellow's infamous "Mentirosa."[44]

As the politics of women in hip-hop is a topic that has generated much debate and a substantial body of writing (namely by Tricia Rose, Joan Morgan, T. Denean Sharpley-Whiting, and Gwendolyn D. Pough within African American contexts and Raquel Z. Rivera in those Latino/a), a queer Latino/a rap presence—and an acknowledgement of that presence—has quite recently surfaced (although Rivera does signal the early intervention of lesbian hip-hop dancer Diana from Dynasty Rockers as well as instances of "lesbian chic" surfacing for male consumption). Contrary to the homophobia espoused by the likes of groups like Cypress Hill and the heteronormativity assumed to fuel hip-hop expression, the emergence of a fittingly titled "Homo-Hop" movement is exemplified by Latino/a artists like the self-identified "gay gangsta, cholo fag, and homo thug" Deadlee (see figure 15), Bay Area lesbian rapper JenRO, and Chicano FTM transgender performer Tre Vásquez (also known as Rigomortis).[45] Alex Hinton's documentary *Pick Up the Mic* (2005)—about queer interventions in hip-hop that features Deadlee—offers an important revision of Richard Montes's documentary *Pass the Mic!* (2002) by title alone.[46] That is, whereas queers have traditionally been overlooked in the passing of the mic, they are compelled nonetheless to pick it up on their own terms. An earlier queer Chicano perspective in hip-hop, however, can be traced to the Summer/ Fall 1993 issue of the magazine or journal *Changing Men: Issues in Gender, Sex, and Politics.* Containing Ricardo Avila's lyrics to a rap song performed with the band The Merkins entitled "Homo/Latino," the message

FIGURE 15 Deadlee. Photograph reproduced with permission by Michael Gregg Michaud.

is a powerfully articulated statement on Chicano gay male identity. Avila raps or writes: "Sometimes I wish I was a white man/Well, this simply can't be/'Coz I'm a faggot/And a Mexican American/I got chubby cheeks/ And I go down on a man's dick/I was raised Catholic/Traditional/ . . . So can you see why/I'm all mixed up/And caught between these rivaling identities." Including a "reggae rap interlude," the backup singers or go-go dancers also chant: "He's a Homo! Latino!/I said a Ho-Ho-Homo Latino!/He lick your boo-tay/And stick it in good/He love the Virgin of Guadalupe" (Avila 1993, 23). Avila's rap was clearly a response to the heteromasculinist desires grounding the work of most Chicano male rappers during the early 1990s.[47]

Chicano rap and many strands of Chicano popular culture have centralized the tough and street-wise homeboy so often that he typically becomes the authentic cultural representative par excellence and a fetishized hypermasculine commodity. Yet in his work Deadlee has uprooted this image by rearticulating it in his music within blatantly queer scenarios. Despite the pan-ethnic masculinist adoption of "gangster subjectivity" (notwithstanding the ability to lay claim to actual gangs), the rise of the "homeboy aesthetic" almost always signifies heterosexuality. With the work of those artists named above—as well as that of an artist like Héctor Silva who has collaborated with Deadlee at cultural events throughout the Los Angeles area—interrogating this aesthetic is part and parcel of challenging the masculinity and heteronormative tenets that would repudiate queer existence in the first place.[48] Deadlee's powerful video, *Good Soldier II* (2006), directed by Johnny Skandros Reyes and featuring African American singer Micah Barnes, forcefully articulates and contests such repudiation within a family-based context. "Sentenced to death" by his father for his inability to be "a good solider" (that is, a good straight family man), the son in the video and in the rap narrative refuses to conform to heteronormative demands and instead embraces his gay identity and sexuality.

The patriarchal impulse of Chicano rap, as reflected in the ways that kinship discourse has been deployed by its (god)father-like figures, need not always limit the possibilities of cultural nationalism and the family serving as mobilizing forces. Indeed, while continuing the critique of this impulse, it is still possible to highlight its strands of resistance and empowerment even within the very terms of kinship. In his essay "The State of Rap: Time and Place in Hip Hop Nationalism," Jeffrey Louis Decker insists that, with regards to African American rap and nationalism:

> Hip hop nationalism is particularly adept at interpreting the past in a manner that develops black consciousness about alternatives to the hegemony of U.S. nationalism. Yet, for black nationalism to be a sustained vehicle of social change, its conservative tendencies need to be addressed and transformed. The point I am trying to make is that within nation-conscious rap 'a certain sort of regression' . . . that manifests itself in a nostalgia for ancient Egypt or a romanticization of sixties black power, is not the only available form for reimagining the time and place of a new black militancy. (1993, 80; see also Zook 1992)

These insights are informative in this context given how strands of Chicano rap consciousness derive power from movimiento discourse. Like the cultural productions of the movement era, which stood "outside the official cultural apparatus," the nationalist sentiment in rap narratives also holds the potential to counter commercializing and regulating popular cultural forms and practices, insisting upon the value of cultural affirmation rather than market demands.[49] Take, for example, Pebo Rodríguez, a writer for *Low Rider Magazine* and distributer of Thump Records, who confesses: "I have to say, when the Chicano rappers are rapping about Chicanismo and being brown and proud, not everybody wants to hear that. Unfortunately, they segregate themselves and limit their audience. When record companies don't see big sales they want, they tend to think maybe it's just a fad. I told a lot of rappers that it's cool to be brown and proud, but not everybody wants to *hear* about that" (Ali 1993, 69; see also Raquel Z. Rivera [2003] for a discussion of commercial failure and the blame placed on cultural pride narratives). Rodríguez's comments highlight how cultural affirmation (and even resistance to domination) in Chicano rap are taken as roadblocks on the path to *economic* success. Thus, one can grasp the potency of Proper Dos's Frank V.'s words when he says: "I wasn't gonna be caught up in people telling me, 'Don't say Mexican, say brown, so you can appeal to everybody'. I just straight-out said 'Mexican Power'. I knew that would limit a lot of record sales, but it was about time somebody would say it, 'cause people were beating around the bush. We can't appeal to everybody. I think we gotta break some ice here" (Ali 1993, 69). While cultural nationalism is never immune to commodification or appropriation, Frank V.'s refusal to hide his "Mexican pride" is an important break from the conventional desire to break into the mainstream and rap for the sake of commercial profit.

The nationalist current that fuels this Chicano poetic consciousness is, to be sure, an important one, and we must not lose sight of that. In fact, I would insist that this current exemplifies one version of what David Lloyd calls "nationalisms against the state." As such, "the possibility of nationalism against the state lies in the recognition of the excess of the people over the nation and in the understanding that that is, beyond itself, the very logic of nationalism as a political phenomenon" (Lloyd 1997, 192). Chiefly in working-class contexts, where Chicano rap has been most instructive, this nationalism "from below" could be the stuff of empowerment and survival. As Frantz Fanon observes in his essay "On National Culture":

I am ready to concede that on the plane of factual being the past existence of an Aztec civilization does not change anything very much in the diet of the Mexican peasant of today. . . . But it has been remarked several times that this passionate search for a national culture which existed before the colonial era finds its legitimate reason in the anxiety shared by native intellectuals to shrink away from that Western culture in which they all risk being swamped. Because they realize they are in danger of losing their lives and thus becoming lost to their people, these men, hotheaded and with anger in their hearts, relentlessly determine to renew contact once more with the oldest and most pre-colonial springs of life of their people. (1963, 209–10)

Indeed, "these men," who, in a contemporary context, might be likened to Chicano male rappers and their audience, feel the need to hold on to the Aztec past that would at once help them retain, via "cultural memory," a sense of historical being while countering the positions of powerlessness they and their listeners are frequently placed in.[50] In other words, rap music may provide the soundtrack for struggle against the oppressive forces circumscribing Chicano and Latino lives.

In his article "Rap and La Raza," Marcos McPeek Villatoro (1994) documents the everyday lives of the González brothers, a working-class Chicano family living among racists in a northern Alabama town. Often referred to as wetbacks, light-skinned niggers, and tacos, the González family finds solace in la familia and, by extension, in rap music by performers such as Cypress Hill, Ice Cube, and Snoop Dogg. In a discussion with McPeek Villatoro about Cypress Hill's classic tune "Latin Lingo" (1991), Ricardo González puts it like this: "I listen to this rap because it talks about la raza. . . . Some people get into fantasy music, stuff that's not real. That's fine, but not for me. This music talks about our world, what we put up with day after day" (McPeek Villatoro 1994, 81). Cypress Hill is a favorite of Ricardo's since "they're Latino. Son carnales, man, they talk about what it means to be us." As such, "this music culture supplies a great deal of the courage required to go on living in the present" (Gilroy 1993a, 36).

Clearly there is no single version of the family in Chicano rap music. Indeed, it has been remixed and extended, scratched and played in multiple versions. And as it presents itself as both necessary and problematic for radical change, la familia persists as a site from which to wage struggles for unity, hence the need for Chicano rap discourse to consistently invoke it for the sake of political thought and mobilization. We might push further, however, to flesh out the possibilities of a reconfigured view of kinship within not only a hip-hop context but a public sphere, where popular culture too often falls short in taking issue with the ideological presuppositions that mediate and determine its wide-reaching capacity. This reconfigured view might indeed be one that seriously gauges the promise of democracy across differences *within*, exposing, for example, how the perpetuation of homophobia, heterosexism, and misogyny in Chicano contexts serves only to promote the hierarchical arrangements upon which authoritarian social institutions depend.

Four

Carnal Knowledge

> to the world
> we are nothing
> but here together
>   you & I
> are the world
>
> • • • Francisco X. Alarcón, "Dialectics of Love" (1985)

T he previous chapters, in their own way, have considered the ramifications of exclusion and inclusion of sexual minorities within
the conjuncture of family and nationalism in Chicano cultural-
political empowerment projects. This chapter, however, will directly focus on curiously ambiguous responses to Chicano gay male sexuality by
advocates of heteronormative kinship arrangements, as well as on how
Chicano gay men implicitly take aim at such responses through various
modes of self-representation that form an archive too often said not to exist. Such responses are formed by acknowledgment and repression; they
straddle the border that divides admittance and disavowal in the struggle
and negotiation to determine kinship. Curious ambiguity hinges upon the
assumption of a "reproductive futurism" for Chicano politics that finds
homosexuality's adoption difficult, if not impossible, given heteronormative prerogatives of *la familia* in its cultural and historical deployments as
an organizing principle.[1] Yet, as I take up such an engagement, I will begin
to show that it is virtually impossible to suggest that kinship discourse
and practice—and their ability to generate a collective consciousness—
are of no use to racial and ethnic sexual minorities. Understanding Chicano

gay male articulations of identity, desire, and experience in relation to this discourse throws light on the impulses behind the simultaneous embracing and resignifying of "family" narratives, such as *carnalismo*, that contribute to the constitution of Chicano gay male consciousness and desires; that is, the recognition of one's self in relation to a community—a brotherhood—of men whose sexual fantasies involve men, the generation of a "dialectic of love," as Francisco X. Alarcón might call it, that functions as a "world-making" endeavor disproving invisibility and silence.[2]

Before addressing these curiously ambiguous responses, I will begin by engaging with scholarly attempts to track the presence of Chicano gay men in the realm of literary and cultural production. In "The Place of Gay Male Chicano Literature in Chicana/o Cultural Work," Antonio Viego (1999, 117) maintains that it "has become a fairly rote observation to make in Chicana/o and Latina/o Studies of gay male Chicano, Latino literary work that there is not enough of it being produced" in contrast to "the plenitude of lesbian Chicana literary work." For Viego, it behooves us not to compare Chicana lesbian cultural production to Chicano gay male cultural production (or the lack of it) given the different social and historical trajectories from which they evolve. He insists that to stake a comparison "demands that the gay male Chicano, Latino subject emerge in cultural, literary work according to the same grid of experiential categories through which lesbian Chicana, Latina cultural, literary work instantiates a lesbian Chicana, Latina subject in narrativity" (118). Viego then asks, "Is gay male Chicano, Latino cultural intelligibility wedded to an analysis of lesbian Chicana, Latina cultural, literary work?" Historically, the answer has been a resounding "yes," reflected in the way two influential queer commentators, Tomás Almaguer and Cherríe Moraga, lament Chicano gay male consciousness in contrast to that tangibly—or rather, textually—forged by Chicana lesbians. Yet one of the dangers implicit in this comparison, Viego persuasively argues, is that "gay Chicano and Latino men are often figured as the weak links in political movements for Chicana/o, Latina/o ethnic, racial empowerment" (120). While it is true that Moraga's and Almaguer's lamentations can indeed function as an alarm call for Chicano gay men to "speak up," the ways in which gay men are rendered "weak links" through their purported silence do not assist in challenging the tendencies, on which I elaborate below, to cast gay men as nonproductive and, ultimately, passive.

The most troubling aspect of Moraga's and Almaguer's presentation of Chicano gay men is that certain modes of presentation are assumed to inaugurate the means by which they, in the first place, must speak. Chicana lesbian discourse, Viego declares, is a "discourse [that] has emerged in academic discourse to the extent that it has narrativized *experience* by engaging racial, sexual, cultural, and class histories in order to produce a recognizable, readable subject" (123). Claims such as "Being the first to shatter the silence on the homosexual experience of the Chicano population" (Almaguer) and "In the last few years, Chicano gay men have also begun to openly examine Chicano sexuality" (Moraga) assist in scripting Chicana lesbians as "the original" queer, speaking subjects while resolutely discounting the historical moments in which homosexuality could be broached outside the realm of assumed, charted contexts. To be sure, "that gay Chicano men are simply not talking, not writing, not being open enough about their sexuality, and the proof for these facts may involve no more rigorous a task than the simple statement of these facts" (Viego 1999, 127) are statements which, made in the context of books and articles, wield an authority determining suitable forms of being.

Viego is also on the mark when he questions why "certain academic disciplines seem currently to be so fond of the Chicana feminist lesbian subject" (122). Certainly, these are the very quarters that have provided, albeit marginally, the constitution of a recognizable Chicana lesbian consciousness. In no way do I wish to fault Moraga and Almaguer for intentionally silencing gay men, nor do I want to devalue the influence Chicana lesbian work has had on both men and women. Rather, like Viego, I am arguing for the recognition of generative moments that exceed conventional textuality and may be performed in alternative, peripheral, or unaccounted-for spaces.

The issue of literary representation is important as far as who gets to count in the conjugation of queer and Chicano/a. Along with the recognizable body of Chicana lesbian literature, a handful of works written by both Chicano heterosexual men and gay men have served as the springboards for discussing queer sexuality. While the presence and circulation of Chicana lesbian texts are credited as single-handedly promoting Chicana lesbian visibility, Chicano gay men have not been exempt from consideration within Chicano/a literature and literary history and criticism. Juan Bruce-Novoa's "Homosexuality and the Chicano Novel" (1986) initiated

critical conversation about gay male sexuality in Chicano literature, spe-
cifically in the work of José Antonio Villarreal, Rechy, Floyd Salas, Oscar
"Zeta" Acosta, and Arturo Islas. More recently, Ricardo L. Ortíz ("Sexuality Degree Zero: Pleasure and Power in the Novels of John Rechy, Arturo
Islas, and Michael Nava" [1993]), Carl Gutiérrez-Jones (*Rethinking the
Borderlands: Between Chicano Culture and Legal Discourse* [1995]), and
John Cunningham ("'Hey, Mr. Liberace, Will You Vote for Zeta?': Looking for the Joto in Chicano Men's Autobiographical Writing" [2002]) have
investigated, to varying degrees, homophobia and homosexuality in the
writings of gay and straight Chicano authors.

Despite the ability of these writings to broach the subject of Chicano
gay men, such work, in the final analysis, is insufficient for those like
Moraga and Almaguer who insist "on a gay male Chicano narrativity that
yields the fact of 'cultural dissonance' Chicano gay men experience in reconciling Chicana/o cultural-symbolic pressures and 'sexual deviancy'"
(Viego 1999, 130). That is, most of these literary texts do not match the
work of Chicana lesbians because they fail to adopt an explicit "Chicano"
agenda that grapples with the "cultural-symbolic pressures" that govern
not only the everyday life practices of Chicano/a populations, but which
also root the interlocking discourses of family, nationalism, and community that have come to define Chicano/a cultural politics.

While he does not completely grasp the social and historical contexts
from which Moraga's and Almaguer's arguments evolve (namely, Chi-
cano/a studies and Chicano movement discourse), Viego is keenly aware
of the cultural politics that have come to frame much of Chicano/a studies. Quoting Almaguer (1991, 257), Viego writes, "Almaguer faults [Rich-
ard Rodríguez and Arturo Islas], specifically, for not sufficiently narrativ-
izing the 'cultural dissonance that Chicano homosexual men confront in
reconciling their primary socialization into Chicano family life with the
sexual norms of the dominant culture'" (Viego 1999, 122). Viego's point
is well taken when he disputes Almaguer's demand for gay men to speak
in a manner akin to Chicana lesbians (based on the assumption of "queer
kin," as Viego puts it), but I also agree with Almaguer given the crucial
significance of the family institution—within both public and domestic
spheres—for Chicano/a sexual politics, and given how Chicano men must
"lift the lid on their homosexual experiences and leave the closeted space
they have been relegated to in Chicano culture" (Almaguer 1991, 97). Yet

Almaguer's claims short-circuit when we consider unaccounted-for cultural forms to begin, as he insists, "interpreting and redefining what it means to be both Chicano and gay in a cultural setting that has viewed these categories as a contradiction in terms" (97). Recognizing that "the gay Latino community is characterized by an absence of traditional texts," Manuel Guzmán (1997, 215) maintains that "consequently, for this community, inhabited spaces should become the location par excellence for the objectification of its generative schemes—the principles on which the production of thought, perception, and action are based." I read "inhabited spaces" loosely here, insisting that Chicano gay men inhabit spaces that haven't been easily detected, spaces that exceed readily accessible literary texts but are nonetheless spaces where "family life" has necessarily been addressed. Chicano gay male articulations of experience, identity, and desire that forge a Chicano gay male consciousness do indeed exist—and have existed—yet they take form mostly in nontextualized, noncanonical arenas. Furthermore, while gay men were being written out of the Chicano family narrative by poets and essayists who were writing from movement trajectories, they were also scripted—in curiously ambiguous ways—as antifamily and rendered as such because of their inability to procreate. In other words, the "value" of gay men to Chicano cultural politics was curious at best since gay men always fail to properly produce or reproduce the family.

As much as his critique of comparing the work of Chicano gay men and Chicana lesbians yields crucial insights, Viego's refusal of "analogical thinking" ultimately prevents any consideration of how the cultural productions and practices of both queer Chicanas and Chicanos are included in a field called Chicano/a studies, but—most significantly here—how they occasionally strive for a sense of collective consciousness. Moreover, one needs to recognize that the cultural production of Chicano gay men is both in the emergent stage as well as contingent upon "recovery work." To establish a similarly solid body of work, projects must be pursued which would: 1) recover and compile materials that are out of print, unpublished, or published in obscure journals and periodicals; 2) conduct and amass oral histories of Chicano gay men (perhaps even writing the histories of those lost to AIDS with the help of family and friends); 3) promote and distribute recent writing, visual art, and film and video (for example, through curatorial efforts, festival acquisition, and the publication of literary anthologies); and 4) critically examine the representations of Chicano gay men in various social and cultural contexts (such as in literature and film) to unveil their positionings therein.[3] The aim of this chapter is twofold in that I see it as part recovery project, part critical analysis, a genealogical effort that stakes claims for Chicano gay male recognition within Chicano/a cultural history.

CURIOUS AMBIGUITY AND THE
CHICANO GAY MALE ARCHIVE

In their introduction to *Chicano Renaissance: Contemporary Cultural Trends*, editors David R. Maciel, Isidro D. Ortíz, and María Herrera-Sobek (2000, xvi) list the sociopolitical struggles that, as they would have it, "contributed in no small part to inspire Chicana/o artists" during the Chicano movement of the 1960s and 1970s: "the drive by César Chávez and Dolores Huerta to unionize the farm workers; the land struggle of Reies López-Tijerina; the formation of the La Raza Unida Party; the Crusade for Justice; the sit-ins, love-ins, and marches against the Vietnam War; the feminist movement; and the gay and lesbian liberation movement." Although Maciel, Ortíz, and Herrera-Sobek do not specify how "the feminist movement" and "the gay and lesbian liberation movement" inspired Chicano and Chicana artists, their inclusion of these struggles suggests an affirmative influence at this particular historical juncture. While mentioning lesbian writers Cherríe Moraga, Gloria Anzaldúa, and Alicia Gaspar de Alba who, we're told, "battle against what *they perceive* to be a homophobic and antilesbian society" (xix, emphasis mine), the editors nevertheless return us all to a politics of solidarity. While such movements indeed contributed to the growing influence of feminist, gay, and lesbian politics for Chicano/a social and cultural projects, they also influenced others to express a curious ambiguity—if not at times an outright resistance—toward those movements' members who might perhaps be part of the Chicano movement as well but nonetheless troubled the conventional family narratives it promoted. Indeed, gay, lesbian, and feminist struggles were often seen as antithetical to Chicano liberation.[4] Feminism and gay and lesbian rights, after all, presented a challenge to prescriptive kinship formations, the normativity of heterocoupling, conventional gender roles, and heterosexual male privileges and desires. By invoking these movements, Maciel, Ortíz, and Herrera-Sobek raise the stakes of a revisionist solidarity that potentially forecloses discussion on the contradictory reception of feminist, gay, and lesbian issues in movement-era and movement-influenced cultural production.

Ramón Gutiérrez's essay, "Community, Patriarchy and Individualism: The Politics of Chicano History and the Dream of Equality," incisively offers two important historical flashpoints. First, Gutiérrez (1993, 45) writes that 1960s and 1970s Chicanismo hinges on "the cultural assertion of masculinity by young radical men." For Gutiérrez, "Chicanismo meant identifying with la raza (the race or people), and collectively promoting the interests of *carnales* (or brothers) with whom they shared a common language, culture, religion, and Aztec heritage" (46). As outlined in previous chapters, brotherhood in movement discourse was regularly synonymous with la familia. More often than not brotherhood was an allegiance between heterosexual men, excluding women and gay men who threatened the potency of the homosocial—not homosexual—bond. Yet brotherhood, like la familia, is not always predicated on exclusion as Gutiérrez would have it. Could it not function as a bond between gay men—brother to brother, *carnal a carnal*—who would seemingly exist outside the word's realm of signification? And might it be worth promoting a politics of brotherhood that does not rely strictly on a gay or straight bond but rather aims to bridge the interests of Chicano men despite sexual identification?

The other important critical strand in Gutiérrez's essay is his mapping of the emergence of Chicana resistance to Chicano patriarchy by highlighting a feminist counternarrative of the Chicano movement that utilizes poetry as an alternative historiography. In the spirit of Gutiérrez's work, I suggest that poetry and other cultural forms—especially those awaiting recovery from newspapers and limited-edition, out-of-print anthologies—must be considered important archival documents that offer vital information about the complexities of Chicano movement history and the cultural discourses it evokes. As I hope this chapter makes clear, noncanonical poetry and "nontraditional" documents (or "ephemera as evidence," as José Esteban Muñoz [1996] might put it) must be read and analyzed for the purpose of unraveling the politics of gender and sexuality—especially relating to Chicano gay men—which are subjects too frequently taken for granted as "presentist," here signifying either materialization in the "recent present" or after the fact of Chicana lesbian literary production.[5] Texts that may have originally circulated in limited quantities and were published in venues that made their canonization virtually impossible are still key documents that can not only reflect the sentiments of their authors, but also speak to the not so "imagined" communities fashioned by and through such publications.

One such poem that has gone unnoticed and expresses a curious ambiguity toward gay male sexuality is Joe Olvera's poem, "Gay Ghetto District." Read at a *"flor y canto"* festival either in 1977 or 1978, Olvera's poem was subsequently published in José Armas's and Bernice Zamora's edited collection *Flor y Canto IV and V: An Anthology of Chicano Literature* (1980, 111). Since the beginning of the Chicano movement, flor y canto festivals were important components of cultural and political events; they also constituted a tradition on their own as "oral literary symposia" in which "a national character, *chicanismo*" was conveyed (10). "Literally translated as 'flower and song,'" writes Cordelia Candelaria (1986, 34), "the phrase *flor y canto* has become synonymous with Chicano poetry itself."[6] Fittingly, within her discussion of the meanings of flor y canto, Candelaria writes: "Every *familia* is a collection of different individuals, habits, and interests which—despite the differences and even contradictions—are nevertheless bound together as one unit sharing aspects of a common identity. So, too, is Chicano poetry in its multiplicity and concomitant unity" (34). This claim may hold true, that is, until homosexuality's entrance on the scene. Indeed, Olvera's poem precisely shows how gay men are virtually impossible to assimilate into the plural singularity (read "familial framework") of Chicano poetry's "common identity" that Candelaria assumes.

The curious ambiguity of Joe, the narrator of "Gay Ghetto District," is revealing given how his poetic presentation of a gay couple—Ricardo and Michael—at first appears gay affirmative but ultimately discloses homosexual panic.

Hand to hand—'neath peaceful blue 'Frisco skies—
Trees swaying gently to ocean breeze—
Ricardo y Michael's hideaway is beautiful
tree-lined home at top of hill—Eureka!

"Thar's gold in them thar hills"—or some such
nonsense of old greed—gold's the answer to Livermore—

Also Gay men walk streets and arms around one t'other—
so that Rosa sees and says, "How cute."
Er you kidding, Rosa? Because one thing these
here folks don't need is more put-downs.
Anita Bryant is Elmer Gantry look-alike wants
to save the folk from their own proclivities—sexual
or sensual—or otherwise—dig?

Who is this Anita Bryant by the way?
Has she evuh felt the prick on shrunken
vagina? Is homosexual love her loss or
Plato's gain? (Olvera 1980, 111)

The first stanza of the poem provides a critical historical context in which racial and sexual politics could either be compared or conjoined. With the line, "Thar's gold in them thar hills," the speaker adopts the accent of the American opportunist who, fueled by "old greed," is lured to the "Golden State" (California) by the discovery of gold in 1848 and the "availability" of property thereafter. At this moment in history, Mexicans and Indians are robbed of their land (which, of course, was initially Indian land) while the Gold Rush, according to Les Wright (1999, 165), transforms San Francisco "from a sleepy backwater to international port and cultural capital of the American West" that is "an estimated 92 percent (or higher) male." As a reversal, the gold in the hills in the contemporary scenario is the City's "hideaway" of two gay lovers. The analogy painted here is complicated, however, since the association of San Francisco as gay Mecca for Ricardo and Michael and San Francisco as Mecca for greedy settlers—even if male—is curious at best. Yet Joe goes on to cast Anita Bryant—the entertainer turned born-again Christian who in 1977 spearheaded the widely supported campaign entitled, appropriately enough, "Save Our Children"—as a modern-day opportunist desiring to take away Ricardo's and Michael's "golden moment." Likening her to Elmer Gantry—the greedy salesman turned preacher of the eponymous Sinclair Lewis novel and 1960 film—Joe desexualizes Bryant, "shrunken" from the realm of both heterosexual and homosexual desire, and counters her antigay platform with ancient Greece via Plato, a (mythologized) historical moment in which homosexual relations epitomized true love.

In the final two stanzas of the poem, however, the speaker overtly reveals his discomfort with male homosexuality, particularly when the line of demarcation between gay identity and his heterosexual proclivities is blurred.

> Anyway—Ballyhoo—Ricardo and Michael—arms
> around each other smile and ask of me:
> "What makes you think we're gay, Joe?"
>
> Why it's so obvious that even liberal as I is—
> must move on—cannot truly dig alternative
> life-style. Oh yes—can dig it for them—but not
> fer me is fat arse arisen to air in full
> fucking position—oh blasted sex—why the blight? (Olvera 1980, 111)

The question, "What makes you think we're gay, Joe?" functions as a pivotal moment. If Joe does not (and cannot) possess the knowledge to determine who is gay and "straight," how, then, does he know *he's* not gay? To sharply distinguish between himself and Ricardo and Michael, Joe turns the gay men into caricatures (indeed, they are ballyhoos with arms around each other, smiling) and conjures up "a fat arse arisen to air in full fucking position," the readily penetrable anus, the commonly phobic-postulated site of gay male sexual pleasure recognized as "the vanishing point of allowable male behavior and of representation" (Leo 1989, 34).[7] Despite admitting his "liberal" perspective (he supposedly "can dig it for them"), Joe insists he "must move on"—he "cannot truly dig alternative life-style." This alternative lifestyle, in other words, runs counter to permissible, normative sexual practices and the naturalized technique for procreation, the basis of "the family." (Even though, by beginning with a vision of their home, he potentially sets up Ricardo and Michael *as* a family.) For Joe, gay identity—an "alternative life-style" to be sure—is seen as a wavering of male potential to rule and reproduce, especially since it is premised on receptive anal sex. Within the poem, the act of getting fucked falls in line with the cultural and historical consequences attached to this practice.[8] In this view, evoking late-nineteenth-century California history makes sense given how "the phallocentric sexual economy of Gold

Rush era San Francisco suggests that we distinguish between penetrative-masculine and receptive-feminine roles in male-male sexual encounters" (Wright 1999, 165).

In paraphrasing the work of anthropologist Roger Lancaster, Tomás Almaguer (1991, 78) notes that in the contemporary Latin American context, the "penetrator" in homosexual acts embodies "a superior masculine power and male status over the other [the "penetrated"], who is feminized and indeed objectified."[9] While *giving* always places a man in a preordained position sanctioned as male, a man who *receives* is understood as rendering himself female. A penetrated man, however, is always a failed woman because a man who receives cannot procreate. As a nonfertile recipient, he signals the end of reproduction. And by refusing to claim his right to patriarchal authority, he cuts all ties to the naturalized family. Since, according to Guy Hocquenghem, "homosexual desire challenges anality-sublimation because it restores the desiring use of the anus" (1993, 98), it follows that "homosexual desire is the ungenerating-ungenerated terror of the family, because it produces itself without reproducing" (107).[10] The homosexual, in other words, is rendered a "blight"—an impairment—for those who propagate the family genealogy. In Olvera's poem, it is not simply gay "blasted sex" that repels Joe; it is his comprehension of "passive" gay male sex as—to borrow from Leo Bersani in "Is the Rectum a Grave?" (1988)—abdicating power. Thus, to "move on" for Olvera means to resist passive subjugation for the sake of generating Chicano progeny *and poetry* (or any form of literature for that matter).

Within the terms of Chicanismo anchored by machismo, the integration of gay and lesbian sexual politics complicates nationalist projects that are "family" based. The terms of these complications correspond with dominant cultural ideas of what counts as family given these projects' demands for nuclear, patriarchal, and heteronormative kinship arrangements. In his 1975 essay "Machismo," José Armas attempts to rescue the macho and his or her "machismo traits" from those whose slogan is "Smash Macho!" For Armas, women's and gay liberation movements are adversary struggles that chastise the values of a machismo that "equipped people to face the challenge of exploitation, discrimination, racism, sexism, classism with self confidence, determination and dignity" (Armas 1975, 64). Armas argues, "In contemporary times, the White women's liberation and the gay liberation movements condemn the macho as a cold chauvinistic person incapable of humanistic exchanges" (52). But while these movements are rendered as "Anglo" phenomena and irrelevant to Chicano struggles by Armas (not to mention that he conflates women's liberation with gay liberation), the point is not merely that whites are imposing their belief systems on Chicanos. In fact, certain white men like Ernest Hemingway are said to embody a brand of machismo very similar to that of Chicanos.[11]

The notorious fear that feminism and homosexuality strive to undermine the heteronormative prerogatives of familia (which are seen as absolutely necessary for political action) is perhaps the more salient point articulated in Armas's desire for machismo. Gay liberation and feminism are, as he sees it, antimacho and, as a result, antifamily. He writes:

> The failure of the white women's liberation movement to attract a mass following from the Chicana woman indicates something important. This is apart from the fact that the family is the basis for all social development in the Chicano community and the woman plays the key role in that development. The white women's liberation has little regard for the family as an institution. At least in the Chicano sense. (Armas 1975, 62–63)

If, by "in the Chicano sense," Armas means the way family is articulated in his *La Familia de La Raza*—that is, an extension of private domestic family relations to public communal kinship politics—one must argue otherwise when considering the complexities of "the women's movement." However, I understand Armas as suggesting that the women's liberation movement and the gay liberation movement hold little regard for the family as an institution because of their outright rejection of machismo as a sign for male heterosexual superiority.[12] In his defense of machismo, Armas denies that it is "a negative, violent and destructive trait . . . a sexist trait and . . . a definition that is used as a distinction between men and women" (53). And yet, in a move that signals a curiously ambiguous impulse behind staking claims for machos, that is, recognizing the importance of resisting patriarchy only to chastise feminism's growing significance for galvanizing women, Armas concedes that sexism is a subjugating force with which Chicanas must contend, admitting to the "chauvinistic and sexist attitudes that arise and do exist in the Chicano culture" (62). The white women's liberation movement, however, is rendered as incapable of attending to the needs of Chicanas, thus Chicanas should look to la raza in order to solve the problem. To remain faithful to a Chicano nationalist ideology, the problems of the community must be kept *entre familia*, solvable within the community.

In chapter 1, I noted how Armas, in *La Familia de la Raza*, argues that women, too, can embody machismo. In "Machismo," Armas (1975) fittingly reveals that he was raised solely by his mother, a "macho" woman. "Sometimes we had a stepfather," he writes, "but mostly she raised us alone." Despite the lack of a father figure, Armas insists that he was raised to be macho as were his three brothers. "A family of machos raised by a woman alone. A woman, a mother who raised machos!" (Armas 1975, 64). Yet, the macho woman must always be a mother, a woman never lacking femininity. Armas maintains: "My mother, who was extremely feminine when she dressed up, taught the girls to dance and the nonverbal language of feminine communication" and, contrary to white culture's perceptions of machismo, his two sisters, "who are today as feminine as my mother, also have machismo" (63–65). In short, machismo is an essentialist trait embodied by all Chicanos despite sexual differences. However, circumscribed by what Armas calls "a total nature which makes the whole (i.e., the Chicano nature)" (61), machismo is ultimately disseminated through reproductive futurism and rests upon the hubris of traditional gender roles. While he implicitly suggests sexism can be addressed through the macho and familia framework, what about gay liberation and its tense relationship with machismo that Armas mentions at the start of his essay? Although Armas deals a blow to the myth of the macho superman by noting "it is not uncommon to see Raza men greet with a hug and walk with arms around each other" (58), given the heterosexualized contours of masculinity and family established within his work, it would be impossible (not to mention culturally sacrilegious) for him to identify these Raza men as gay. After all, figuratively echoing Joe Olvera's poem, Armas insists that "passivity is not permitted" (59).[13]

CRUISING (THROUGH) CHICANISMO

Thus far I have examined texts charged with the political currents of the Chicano movement. But unlike many scholars who use the 1960s and 1970s as bookends to bracket Chicano movement discourse, I want to insist that such periodization does not always account for the rhetorical force of Chicanismo that bleeds into the 1980s—and into the present for that matter—as evident in popular culture. In "Ondas y Rollos (Wavelengths and Raps): The Ideology of Contemporary Chicano Rhetoric," José Angel Gutiérrez argues that movement figures like César Chávez, Reies López Tijerina, Rodolfo "Corky" Gonzales, and himself

> embarked on a course to legitimate Chicanismo, an operational working definition of Chicano culture. In their speeches, these men utilized new words to give life to the social protest movements of the 1970s. These words—Chicano, Aztlán, La Raza, La Causa, Huelga, Carnalismo, for example—broke with assimilationist thought because they set up an ideological framework of action against the Anglo system. The Chicano slogans called for goals that would result in independently created Chicano social institutions. The words and slogans became self-identifiers that represented pride, cultural identity, political militancy, and concerted, collective action. The young, the women, and the poor saw themselves as the authors of their own advocacy and destiny. (Gutiérrez 1985, 147–48; see also Powers 1973)

Such words and slogans—part and parcel of Chicano movement discourse—persisted throughout the 1980s and 1990s in cultural forms like poetry, music, and media culture. New Chicano left movements also adopt (often with a difference) the lexicon of Chicanismo typically deemed a 1960s and 1970s phenomenon. A particular example of Chicanismo's impact within a more recent popular frame is evident in the culture of car customization, or—as the subtitle of Rick Tejada-Flores's documentary film *Low 'n' Slow* (1983) announces—"the art of lowriding."[14]

In 1981, the lowriding magazine *Firme* from the Los Angeles suburb of San Gabriel initiated discussion on homosexuality in its fifth issue among a predominantly working-class Chicano readership by publishing an interview with "a gay Chicano" named Victor.[15] Entitled "A Gay Life Style (Only if La Familia Approves)," the interview not only sought to inform its presumably heterosexual readership about gay male identity and sexual practices, but it juxtaposed two seemingly opposite identificatory terms at that historical moment: Chicano and gay.[16] Moreover, this rather obscure article from the Chicano/a queer archive is but one example of how debates about gay identity were taking place within working-class Chicano communities, and it serves as evidence of how heteronormative impulses underscored familial/nationalist politics.

Produced by the Mexican-American Ventures Corporate Operations,

Inc., *Firme*'s first issue was released in early 1981. *Firme* published six issues in 1981, two in 1982, and disappeared until almost a decade later when in 1993 it reappeared as a "double-feature" publication, back-to-back with (*Firme* Magazine Presents:) *Chicano Arte*. In 1994, the magazine became *Q-Vo* (although the title *Firme* still appears in various locations throughout the magazine), the publication that *Firme* absorbed back in 1982. Over the years and despite its numerous changes, Benjamin Francisco Hernández remained the publisher. At first glance, *Firme* is comparable to the format and general content of the widely recognized *Lowrider Magazine* (whose premiere issue appeared in January 1977) mainly because both appeal to a young Chicano male readership and highlight car culture (either customizing or cruising). Evident by the simple fact that both magazines emphasized the term "Chicano," *Lowrider* and *Firme* stressed Chicano cultural pride informed by *el movimiento*.[17] A closer inspection, however, reveals that while *Lowrider* stresses the art of car customization first and foremost, *Firme* featured a wide range of Chicano artistic forms and practices.

Unlike *Lowrider*, *Firme* did not succeed on a national or international level. Yet in the early 1980s, while *Lowrider* was receiving complaints from readers for selling out the community in the name of business expansion (as a concerned incarcerated reader put it in a penetrating letter to the magazine, "I hate to think you vatos are going capitalist on your own Raza" [cited in Plascencia 1983, 165]), *Firme* remained loyal to the Chicano communities of Aztlán. Although *Lowrider*, too, spoke the language of Chicanismo, it was never clear, as Luis F. B. Plascencia (1983) points out, who owned and operated the magazine and what the magazine's goals were. Thus, Hernández makes sure to inform his readers that *Firme* was "media owned and operated by Chicanos for Chicanos." Moreover, Hernández firmly states: "We must take what belongs to us. The most valuable commodity around is ourselves. We can build a better mas firme barrio society, truly a la brava. The success of this magazine stands on this." *Firme*, too, published business advertisements, but it is evident that the magazine was less concerned with selling items like cars and car parts to Chicanos than with the multifarious dimensions of, as the magazine's subtitle declares, "Chicano Life" through coverage of politics, art, music, film, and community happenings. Additionally, a regular section entitled "Barrio Chicanada" displayed photographs in a format that reminds one of a family photo album. Indeed, "Barrio Chicanada," which depicts *Firme* readers and members of the Chicano/a community in general, almost always includes the standard family images of father, mother, and children.[18] In short, the "arte" in *Firme* was more than cars; art was also the practices of everyday life. As Hernández states in his "Note From the Publisher" column in the second issue:

> We all know the creative Chicano mente. "Cars as art." A lot of jale goes into a firme ride, and most of the work is done by the owner himself. We like to give credit where credit is due. As for you vatos who disagree, Bueno hay tienen los magazines de los gavas, tu sabes, "Street Chatter," "Hot Chatter," y "Road y Traques," etc. A puro bore! Con nada de estillo! Inside the pages of this issue you will find "puro arte Chicano." Check it out, ese y esa! (B. Hernández 1981a, 7)

As suggested, *Firme* stood apart from car magazines published by "los gavas," or white people, as it remained indebted to la causa and the goals of the movement. And since accusations were flying at the time that *Lowrider* was possibly white owned (mainly because it was unclear at the time who was behind the magazine's operation) or selling out, Hernández's critique is most likely directed at *Lowrider*, their rival publication, not the fabricated titles he lists. Early editions of the magazine contain a subscription ad with a cartoon of a frenzied Chicano wanting to purchase a (sold-out) copy of *Firme* at a newsstand. Appropriately enough, in the background we see a magazine called "Blowrider," adopting the trademark *Lowrider* symbol of a pork-pie hat, dark shades, and a thin mustache that together create a facial silhouette of a pachuco. On the cover of "Blowrider," however, the pachuco's mustache is gone; in its place is a set of feminine lips. The title "Blowrider" and the image beneath it are quite suggestive. Certainly, *Firme* is implying that *Lowrider* "sucks." Figuratively, this insinuates that *Lowrider* is inferior to *Firme*. Literally, for *Lowrider* to suck it must be placed in the passive role of a woman, hence the replacement of a man's mustache with a woman's lips on the *Lowrider* trademark. This gesture underscores the need to render *Firme* "on top" and *Lowrider* "on the bottom."

One aspect that ultimately links both publications, making them virtually indistinguishable, is their display of "*firme rucas*," the scantily clothed women within and on its covers. The common perception among

Chicanos and Chicanas that the communities who "subscribe" to these magazines are sexist and homophobic makes sense given how the provocatively dressed women—which are part and parcel of *Firme*'s "Barrio Chicanada" section—unabashedly cater to male heterosexual desires. A letter to the editor from Macho Man "De Hollywood" in the second issue of *Firme* reads: "You should . . . show more girls showing off their beautiful bronze bodies, make them wear G-strings with their flesh exposed to the camera, make them pose in erotic positions that will make every Chicano proud." Even if this letter is fictional (as some of its letters seem to be), both *Firme* and *Lowrider* have indeed taken Macho Man's suggestions seriously. After all, the success of these magazines does not hinge only on displaying supped-up bodies of cars but also on displaying the "beautiful bronze bodies" of Chicanas.

Chicanas, however, did not remain silent about the exploitation of women in these magazines. From the late 1970s to the more recent issues, various published letters chart the discomfort—and fury—at the way women are portrayed in both *Lowrider* and *Firme*.[19] Despite the published objections to the sexist practices of these publications, no attempt was made to eliminate the images of provocatively dressed women because the reader or viewer was always assumed to be a heterosexual man whose gaze and libidinal desires were being courted.[20] Similar to numerous documented moments in the movement, women's objections were nevertheless occasions for men of la raza to brand outspoken Chicanas as belligerent feminists and, in turn, man-hating lesbians. This was the case in a 1993 issue of *Firme*, crystallized in "Dear Tommy Tapado," a column of fictional letters answered by "Tommy," an abrasive *vato loco* who doesn't hold back. Although intended as comic relief, one letter highlights the serious homophobic impulse of the magazine. It reads: "Dear Firme: Although I know you probably won't print this letter, I have to tell you that your magazine stinks! I bet the publisher is a pompous male chauvinistic pig, who doesn't know the difference between a hole in the wall and the hole in his head and probably has an I.Q. of 3." The letter is signed "Debbie Dyke" from "Hollyweird, Ca." Although Debbie's letter may be based on the letters *Firme* has received throughout the years, it also functions as a warning for those who may be tempted to write in and complain about the magazine's sexism: objecting women will be written off as dykes.

Firme's heterosexist tendencies were firmly established back in 1981, also within the Tommy Tapado letter section. In issue number 4, a woman named "Lupe La Loca" writes: "Dear Tommy: Why is it that you guys at *Firme* always show girls that are always half naked and not guys?" Tommy answers: "Dear Vieja Bomba: We show girls half naked because that's the way we like them and we don't show guys that way because we're no fags!" However, the very next issue features an interview conducted by special projects editor Carlos Hernández with a Chicano gay man named Victor.

In his "Note," which opens this particular issue, Benjamin Hernández writes, "Our interview with Victor shares some alarming and confusing attitudes on sexual identity. On the other hand, *Firme*'s finest of the month is Frank Abundis, a second generation Chicano businessman, who aspires for success and life's pleasurable endeavors" (B. Hernández 1981b, 5). Here, Victor is juxtaposed with *"Firme's* finest," a presumably heterosexual "page-three" male model who appears in each issue of *Firme* (and very similar to the "Page Three Fella" in the tabloid published in the UK, *The Mirror*).[21] Whereas Frank must be lauded for his accomplishments (not to mention his unabashed manliness, as evident in his photo in which he appears shirtless and displays his muscular physique), Victor as a gay man can only offer alarming and confusing perspectives on a contorted sexual identity.

Unlike Benjamin Hernández who dismisses Victor as sexually confused, Victor's interviewer, Carlos Hernández, seems more sympathetic and willing to take seriously what his interviewee has to say. In fact, the manner in which Carlos Hernández begins his piece is not the sensationalized introduction we would have expected to read after Benjamin Hernández's jeering comment in his "Note." The interview begins as follows:

> As Chicanos are a minority in America, homosexuals are a minority within la gente. And, like anyone who is different from the majority, gays sometimes find they are misunderstood and disliked. However, according to Victor, a gay Chicano, attitudes are slowly improving toward gays.
>
> *Firme* is publishing an interview with Victor to give insight into the gay life style and beliefs. Nevertheless, it's important to remember that Victor is just an individual and not necessarily reminiscent of all gay Chicanos. (C. Hernández 1981, 18–19)

Contrary to José Armas who understands Chicanos and homosexuals as disparate subjects, and thus refuses to recognize the existence of Chicano homosexuals, Carlos Hernández acknowledges the presence of Chicano gays as a "minority within la gente." He also aligns homosexuals with other disenfranchised groups, "like anyone who is different from the majority," and not as the enemy of Chicanos (as is typically the case). If we can agree that the interview is conducted in good faith (that is, operating from an antihomophobic premise), then it is possible to see Carlos Hernández as part of a contingent whose "attitudes are slowly improving toward gays."

The questions Hernández asks Victor are wide ranging, extending from the essential to the dubious (and perhaps I'm being overly critical of someone who wants to know if a gay man would court a "transsexual who, because of a sex operation, turned himself into a beautiful woman"). Yet for those who want to learn about "the gay life style and beliefs," Hernández's questions such as "Are you one of those people who feels you were born a homosexual?" and "How does your family feel about your being homosexual?" are nonetheless crucial. To his credit, Hernández also provides important, critical background information after some of the questions he asks and that Victor answers. For example, Hernández asks Victor: "When you first started 'coming out,' as they say, was there anyone who told you that being a homosexual was wrong?" Victor answers: "Well, I went to Catholic school all my life, and of course they teach you from the Bible what things are wrong. But, in answer to your question, I would say it was one of my school teachers that I first heard say it was wrong." As an aside, Hernández offers the following insights:

> Gay Christians admit that the Bible condemns sexual relations between two people of the same sex, calling it an abomination. But because the Bible also calls camels and eagles abominable things (Leviticus 11) and condemns to death stubborn children as well as any man who picks up sticks on the Sabbath (Deuteronomy 21; Numbers 15), gay Christians say the Old Testament prohibitions cannot be rashly quoted or easily understood outside their historical and cultural contexts. Furthermore, gay Christians state that nowhere in the New Testament does Christ condemn homosexuality, and that St. Paul warned against idolatrous sexual worship practiced by pagans but was not referring to true, Christ-believing homosexuals. (18)

Hernández's gloss on the Bible, and the contradictory interpretations of it, illuminates how dismissals of homosexuality as a "sin against God" do not hold when considered within a more comprehensive and judicious historical frame. Hernández diligently seems to be carving out a space for Victor within Chicano religious and popular cultural contexts traditionally unaccustomed to housing queers.[22]

The recuperative aspects of the interview, however, exist in tension with the larger, ideological premises of heternormativity, highlighted in the formalistic presentation of the interview with regard to accompanying images, title, and, of course, Benjamin Hernández's casual dismissal of Victor's perspectives as "confusing" and "alarming." Printed alongside the text are two noncredited drawings. The first is of a "made-up" man adorning "women's" clothing. That he looks white evokes the idea that only white men can be gay or that gayness is a "white thing." He wears heavy makeup, large hoop earrings, and string (a necklace? a dog collar? a whip?) around his neck. Decked out in a corset, black panties, and stockings supported by a garter belt (one gets the sense he is into s/m given the style of clothing and the absence of his hands—they are presumably tied behind his back, thus accentuating his "passivity"), he is displayed as effeminate (in spite of having a penis—of which the outline through his underwear *and* corset is curiously accentuated by the artist—and a muscular, clearly male, chest). The second image is in the same vein as the first, although here, along with what looks like a carbon copy of the above-described transvestite, we are also presented with what appears to be a transsexual. Similar to her counterpart based on facial features, the distinction lies in the fact that she has large breasts (sustained and covered by suspenders). Are these figures supposed to provide us with an idea of what Victor looks like? Or are they merely exaggerated representations sketched by a phobic imagination?

Although Victor admits to "doing drag," he insists that he is gay and not simply a "transvestite." (Hernández asks Victor if he would consider himself a transvestite, to which Victor answers, "No, not really. I'd rather be considered gay.") This point, however, is subsequently buried by the signifying force of these salaciously deviant images that crudely collapse transvestites, transsexuals, and gay men. In short, these images conjure up well-worn perceptions of gay men as effeminate and wanting to be women. (One cannot help but think of the exaggerated aspects of lowrider aesthetics in which women's femininity and sexuality are juxtaposed against the hardness of "real" men.)

The title, "A Gay Life Style (Only if *La Familia* Approves)," is provocative. But to which familia does it refer? When asked about how his family feels about his being gay, Victor answers, "Well, it was about a year ago that I first told my parents that I was gay. My dad said, 'Oh, I kind of figured that a long time ago'. But my mother was in shock and wanted me to see a doctor because she thought I wasn't normal" (C. Hernández 1981, 18). Although Victor's parents' responses are far from congratulatory, they do not appear to be preventing him from asserting his gayness. In other words, his family's consent (or lack thereof) does not necessarily deter Victor's leading "a gay life style" as the title of the interview suggests it would. What is meant by "la familia's approval," then, is that which is conceived and wielded by *Firme Magazine*. "La familia de la raza" would most likely object to Victor's lifestyle since it conflicts with the principles to which this particular family adheres. The accompanying drawings of hyperfeminine transvestites and transsexuals assist in the prohibition of Victor—whose words presumably breathe life into these drawings—from the "Barrio Chicanada" section, with the male-female couples and nuclear families, given "la familia's" obligatory disapproval of his gay lifestyle. Moreover, despite the detectable "good intentions" of Victor's interviewer, the capacity to include Victor as part of the *Firme* scene—a scene that is undeniably familial—is undermined by the normative tenets of Benjamin Hernández's, and *Firme*'s, Chicano cultural politics.

The final question posed to Victor, "Do you ever plan to marry?," is not meant as an inquiry into whether Victor ever plans to marry a man. Instead, it returns to a previous question, "Have you ever thought of going straight?," thus foreclosing any possibility in shifting the terms of not only conjugality but, more imperatively, familial constitution. When Victor answers, "No, I haven't [thought of going straight]. But I've thought of having children," a perplexed Hernández asks, "Having children? How?" Victor responds, "Yeah, you know. Maybe in the future I can adopt or acquire one through artificial insemination (a surrogate mother). Any which way really, as long as I wouldn't have to get down with a woman" (C. Hernández 1981, 19). Unfortunately it seems that both Carlos and Benjamin Hernández *do not* know, nor do they desire to reconsider the sanctioned terms of family organization. No matter how many times

Victor declares he is not sexually attracted to women, Hernández is unable to disentangle conventional and alternative conceptions of gender roles and the family. The institution of "marriage" and its attendant accessories (namely spouse and children) are tangible only within *Firme*'s heterosexual matrix. Those like Victor who challenge or refuse to adhere to the matrix are, in the final analysis, written off as confused (and not only by magazine editors). Clearly, he could never qualify for inclusion in the magazine like the "real" barrio chicanada who are eligible to partake in (the section) "A Memorable Firme Wedding."

Victor's candid comments about his sexual identity and practices cannot help but establish an undercurrent of heterosexual anxiety. This anxiety is not unlike the sentiment conveyed in Joe Olvera's "Gay Ghetto District." In both texts, Chicano gay men function as a fetish for straight men, apparent in their interest in, and curiosity about, what gay men do and how they do it. But like any fetish, this harbored interest and curiosity must always result in disavowal, here the disavowal of (homosexual) desire.[23] As I have shown thus far, any affirmative constitution of gay male identity that holds the potential to short-circuit the nationalist ambitions resting upon heterosexual presumption and reproduction must be renounced. Thus, in order to sustain the primacy of fixed notions of manhood, nation, and family, gay men must be seen as failed men, literally and figuratively converted into failed "women"—subjected to a nonreproductive, sexually submissive (that is, anally receptive) role, simultaneously branded as confused men who require that necessary sex change to become women. In either case, they are understood as thwarting the generation of la familia and its heteronormative codification.

YA VAS, CARNAL

Despite, or because of, the ambiguous aura surrounding the *Firme* interview, I want to read "Victor" as a precursor to Chicano gay male historical consciousness articulated not only by writers, but also by painters, photographers, filmmakers, and video artists. His self-assured stance reverberates well beyond the curious ambiguity containing and disciplining his unabashedly queer desires. But what does one make of his willingness to be included on the pages of *Firme?* I understand Victor to be engaging his brothers—his familia, as it were—about himself not only as a gay man but as a Chicano gay man within and beyond the boundaries of a preconceived community. To be sure, this is merely one hypothesis about why he grants the interview. Victor knows his inclusion within "Barrio Chicanada," so to speak, will always be thwarted by those "brothers" who do not embrace him. Yet as the Chicano gay writer Eric-Steven Gutiérrez (1992, 244) states, "Our families may reject us but we belong to them nonetheless. . . . We must not abandon them. They are ours. Even if it is impossible to stay, they remain ours for as long as we claim them; for as long as we attempt to reconcile our queer and Latino communities and identities." To my mind, Victor is, to paraphrase Gutiérrez's essay, a Chicano gay man "claiming la raza." He is like the activist Rodrigo Reyes, based in San Francisco and founder of the historic Gay Latino Alliance, whose essay "Latino Gays: Coming Out and Coming Home" appeared the same year as the *Firme* interview in the Latino magazine *Nuestro* (Spanish for "us") and who insisted on working "side-by-side with [our] heterosexual *vecinos*, serving the community in which [we] feel [we] rightly belong" (R. Reyes 1981, 44). These are not simple bids for inclusion into heteronormative "family" arrangements but desires to recast the terms that conventionally define what counts as la familia.

Nearly twenty years later, car culture and the magazines that promote lowriding have surfaced within Chicano gay male cultural production as iconography that is not simply contested but—quite like la familia—reconfigured in the name of challenging old, and creating new, collectivities. Augie Robles's documentary video *Cholo Joto* (1993) employs shots of *Lowrider* and family photographs (many of which could be included in *Firme*'s "barrio chicanada") after a young gay man, Valentín Aguirre, waxes critically on the narrow nationalism of Chicano movement ideologues in his native San Diego neighborhood of Logan Heights. Aguirre calls out the sexist and homophobic nationalists, telling them, "You might as well be in the sixties, still listening to 'Angel Baby' and thinking you're on the cover of *Lowrider*." In his reading of this scene (which emphasizes Aguirre's commentary on a mural of Ché Guevara), José Esteban Muñoz (1999, 15) rightly argues that Aguirre's "performance does not simply undermine nationalism but instead hopes to rearticulate such discourses within terms that are politically progressive."[24] Fittingly, Aguirre confesses, "I love *Lowrider*, but, I mean, I'm not on the cover!" While men generally don't appear on the cover of *Lowrider*, Aguirre is stressing his absence from the magazine's cover as a gay man. I read Aguirre's commentary—after Gutiérrez, Reyes, and Muñoz—as his declaration of love for la raza, and his desire for inclusion in a community whose embrace is, nonetheless, always without guarantee.

Al Lujan's video *S&M in the Hood* (1998) takes Aguirre's exclusion seriously and addresses it with a touch of queer humor. In an opening shot that flashes what may as well be the "Blowrider" symbol described above but with an added beautifying facial mole á la Marilyn Monroe, the logo, also used by the San Francisco-based gay comedy troupe Latin Hustle (to which Lujan belongs), recasts the heteronormativity of lowrider culture in a Chicano-specific context of queer world making. The presence of the image, I would argue, sets the stage for a provocative depiction of eroticism, cultural identity, and humor within the contours of a gay-affirmative Chicanismo. The way in which the tape scrambles "traditional" cultural discourses—gay male s/m, lowrider iconography, and a Chicano or Mexicano piñata-breaking contest (we must remember that piñatas are most often found at family gatherings such as birthdays)—mirrors the strategies undertaken by Chicano gay men like Victor, Gutiérrez, and Aguirre who strive to create and define complex yet historically specific identities and communities.

Along with video, painting is another medium where family politics and Chicano gay male consciousness have been broached. Oxnard native and current San Francisco resident Eugene Rodríguez is a painter, video artist, curator, and educator whose path-finding work is also crucial for discerning the experiences of Chicano gay men and la familia. In his "Artist Statement," he writes:

> My artwork explores the familial and cultural effects of alienation and follows it generation by generation on both a micro and macro level. I examine the forces of class, ethnicity, location, and sexuality. This exploration comes out of my experience of growing up in a working class family striving to be middle class in the 1960s and 1970s. On the macro level my work explores the construction of identity conveyed through cultural icons and archetypes but filtered through the lens of the media. Visually my art is a hybrid of U.S. soap operas, prime-time TV, and Mexican telenovelas with a touch of theater, neo-realism and surrealism. (Rodríguez 1999)

A collection of twelve paintings entitled "Interruptions" explores "gender roles in the Latino family, personal relationships, and how we perceive media images, stereotypes, and the distance between the ideal and the actual."[25] Within these paintings, Rodríguez reconfigures traditional family iconography by juxtaposing family photos with images of Chicano gay men. These stunning paintings provide a pointed commentary on masculinity and its impact on relations between men.

Rodríguez's life history also provides a significant context in which to situate and understand his work. As he was growing up during the 1960s and 1970s in a working-class family of sharecroppers, Rodríguez witnessed firsthand an emergent political and cultural consciousness embraced by (former) Mexican Americans. Indeed, Rodríguez was touched by the force of the Chicano movement. While moved by its liberationist rhetoric, Rodríguez's relationship with the Chicano community was, at best, strained. This was in large part due to his being openly gay:

> Growing up I had a very odd relationship with the Chicano movement. I felt a lot of angst and my wanting to hide came from knowing I was a homosexual. It was all about not knowing how to be in the world and also not seeing anybody like myself with that experience out there in the Latino community. I was in high school when I came out, so it was not very comfortable. Most of the Chicanos then . . . the men . . . were extremely macho. There were a couple of men who I really liked that I thought were right, but for the most part it seemed like it was kind of a macho mafia. (Rodríguez 1998)

Unlike many of his male classmates, Rodríguez did not take up "cholo styles" or standard masculine affectations. Rather, he "was at odds with the Pendelton shirts and the very baggy clothes" given his penchant for glam rock. Adopting an aesthetic largely influenced by glam rock, epitomized by the likes of David Bowie, Rodríguez was bound to stand out like a sore thumb. This, of course, led to his alienation from a movement that had little room for androgyny and flashy clothes.[26]

After moving to Los Angeles shortly after graduating from high school, Rodríguez began to establish relationships with other Chicano gay men who had been kicked out of, or estranged from, their blood families. Rodríguez recognizes these relationships as attempts at "redefining family," that is, the need to establish support networks that provide protection from the homophobia of traditional families and society at large and the racism of the dominant culture and a largely white gay subculture. Rodríguez, however, refuses to romanticize these "new families" considering how, when he now looks back, many of his would-be kin reproduced the alienating effects that were part and parcel of one's inherited family. He can recall the jealousy, contempt, dishonesty, and insecurity harbored by many of his Chicano gay "brothers" who were to presumably provide unconditional love. Despite these conflicts and tensions, these alternative kinship networks did nonetheless provide a space in which to bond over shared experiences and, for some, to ultimately develop the facility to navigate antagonistic arenas.

It is fitting, then, that Rodríguez's paintings conjoin images of various Chicano gay men with the men with whom he grew up. Noting the role that family photography played in his life ("In my home we had family photographs everywhere, so if our history was not always talked about it was always shown. And you could ask questions from photographs!" [Rodríguez 1998]), Rodríguez reproduces these images in his paintings to establish what Marianne Hirsch calls "familial looks." For Hirsch, familial looks signal the ways that domestic photographs command looking practices "that both create and consolidate the familial relations among the individuals involved, fostering an unmistakable sense of mutual recognition" (Hirsch 1997, 2). Familial looking, however, must not be considered a passive practice. Although a sense of mutual recognition may be established through familial looking, Rodríguez refuses to fashion looking relations in accordance with patriarchal and heterosexist ideologies. In fact, when Rodríguez superimposes scenes depicting sensual situations between Chicano gay men, he complicates any simple understanding of family by shifting the terms of conventional looking relations.

In *Fathers, Sons, and Sometimes Lovers* (1999), a painting composed of five panels, Rodríguez links a reproduction of a photograph of his father with several scenes depicting Chicano gay men (see figure 16). These scenes show two men in different states of slumber and a close-up of a couple engaged in a passionate kiss, along with a reproduction of a frame from his video *Buried and Unseen: Chiaroscuro* (1998) in which two men—Dario and George—are engaged in a discussion about their attempts to establish a long-term relationship. Strategically placed at the center of the painting, the father here signals the paternalism that, without fail, affects the bonds between men, particularly gay men. But Rodríguez also interrupts the presence and authority of the father by including a visible crack in the center of the panel that would otherwise connect to

FIGURE 16 Painting by Eugene Rodríguez, *Fathers, Sons, and Sometimes Lovers.*
Collection of Marty and Nancy Melzer. Reproduced with permission by the artist.

make his image, and the painting, "whole." The crack also distances the
father from the beer bottles representing the alcohol the artist associates
with his father that, as Rodríguez insisted during an interview, helped his
Father cope with the pressures of manhood. While one could (and should)
read *Fathers, Sons, and Sometimes Lovers* as a tribute to Chicano men, it
must also serve as a cautionary reminder that male relationships—gay
and straight—must always confront patriarchy's damaging interruptions.

Similar to *Fathers, Sons, and Sometimes Lovers, ¡Mira!* (2000) reproduces an image from the Rodríguez family photo archive (see figure 17).
The photo here shows two adult male relatives standing side by side. In
between them stands a young boy (Rodríguez perhaps?) who looks up,
admiringly, at one of the men. It is hard not to read this image as a family
portrait. While one immediately thinks of Grant Wood's famous *American Gothic, ¡Mira!,* however, resituates domestic iconography and, by
extension, the family, in a gay male frame. Behind the couple stands a
house—that unequivocal symbol of domesticity—above which looms an
image of two men making love. These two "men" are in fact G. I. Joe dolls

FIGURE 17 Painting by Eugene
Rodríguez, *¡Mira!* Collection
of Marty and Nancy Melzer.
Reproduced with permission by
the artist.

whose conventional masculine function is undermined by turning the
doll's hypermasculine, heterosexual persona on its head, casting him as a
potential male role model who desires men.[27] Furthermore, the pointing
finger that emerges from the bottom center of the painting prompts the
two men (and the painting's spectator) to look—*¡mira!*—at the action taking place between Joe and his lover, perhaps to see heteronormativity dis-
mantled, giving way to the world-making efforts of Rodríguez's canvases.

In her essay "Queer Aztlán: The Re-formation for Chicano Tribe," Cherríe Moraga (1993b, 160) suspects that "heterosexual Chicanos will have
the world to learn from their gay brothers about their shared masculinity." Rodríguez in fact sees his work as initiating a necessary dialogue between men—both gay and heterosexual—about their shared masculinity
and its influence on their lives within la familia (that is, within both its
bio- and sociocommunal contexts). Rodríguez notes:

At the artist's talk at Encantada [Gallery of Fine Arts] there were so many types of people who showed up. Women and men, queers and heterosexuals, people of color and white people. But I was struck by the dialogue between the Latino gay men and the heterosexual Latino men. It was so exciting to have this dialogue about sexuality and gender roles in the Latino family. It was reflective of the dialogue I try to initiate in my paintings between the men of the 1920s, '30s, and '40s with gay men of today. I want that conversation to take place in the paintings and between the men who see my work. In these discussions it is important that we not leave out homosexual desire or homosexuality as is what usually happens in the Chicano family and community. Sometimes it's like, yes, you can come to the party but you have to sit out in the lobby. I want to have a conversation in full, and I don't want to edit or limit anything for fear of the norm of heterosexual patriarchy in talking about Chicano masculinity. (E. Rodríguez 1998)

While Rodríguez asks gay men to break the silence around issues of sexuality and collectively speak out against their subordination within la familia and Chicano nationalist projects, he also calls upon heterosexual men to assist in contesting the inequalities within traditional family mo(ve)ments with which they're often complicit. Like Moraga, Rodríguez's return to the family had much to do with his initial alienation from it:

The use of the family for me is to return to the family after having abandoning the concept out of pain from the homophobia I experienced and then, in the 1970s when my father killed himself and my mother died of cancer. And coming out of the closet as homosexual, I wanted to run from all of it because I wasn't accepted by my family. So I felt as though I would . . . being seventeen, and arrogant, thinking that I would in one swoop be able to rewrite history and delete the word family from my dictionary as well as from cultural practice, if possible. I also didn't understand in terms of my pain where that came from, and why I would feel that way about the family. So I think having lived throughout the eighties in Los Angeles trying to find where I fit into society as well as trying to find love. I think the work is, at this point, all about trying to return to family, because, for myself, it is a necessity and a very strong thing. Yet while it can be very nurturing, powerful, and comforting, it is not perfect. It is certainly problematic at times with regards to sexualities and gender roles. So, in terms of the work I do, I try to look at those questions of, How do Latino gay men form family without abandoning their family of blood? How do they include their blood family with their family that they've made regarding their "marriage," so to speak, to other Latino gay men? (E. Rodríguez 1998)

Clearly, Rodríguez's work about the family is complex, at times even contradictory, yet it is very clear about its desire to create community between Chicano men, as well as between Chicanos and Chicanas, across genders and sexualities. Certainly a means for dealing with the racial, sexual, and economic subordination of the nation-state, the family for Rodríguez also operates as an arena in and through which cultural and political empowerment becomes possible.

I will end this chapter with a poem by activist Rodrigo Reyes, whose work with the San Francisco–based Latino/a queer organization GALA (which he founded) will be further discussed in this book's conclusion in relation to the documentary ¡Viva 16! Allow me, however, to say a few things about Reyes that I believe give his poem and my reading of it a suitable historical context. Reyes was deeply involved in the Chicano movement during the 1970s, reporting extensively on it for KPFK, the Bay Area's Pacifica Radio station (Roque Ramírez 2004, 33–34). His LGBT community ties were ultimately woven in with his ties to the Latino community, thus giving way to GALA's formation. A prolific and highly influential activist during his lifetime, on January 19, 1992, Reyes passed away from complications due to AIDS. In her "Tribute," published in *The Last Generation*, Cherríe Moraga (1993, 175–78) writes, "Last night at the service, I kept thinking . . . Rodrigo loved his own kind, his own brown and male kind. Listening to the tributes made to him, it was clear that the hearts he touched the most deeply were his carnalitos. And each one, as lovely as the one preceding him, spoke about Rodrigo, 'mi 'mano, mi papito, mi carnal, ese carbon . . . ' con un cariño wholly felt." Although Moraga confesses to not always feeling recognized as a sister by Reyes and questions his dedication to his sisters (attributing this to "all the wounds of family betrayals and abandonments"), she nonetheless identifies him as a brother and, more to the point here, acknowledges his impact on his Chicano and Latino gay male *carnales*. So much so she ends her tribute with the following verse:

He did make space for them, his brothers
he did plant seeds,
he did lay ground.

And this is where the young ones pick up . . .
¡Adelante 'manitos! (178)

Reyes is one of many Chicano gay men no longer with us who indeed inscribed his experiences as a Chicano gay man not only in the public sphere where he made his presence known as an activist but also in his writing, which is in need of redistribution and recirculation. In his writing, it becomes clear that his "'manitos" were the objects of his desire, a desire charged with both a crucial sexual current as well as a bond that extends beyond heteronormative kinship.

Appearing in 1985 with Humanizarte Publications in San Francisco and now out of print, a collection of Chicano gay male poetry entitled *Ya Vas, Carnal*—which I translate from the Chicano Spanish as, "Go on, brother!"—featured the work of three gay Chicano poets: Francisco X. Alarcón, Juan Pablo Gutiérrez, and Rodrigo Reyes. (This is also where Alarcón's poem, which serves as this chapter's epigraph, appears.) "Carnal Knowledge," Reyes's poem that opens the collection is, as I understand it, about Chicano gay consciousness, desire, and brotherhood, the stuff about which this chapter has been concerned. I cite it in its entirety:

Carnal,
ése,
sabes qué,
don't I know you?

Didn't we meet
eyes, una vez,
didn't I kiss
your heart
once? Calmado.
I am sure
I know you
Oye carnal,
didn't you
use to live
next to me,
a un ladito?
I remember

that if I

reached out

I could touch

you.

It was a long time ago

Then you split.

Querías conocer mundo.

Te acuerdas?

Simón, I'm sure

it was you.

Do you know

me,

carnal? (Reyes 1985, 8–9)

Who is this carnal, this brother? Not simply his *hermano* ("proper" Spanish for brother, usually connoting a biological kinship brother), this *carnal* (Chicano Spanish for an extended kin-like brother) is the speaker's lover. Perhaps an MSM with whom he has made love, or perhaps an openly gay man who has turned his back on him, the carnal in question is being asked to acknowledge the speaker, with whom he not only shares the experience of bodily contact—carnal knowledge—but also the knowledge of brotherhood, a knowingness exchanged between carnales. In this poem, Rodrigo Reyes helps flesh out a history of gay consciousness between Chicano men in which to love a "brother" fuels the ability to mobilize "brotherhood" in queer political projects informed by desire. This stance, I believe, is akin to the group of African American gay men whose influential writings appear in the groundbreaking collection *Brother to Brother*, influenced by the well-known declaration, "black men loving black men is the revolutionary act," from Marlon Riggs's documentary *Tongues Untied*. So the question at the end of Reyes's poem—"Do you know me, carnal?"—is not merely a one-way, interpellative inquiry; rather, its provocative impulse stimulates a generative request for mutual recognition: as I call you, my brother, acknowledge me as yours.

Afterword Making Queer *Familia*

> These spaces of *familia* have all made this moment of conclu-
> sion possible; they have taught me almost everything I now
> know about queer, about desire, about bodies on the margins,
> and dance floors creating momentary centers.
>
> • • • Juana María Rodríguez, *Queer Latinidad: Identity Practices,*
> *Discursive Spaces* (2003)

I n her foundational essay, "The Traffic in Women: Notes on the 'Political Economy' of Sex," anthropologist Gayle Rubin (1975, 169) maintains that kinship is not "a list of biological relatives" but rather "a
system of categories and statuses that often contradict actual genetic relationships." While this book has detailed at length the ways in which *la*
familia has been deployed as a means of maintaining normative kinship
arrangements, I want to close by illustrating how reconfigured kinship arrangements need not be established in mutual exclusivity from biological
relations. Kath Weston has identified this as enacting "chosen families."
For Weston (1992, 137), "chosen families do not directly oppose genealogical modes of reckoning kinship. Instead, they undercut procreation's
status as a master term imagined to provide the template for all possible
kinship relations." Indeed, chosen families lie at the heart of Chicano/a
queer politics so much so that it has become virtually impossible to articulate notions of community without signaling their import. And while
this afterword aims to show how "queer familia" as a chosen family might
contest the heteropatriarchal stronghold on communitarian thought in
Chicano/a cultural politics, it must also end with a cautionary note given
how "queer" reconfigurations are always provisional.

Let us return, then, to the work of Cherríe Moraga broached in this book's introduction as an important guidepost for charting its conceptual terrain. As a way of making more tangible her dream for "Queer Aztlán," Moraga adopts la familia to foreground its potential for collective empowerment and social change. Her comprehension of empowerment, however, does not focus exclusively on the blood family entrenched within the domestic sphere, nor does it substitute such a family with a sociosymbolic kinship network mobilized within the public sphere. Instead, as Moraga's reworking of la familia breaks from the heteropatriarchal expectations that characterize the typical desires to utilize "private" matters for "public" values, she additionally scrambles kinship with the family to formulate a radical dialectic. Moraga, I believe, succeeds in disengaging their usual hard-and-fast categorization that also separates the private from the public by situating la familia within a genealogy conjoining individuals relatively immediate and socially extended.

Coterminous with her critique of Chicano nationalism, Moraga (1993b, 157) points out that "the preservation of the Chicano familia became the Movimiento's mandate and within this constricted 'familia' structure Chicano políticos ensured that the patriarchal father figure remained in charge both in their private and political lives." Yet Moraga's insistence on utilizing the idea of la familia shows how belonging to *la raza* need not be contained by a male nationalist desire. Thus her troping of the family frequently shifts between her biologically given family and her sociopolitical family of choice, privileging neither relation over the other in the final analysis but rather animating the notion of a "chosen family." Importantly, Moraga's deployment of the family always reveals a radical departure from conventional nationalist appeals found in early movement texts.

For Chicana/o queers—as Moraga has shown—disinheriting one's biologically given family is a near impossible task considering how blood ties often prove invaluable. As Sunil Gupta has remarked in the case of Black and Asian gay men in Britain,

> the family was the source of both material and communal well-being. In a hostile white environment, for the first generation the community was their only hope of comfort and security. To turn your backs on it was to cut yourself off from both this security in real terms and from a sense of identity that was/is separate from the whites. (1989, 176)

In response to the exclusionary practices of white queer communities, the work of Moraga echoes Gupta in its desire to maintain family connections. Moreover, Moraga (1993b, 147) acknowledges finding a "sense of place among la Chicanada," which, "not always a safe place . . . is unequivocally the original familial place from which [she is] compelled to write, which [she] reach[es] toward in [her] audiences, and which serves as [her] source of inspiration, voice, and lucha." In turn, Moraga's "Queer Aztlán" amplifies this family relationship and recasts it within the public sphere as a strategy for contesting the inequalities faced by queer members of la raza. Despite the questions it provokes and, indeed, its limitations and exclusions, Moraga's new nationalism does part ways with conventional demands for national consciousness since it is premised on a democratic egalitarianism for Chicanos and Chicanas in spite of—or most likely because of—class, gender, and sexual differences.

While Moraga insists that "la Chicana Indígena must stand at the center" of her new nationalism, "Queer Aztlán" nonetheless encompasses heterosexuals (who are no doubt rehabilitated) as well as gay men. Indeed, her nation-based kinship network is fundamentally concerned with the role of Chicano gay men in enacting a liberatory politics. Although critical of gay men and their inherent male privilege ("Being gay does not preclude gay men from harboring the same sexism evident in heterosexual men" [1993b, 161]), Moraga nevertheless closely aligns them with lesbians given their shared marginalization from blood families and the Chicano community at large. "When 'El Plan Espiritual de Aztlán' was conceived a generation ago," she writes, "lesbians and gay men were not envisioned as members of the 'house'; we were not recognized as the sister planting the seeds, the brothers gathering the crops. We were not counted as members of the 'bronze continent'" (159). Here Moraga signals a bond between the queer outcast "siblings"; yet she simultaneously puts pressure on Chicano gay men "to recognize and acknowledge that their freedom is intricately connected to the freedom of women." By doing so, "gay men can do their part to unravel how both men and women have been formed and deformed" by racism, misogyny, and homophobia (162).

Various cultural productions reveal that Chicano/a queers have taken up and extended Moraga's attempt to recast and conjoin our understanding of kinship and the family (albeit at times confirming her point about the gay male potential to wield power over women). To provide illustration, I want to engage with Augie Robles's and Valentín Aguirre's 1994 documentary video, ¡Viva 16! Yet let me briefly digress to discuss John D'Emilio's influential essay "Capitalism and Gay Identity" (1983), which importantly illustrates how the conjugal relationship of capitalism and family tends to suppress gay and lesbian identities yet simultaneously enables their emergence via new modes of kinship.

D'Emilio suggests that gay and lesbian communities exist on terrain beyond the boundaries of the heterosexual family, on terrain where social and sexual collectivity and collaboration become possible. Noting the declining centrality of the family's economic stronghold given men's and women's participation in the capitalist free-labor system, D'Emilio traces the emergence of literary societies, private social clubs, drag balls, and bars as social spaces where gay men and lesbians ultimately came together in the early twentieth century. A parallel socioeconomic phenomenon, of course, holds true in the late twentieth and early twenty-first century for Chicano/a and Latino/a queers, particularly those migrating to, and residing and working within, urban spaces in the United States. Indeed, for as much as D'Emilio's historical account is insightful, especially when translated for a context in which queer communities of color and their specific experiences take center stage, it is important nonetheless to signal his essay's blind spots. Scott Bravmann (1990, 70), for instance, observes how the "newly gay identity and social action" tracked in D'Emilio's essay ultimately "reflect the same differentiation based on gender, race, and class that pervades capitalist societies." In other words, in D'Emilio's conceptual frame, "when it first emerged, gay life was the domain of middle-class urban white men." While Bravmann is also right to note that "the formation of a modern gay identity must have depended on the subjugation of people of color" (71), it is imperative to grasp how gay identity formation depended upon a split from the families from which these gay men once belonged. Alan Sinfield's discussion on the rise of "metropolitan gay identities" in his book *Gay and After* resonates with D'Emilio's project, yet parts ways with it when he correctly argues that the "metropolitan disaffiliation from family does not suit members of racial minorities" (1998, 7). Thus when considering the convergence of metropolitan identities of racial-ethnic gay men and lesbians, one must always consider the sustained relevance of family and kinship in their discrepant articulations.

This is evident in ¡*Viva 16!* (1994), Augie Robles's and Valentín Aguirre's video documentary "focusing on the queens, drag performers, and homeboys of San Francisco's gay Latino strip," the Mission District.[1] Along with spotlighting two neighboring gay bars—Esta Noche and La India Bonita—that lie on 16th Street (hence the video's title), the documentary maps the emergence of a San Francisco queer Latino community coterminous with—and not necessarily exclusive from—the Chicano movement.[2] ¡*Viva 16!* opens with shots that frame a distinct cultural terrain as well as the iconography particular to the Mission District and other urban Latino hubs (for example, fruit stands, run-down buildings, and Virgen de Guadalupe and Aztec calendar T-shirts). Aguirre and Robles admit that the "primary focus" of the video "is Chicanos" (Brandley 1994); yet the video also brings into focus the overlapping histories and experiences of those composing a diasporic, transnational Latino cultural citizenship.

In the introduction to their edited collection, *Latino Cultural Citizenship: Claiming Identity, Space, and Rights*, William V. Flores and Rina Benmayor (1997, 1) define Latino cultural citizenship as "a range of social practices which, taken together, claim and establish a distinct social space for Latinos in this country. Latino social space is evolving and developing new forms, many of them contributing to an emergent Latino consciousness and social and political development." Extrapolating from the work of Arjun Appadurai, Puerto Rican theorist Juan Flores (1997, 221) argues that though it is important to view "lo Latino ('Latinoness') from the optic of the particular national groups, the social and cultural perspective of each group also evokes some relation to a Latino 'ethnoscape' of transnational dimensions." Although viewed from a Chicano optic, the video ultimately—and necessarily—examines a distinctly Latino ethnoscape given the transnational dimensions of the Mission and the Latino gay scene in general, and the gay bar scene in particular, in San Francisco.[3] Indeed, Andres Camacho Contreras, one of the video's interviewees, points out that Esta Noche and La India Bonita are spaces occupied not only by "Mexicanos" but by Latinos whose roots stem from various regions of the United States (including, of course, Aztlán) and Central and South America (as well as "Americanos" and Filipinos).

To make further sense of these spaces, Avtar Brah's *Cartographies of Diaspora: Contesting Identities* offers an important conceptual frame in which to situate the dynamics captured in *¡Viva 16!* In her book, Brah (1996, 16) employs the "immanent" concepts of diaspora, border, and politics of location, which, taken together, "mark conceptual connections for historicised analyses of contemporary trans/national movements of people, information, cultures, commodities and capital." From this site "a new concept" is initiated: "diaspora space." Diaspora space is, as she argues, "a point of confluence of economic, political, cultural, and psychic processes." Moreover,

> it is where multiple subject positions are juxtaposed, contested, proclaimed or disavowed; where the permitted and the prohibited perpetually interrogate; and where the accepted and the transgressive imperceptibly mingle even while these syncretic forms may be disclaimed in the name of purity and tradition. Here, tradition is itself continually invented even as it may be hailed as originating from the mists of time. (Brah 1996, 208)

"Distinct from the concept of diaspora," diaspora space "is 'inhabited' not only by diasporic subjects but equally by those who are constructed and represented as 'indigenous'" (16). Diaspora space, then, is an effective concept that situates the intersecting local Chicano and transnational Latino community formations evident in *¡Viva 16!*, the Mission, and, most importantly, specific geopolitical moments.[4] Likewise, given the way familial traditions are "continually invented" within diaspora space, we can also register its "new" manifestation in rooted, yet spliced, genealogies.

As with most documentaries, *¡Viva 16!* employs talking heads, voice-over narration, shots of still photographs, and an assemblage of archival footage. Significantly, the video begins with family photographs and a personal memoir of activist and health administrator Diane Felix. She begins with a personal anecdote about the evolution of her lesbianism. We then hear from Chris Sandoval and Ricky Rubio who elaborate on the emergent Chicano/a gay and lesbian community in San Francisco in the early 1970s. When Rubio discusses GALA, The Gay Latino Alliance, the language of kinship central to queer Latino community formation is instantly detected. Rubio declares: "I really didn't want to become a part of GALA, it became a part of me." GALA members also understood "the family" as "their source of strength"—"At the core of GALA's philosophy is not to alienate ourselves from our families and community but to help them come to understand our gayness in a Latino context."[5] In *¡Viva 16!*, Felix, Sandoval, and Rubio collectively detail how GALA was a departure point for the eventual creation of the bar Esta Noche, which endeavored to establish a queer Chicano/Latino counterpublic.[6]

For Michael Warner (2002, 121–22) one of the distinguishing features of counterpublics is that they attempt "to supply different ways of imagining stranger sociability and its reflexivity . . . oriented to stranger-circulation in a way that is not just strategic but also constitutive of membership and its affects." Premised on "imagining stranger sociability," the video reveals how Esta Noche's owners sell their house so as to create a space where, as Felix conveys, "the bar became home and strangers became family." In a related vein, we might invoke Manuel Guzmán from chapter 4 who reads the New York bar La Escuelita as "the house of gay Latino men in the city of New York," a "house" where generative schemes such as "the principles on which the production of thought, perception, and action are based" (1997, 215). *¡Viva 16!* offers a view of queer Latino kinship networks that counter dislocation within the inhabited space of the house-*cum*-bar, hinging on the strategy to forego domestic private property for communal public space.[7] Indeed, throughout the video, the subjects of *¡Viva 16!* elaborate on the pleasures and politics of Latino/a queer bodies in a communal public. To invoke Juana María Rodríguez whose words opened this afterword (words that were fittingly inspired within bars like Esta Noche), such spaces supply a sense of familia because of the ways in which they foster a sense of Latino/a queer belonging. Moreover, the video's overarching narrative recalls Cherríe Moraga's attempt to recast the rhetoric of Chicano/a cultural nationalism in "Queer Aztlán": situating the Chicano homeland of Aztlán in a sexually democratic—that is, an antiheterosexist and antihomophobic—frame. At the start of the video, *¡Viva 16!* fittingly identifies itself as a twenty-first-century Aztlán production. However, the ethnoscape of a transnational queer Latino/a counterpublic begs a rethinking of Chicano cultural nationalist objectives given the more expansive, transnational alliances invariably forged.

Akin to Moraga's scrambling of kinship networks chosen and given, the queer Latino bar is not off-limits to biological family members. In writing about La Escuelita, Manuel Guzmán argues that for men in the bar, "the articulation and the negotiation of sexual desire must perforce blend in the matrix of social interactions found there." Yet,

> while sitting or dancing, men must negotiate their sexual desires in the presence of homosexual women, heterosexuals, and their relatives. Mothers and their mothers, *nuestras abuelas*, are members familiar to the audience. According to Raúl [La Escuelita's co-owner], "we, Hispanics, do not have any shame or *complejos* with regards to our children. We love them as they are. They [Hispanic families] have heard so much about La Escuelita that they come to see where it is their children go to. I know that is the case because I receive them at the door where they always ask for a table." (Guzmán 1997, 215)

Although Raúl claims that *all* "Hispanic families" do not harbor shame or complexes about their gay children (a sweeping claim to be sure), his observations are nonetheless useful to ascertain how Latino/a queer spaces might not always be exclusively queer. Indeed, listed on a flier for GALA's first anniversary dance, along with the traditional features one would expect to find at gay dances such as live music and food, is childcare. As is the case with La Escuelita, the families present at La India Bonita and Esta Noche must ultimately meet the challenges to heteronormativity posed by a queer public culture. Focusing on "the mother of a Chicano drag queen," Ramón García's poem "Miss Primavera Contest," published in *The Americas Review* in 1994—the same year of ¡*Viva 16!*'s release—takes place at La India Bonita. In it, García highlights how a Fellini-like surrealism mixes with the familiar sights and sounds of a queer Latino bar (where "machismo and being maricón are blurred/as the tough cholo dances with the drag queen"); and yet this space does not require detachment from "traditional" family relationships. Within the queer space of La India Bonita, for example, an alternative identification between mother and son emerges. García writes, "Miss Primavera's mother/must have been a little like/Miss Primavera herself, her son/and deep inside this must please her/for her hijo to turn out/so much like her/when she was in the Spring of her life—a little bit loca" (and "*loca*" is, fittingly, a term used by Latino/a queers to refer to someone *as* queer). The mother's identification with her son also offers a refreshing reversal of traditional parent-child sexual difference models, namely the Oedipus complex and the passage it requires in obtaining normative familial and sexual status.[8]

Judith Butler (1993, 124) argues that the rearticulation of kinship by the transgender African Americans and Latinos who comprise the New York subcultural drag ball scene in the film *Paris Is Burning* "might be understood as repetitions of hegemonic forms of power which fail to repeat loyally and, in that failure, open possibilities for resignifying the terms of violation against their violating aims."[9] In other words, it is possible to acknowledge "the force of repetition" as "the very condition of an affirmative response to violation" (124).[10] Importantly, Butler also emphasizes that there are moments in which these strategic repetitions cannot be called subversive. Such a moment in *¡Viva 16!* is when the men are unwilling to understand the necessity of a women's component in GALA. In a moment of finely honed crosscutting, Felix and Rubio elaborate on the tensions between men and women within the group around the creation of a women's component. Rubio insists the group had to be a group undivided, "all for one," as it were, "fighting for one goal." Felix, though, insists that women also required a separate space given the male-dominant composition of the group. Felix relates the situation to that of a family feud, chalking it up to an instance of unconditional love, a moment in which women must negotiate the presence of brothers whose gender socialization affects their relationships with women. Certainly, this moment of a gay-inflected paternalism symbolically keeps the divisive bar in between gay and lesbian communities firmly intact. Furthermore, the space of the bar (like diaspora space, cultural nationalism, or la familia) is never inherently devoid of inequality. Consider, then, how the number of women in this space, as captured in the documentary, is minimal at best in contrast to the number of men. Reflective of GALA's gender politics, women in the bar scenes showcased in *¡Viva 16!* are relegated to secondary status. As Horacio Roque Ramírez's research on GALA has shown, the marginalization of women in GALA extended into the space of Esta Noche (which "undermined GALA's social and political fundraising efforts") since the bar was inevitably regarded as a business and not a political organization, thus destabilizing the potential of democratic kinship in light of proprietorship. Thus women's protest and demand for equal treatment would be further ignored and dismissed (Roque Ramírez 2003, 256). Clearly evident is the provisional status of queer (read here as gay male) constitutions of community, including the fact that nonheteronormative attempts at collectivity are never inherently liberatory or automatically given. Indeed, the gendered hierarchies particular to the domestic sphere can indeed extend into the public domain of a bar that for some might be home sweet home whereas others may desire to burn it down.

This book has sought to unveil the complexities in maintaining la familia as an organizing principle for Chicano/a cultural politics. It is not hard to see why its retention proves difficult given its placement at the heart of heteropatriarchal value systems. Yet the significance of kinship becomes evident when taking into account the myriad forces of subordination faced by Chicano/a and Latino/a communities. In particular, the queer folk within these communities will undoubtedly continue to critically assess and negotiate their relationships with the families to whom they are born as well as to those with whom they are joined by necessity. In his book, *Against Nature: Essays on History, Sexuality, and Identity*, Jeffrey Weeks (1991, 135) argues that it is within the "subterranean social order" that genuine alternative families are created. It is my hope that the Chicano/a and Latino/a subterranean social order reflected in the texts and cultural practices with which this book has grappled precisely illustrates how community is made, and remade, ideally over and against normative familia romances whose hopeful passing will call forth its next of kin.

Notes

INTRODUCTION: STAKING FAMILY CLAIMS

1. Consider Dorothy and Thomas Hoobler's *The Mexican American Family Album* (1994), a general, pictorial history of Chicanos that has on its cover a photo of the "Ramírez family of Nietos, California, around 1890" while the last image in the book is of a "1990s family reunion."

2. In his formulation of the term, Ferguson (2004, 6) draws from Karl Marx in *The German Ideology* who "universalized heteropatriarchy as he theorized property ownership." "For Marx," Ferguson importantly reminds us, "tribal ownership presumed a natural division of labor symbolized by the heterosexual and patriarchal family" (2004, 6).

3. Although "Chicano" and "Chicano/a" may be used interchangeably, the singular use of "Chicano" more often than not foregrounds masculine signification. Also, although distinctions may be made between the two terms, I use "machismo" interchangeably with "masculinity." I believe they fundamentally overlap, particularly when used, as Alma García notes, "within a Chicano context." I will further discuss this issue in chapter 1.

4. Foundational texts that have also influenced this thinking on nationalism and gender and sexual politics include George L. Mosse's *Nationalism and Sexuality: Middle-Class Morality and Sexual Norms in Modern Europe* (1985), Doris Sommer's *Foundational Fictions: The National Romances of Latin America* (1991), and the anthology *Nationalisms and Sexualities* (1991), edited by Andrew Parker, Mary Russo, Doris Sommer, and Patricia Yaeger.

5. Benedict Anderson (1983) distinguishes between nation-states and nation formation vis-à-vis citizenship. See also Frantz Fanon's *The Wretched of the Earth* (1963), John Breuilly's *Nationalism and the State* (1982), Partha Chatterjee's *The Nation and Its Fragments: Colonial and Postcolonial Histories* (1993), James Clifford's "Routes" (1997), Neil Lazarus's *Nationalism and Cultural Practice in the Postcolonial World* (1997), and Emma Pérez's *The Decolonial Imaginary: Writing Chicanas into History* (1999) for more on this point.

6. See also George Mariscal's *Brown-Eyed Children of the Sun* (2005).

7. The book's chapter titles in which he quotes the (same) passage from *El Plan* are, respectively, "La Reconquista" and "A Grudge against the Gringo."

8. See also Herman Gray's "Is Cultural Studies Inflated? The Cultural Economy of Cultural Studies in the United States" (1996) for an illuminating discussion on the politics and functions of cultural studies.

9. See the collection of essays edited by Paul Gilroy, Lawrence Grossberg, and Angela McRobbie, *Without Guarantees: In Honor of Stuart Hall* (2000), for evidence of the transnational impact of British cultural studies. Angie Chabram-Dernersesian's (2000) contribution, "Critical Dialogues on Chicana/o Cultural Studies," is instructive in this context given how it conveys responses by numerous Chicana/o scholars on the relationship between Chicano/a studies and cultural studies.

10. Two illuminating ethnographic studies of gay male "chosen families" are William G. Hawkeswoods's *One of the Children: Gay Black Men in Harlem* (1996) and Peter M. Nardi's *Gay Men's Friendships: Invincible Communities* (1999). Appropriately both texts draw upon Weston's work. For a lively debate on gay and lesbian kinship, see the section "An Exchange with David M. Schneider on Gay and Lesbian Kinship" in the journal *Cultural Anthropology*, which features Schneider's (1997) insightful essay, "The Power of Culture: Notes on Some Aspects of Gay and Lesbian Kinship in America Today." For recent considerations of kinship from an interdisciplinary frame, see the anthology *Relative Values: Reconfiguring Kinship Studies* (2001), edited by Sarah Franklin and Susan McKinnon. Judith Butler's *Antigone's Claim: Kinship between Life and Death* (2000a) and David L. Eng's "Transnational Adoption and Queer Diasporas" (2003) represent important recent work on kinship and queer communities.

REAPPRAISING THE ARCHIVE

1. In recent years the body of scholarship on the Chicano movement has grown tremendously. See, for example, Ignacio García, *United We Win: The Rise and Fall of La Raza Unida Party* (1989); Carlos Muñoz Jr., *Youth, Identity, Power: The Chicano Movement* (1989); Juan Gómez-Quiñones, *Chicano Politics: Reality and Promise, 1940–1990* (1990); Armando Navarro, *Mexican American Youth Organization: Avant-Garde of the Chicano Movement in Texas* (1995); Alma M. Garcia, ed., *Chicana Feminist Thought: The Basic Historical Writings* (1997); Ernesto B. Vigil, *The Crusade for Justice: Chicano Militancy and the Government's War on Dissent* (1999); Armando Navarro, *La Raza Unida Party: A Chicano Challenge to the U.S. Two-Party Dictatorship* (2000); Jesús Salvador Treviño, *Eyewitness: A Filmmaker's Memoir of the Chicano Movement* (2001); Ernesto Chávez, *"¡Mi Raza Primero!": Nationalism, Identity, and Insurgency*

in the Chicano Movement in Los Angeles, 1966–1978 (2002); Lorena Oropeza, *¡Raza Sí! ¡Guerra No!: Chicano Protest and Patriotism during the Viet Nam War Era* (2005); George Mariscal, *Brown-Eyed Children of the Sun: Lessons from the Chicano Movement, 1965–1975* (2005); and Lorena Oropeza and Dionne Espinoza, eds., *Enriqueta Vasquez and the Chicano Movement: Writings from "El Grito del Norte"* (2006).

2. Consider Carlos Muñoz Jr. (1989, 15) who writes: "Chicano youth radicalism represented a return to the humanistic cultural values of the Mexican working class. This in turn led to the shaping of a nationalist ideology."

3. The upholding of patriarchy put forth here might also be linked to Tijerina's use of homosexual baiting as a way to prove one's manhood as revealed in a speech delivered to an audience at the University of California, San Diego: "I don't blame the Minutemen for doing those things, because they have run out of men. Most of them are homosexuals now and very few men are found among them." See "Viva La Raza" in the UCSD student newspaper *Indicator* (January 29, 1969: 4). My thanks to Professor Jorge Mariscal for bringing this piece to my attention.

4. See, for example, Octavio Ignacio Romano-V.'s "The Anthropology and Sociology of the Mexican-Americans" (1968) and "Social Science, Objectivity, and the Chicanos" (1970); Nick Vaca's two-part essay "The Mexican-American in the Social Sciences, 1912–1970" (1970); Nathan Murillo's "The Mexican American Family" (1971); Miguel Montiel's "The Social Science Myth of the Mexican American Family" (1970); and, of course, the path-finding ethnocriticism of Americo Paredes, *Folklore and Culture on the Texas-Mexico Border* (1993a). All of these authors preceded and informed the ensuing work of Chicana intellectuals Lea Ybarra (especially her oft-cited 1977 dissertation "Conjugal Role Relationships in the Chicano Family") and Maxine Baca Zinn (whose 1979 article "Chicano Family Research: Conceptual Distortions and Alternative Directions" stands as an exemplary case in point), which employed a gendered analysis of misrepresentations of the Chicano family in the social sciences.

5. For a thorough reading of these studies, see Richard Griswold del Castillo's *La Familia: Chicano Families in the Urban Southwest 1848 to the Present* (1984). In *Women's Work and Chicano Families: Cannery Workers of the Santa Clara Valley*, Patricia Zavella (1987, 13) importantly notes that a "hearty critique of acculturation theory and functionalism has developed in the past decade and a half, much of it by Chicano social scientists. This revisionist body of work shows that functionalism, as it has been applied to Chicano families, reifies values and norms and disregards change and variation among both Mexicans and Mexican Americans." Maxine Baca Zinn—discussing the limitations of assimilationist analytic frameworks and the potentials in adopting the internal

colonialism framework—argues, "An alternative framework must be adopted. It is necessary to steer analysis away from assimilation and toward a perspective which includes the concepts of oppression, opposition and change" (Baca Zinn, 1975, 15). It is well to note here, in the spirit of foreshadowing a discussion later in this chapter, that Zavella (1987, 13) writes immediately following the mention of this revisionist body of work that: "to the extent that functionalist and acculturation studies have any virtue, it is that they describe the *ideology* of traditional Chicano families." The ideology of traditional Chicano families, of which patriarchy (or "machismo") is frequently part and parcel, was not thoroughly and critically scrutinized by many Chicano (male) scholars, perhaps in fear of acknowledging some valid claims within functionalist and acculturation studies—a move that would indeed align them with those whose work was dismissed as racist and stereotypical. Yet in refusing to acknowledge and challenge male domination, the work of Chicano scholars was not entirely different from those they contested. Furthermore, although these Chicano social scientists wished to emphasize complex and varied experiences of the family, complexity and variety were unassimilable terms for certain brands of movement nationalism.

6. For an exemplary essay on Chicana feminist contestation of the patriarchal paradigm, see Dionne Espinoza, "'Revolutionary Sisters': Women's Solidarity and Collective Identification among Chicana Brown Berets in East Los Angeles, 1967–1970" (2001). Important recent studies that engage with Chicana feminist print culture of the era include Maylei Blackwell, "Contested Histories: *Las Hijas de Cuauhtémoc*, Chicana Feminisms, and Print Culture in the Chicano Movement, 1968–1973" (2003); and Benita Roth's *Separate Roads to Feminism: Black, Chicana, and White Feminist Movements in America's Second Wave* (2003).

7. Some scholars have suggested that Chicanas felt the need to conform to movement ideologies despite their discomfort and subordination so as not to sabotage the efforts of Chicanismo's potential to effect social change. On this point, see, for example, Sonia Saldívar-Hull's *Feminism on the Border: Chicana Gender Politics and Literature* (2000). Saldívar-Hull also offers a pointed critical reading of Baca Zinn's "Political Familism" (1975). Two years after Baca Zinn, Chicana feminist Clara Gloria Castrellón (1977, 7) questioned the paternal codification of familia and raza by claiming that "the institution of marriage is counter-evolutionary" and that "the most insidious group of counter-revolutionary agents" are children who monopolize women's time and stand as "the greatest obstacle to revolutionary thought today." Castrellón's poignant manifesto "Love and Revolution" is from the sole issue of *Capirotada* (1977), a Chicana literary and arts publication from the University of Texas at El Paso.

8. The edition from which I cite has a 1972 copyright and a $1.50 price tag on the back cover.

9. While there is no mention of Armas in the publication, Chicano students at San José State University in California published a serial pamphlet in 1972 first titled "La Familia" but subsequently changed to "La Familia de La Raza." The pamphlet called upon students to organize around the concept of la familia that linked "the immediate *familia*" and "our 'universal *familia*'" so as to deploy "La Familia as a model of action" that would in turn generate carnalismo. The cover image is, appropriately enough, Joaquín Chiñas's *La Familia*, which I will discuss shortly. I thank Dionne Espinoza for bringing the publication to my attention.

10. Numerous books address the myth of declining "family values," before and after the "pro-family" campaigns staged by the Right and Christian fundamentalists in contemporary political culture. The following titles are prime examples: Christopher Lasch, *Haven in a Heartless World: The Family Besieged* (1977); Barrie Thorne and Marilyn Yalom, eds., *Rethinking the Family: Some Feminist Questions* (1992); Judith Stacey, *Brave New Families: Stories of Domestic Upheaval in Late Twentieth Century America* (1990); Stephanie Coontz, *The Way We Never Were: American Families and the Nostalgia Trap* (1992); Judith Stacey, *In the Name of the Family: Rethinking Family Values in the Postmodern Age* (1996); Stephanie Coontz, *The Way We Really Are: Coming to Terms with America's Changing Families* (1997); Hilde Lindemann Nelson, ed., *Feminism and Families* (1997); and Gill Jagger and Caroline Wright, eds., *Changing Family Values* (1999).

11. "I am Joaquín" was originally published in 1967. In this text I cite the Bantam Books edition *I am Joaquín* yet I retain the quotation marks around the title (rather than italicize the title as a book) to connote the genealogy of the poem as a poem. "Since 1967," states the first line of the section "About 'I am Joaquín'" in the Bantam edition, "the Crusade for Justice has published, in mimeographed, photocopied, and printed editions, over 100,000 copies, which have been given away or sold to support the organization" (R. Gonzales, 1972, 2).

12. Edward James Olmos's made-for-cable HBO film *Walkout* (2006) about the East Los Angeles high school blowouts fittingly depicts a recital of the poem at a youth leadership conference. The portion of the poem—as well as the particular version—cited by Fregoso and Chabram, however, does not make reference to Aztlán, although the poem is placed within the context of Aztlán immediately following their discussion of it. It should be noted that even the poem in its entirety, printed as Bantam Book's 1972 *I Am Joaquín*, does not mention Aztlán. Rafael Pérez-Torres also recognizes this point in *Movements in Chicano Poetry: Against Myths, Against Margins*, writing: "Although it does

not invoke the name Aztlán, the poem expresses a number of concerns that Chicana [sic] nationalism articulates through Aztlán" (1995, 69). Indeed Aztlán is undoubtedly a sort of relational homeland and a psychosymbolic space to situate Chicano nationalism, yet the symbolic currency of the family unveils deeper historical implications. For comprehensive discussions on Aztlán, see the Anaya and Lomelí collection *Aztlán: Essays on the Chicano Homeland* (1989). For elaborations on the importance of retaining Aztlán as a signifier for Chicano cultural politics, albeit reconfigured to embrace gender and sexuality, see Daniel Cooper Alarcón's "The Aztec Palimpsest: Toward a New Understanding of Aztlán, Cultural Identity and History" (1988–90) and Pérez-Torres's "Refiguring Aztlán" (1997). Both essays appeared, appropriately enough, in *Aztlán: A Journal of Chicano Studies.*

13. For more on Gonzales and the Crusade for Justice, see Ernesto Vigil's *The Crusade for Justice* (1999) and the collection of Gonzales's writings entitled *Message to Aztlán: Selected Writings* (2001). Juan Haro's *The Ultimate Betrayal: An Autobiography* (1998) offers a critique of the Crusade for Justice in which the author charges the organization with nepotistic practices that benefited only Gonzales's *biological* family.

14. What I appreciate about Limón's discussion of the poem is his understanding that although Joaquín (or is it Gonzales?) recognizes that "repressed Woman, this ephebe is on the verge of crafting such a unified poem of critical androgyny. That such a poem is possible for this male poet is intriguingly suggested by the lines immediately following this female section, when the speaker identifies himself with Woman: 'I am her/and she is me'. But the aggressive nationalist poet does not pursue this androgynous identification and too soon returns to the self-assertive rhetoric of masculine *daemonization.* In lines that ostensibly speak to the social present we find a telling statement of the poet-speaker's relationship to his strong fatherly precursor and his desire to be a strong replacement" (Limón 1992, 127). On the point about youth cultures, see the work of Dionne Espinoza, "Pedagogies of Nationalism and Gender: Cultured Resistance in Selected Representational Practices of Chicano/a Movement Activists, 1967–1972" (1995) and Ernesto Chávez, "'Birth of a New Symbol': The Brown Beret's Gendered Chicano National Imaginary" (1998), which contextualizes Chicano movement activism within a youth cultures paradigm; Elizabeth Martínez's book *De Colores Means All of Us: Latina Views for a Multi-Colored Century* (1998) in which the final section "La Lucha Continua: Youth in the Lead" finds hope in youth movements for social change; and studies by Stuart Hall and Tony Jefferson, *Resistance through Rituals: Youth Subcultures in Post-War Britain* (1976), Angela McRobbie, *Feminism and Youth Culture: From Jackie to Just Seventeen* (1991), Tricia Rose, *Black Noise: Rap Music and Black Culture in Contemporary America* (1994), the essays in the collection *Generations of*

Youth: Youth Cultures and History in Twentieth-Century America (1998) edited by Joe Austin and Michael Willard, and also Victor Viesca, "The Battle of Los Angeles: The Cultural Politics of Chicano/a Music in the Greater Eastside" (2004)—works that address the intersecting discourses of race, class, gender, and youth with regards to popular cultural production and social movements.

15. For more on nationalist discourse in Chicano literature, see Sylvia Alicia Gonzales' "National Character vs. Universality in Chicano Poetry" (1975), Alurista's "Cultural Nationalism and Xicano Literature during the Decade of 1965–1975" (1981), Carlota Cárdenas de Dwyer's "Cultural Nationalism and Chicano Literature in the Eighties" (1981), and Roberta Fernández's *"Abriendo caminos* in the Borderlands: Chicana Writers Respond to the Ideology of Literary Nationalism" (1994). Alurista's essay briefly mentions "I am Joaquín." For further readings of "I am Joaquín" in particular, see Cordelia Candelaria's *Chicano Poetry: A Critical Introduction* (1986) and Juan Bruce-Novoa's *Chicano Poetry: A Response to Chaos* (1982), especially for discussion on the role of women in the poem. Both of these studies are discussed, affirmed, as well as taken to task, by Limón. Consider as well Rafael Pérez-Torres's *Movements in Chicano Poetry: Against Myths, against Margins* (1995) on how the poem "prefigures" Aztlán in its spirited advocacy for Chicano cultural nationalism; his reading helps shed light, from a different angle, on the argumentative position taken by Fregoso and Chabram.

16. In her essay "And Yes . . . the Earth Did Part: On the Splitting of Chicana/o Subjectivity" (1993), Angie Chabram-Dernersesian mistakenly credits Chiña's print to "Walter Baka" [*sic*]. Although Walter Baca drew the images dispersed throughout *La Familia de la Raza*, the cover image is undeniably Chiñas's as identified by Cesar A. González (1982). To her credit, Chabram-Dernersesian, in a footnote to her recent article "En-countering the Other Discourse of Chicano-Mexicano Difference" (1999, 286), writes "The artwork for *La Familia de La Raza* is credited to Walter Baca, although I have not been able to confirm whether the cover of this essay is also his production." Rosa Linda Fregoso, in her 2003 book *MeXicana Encounters*, also incorrectly identifies the artist and the title of the image: "Entitled 'La Raza' by its author, the muralist Walter Baca, the drawing was recently brought to my attention by the historian Lorena Oropeza, whose analysis sparked my own early memories of this image, which in poster form hung on the wall of the Mexican American Youth Organization's headquarters in Corpus Christi in the early seventies" (74). In 2002 I published a version of this section in *Aztlán: A Journal of Chicano Studies* where I provide evidence of the artist's identity. See "Serial Kinship: Representing La Familia in Early Chicano Publications."

17. Those acquainted with Chicano/a movement history will realize that Enriqueta Longeaux y Vásquez's thought requires a much more thorough unpacking, and

they may feel that I am creating a straw(wo)man who is the purveyor of "passive female sentiment." Professor Dionne Espinoza, who has written extensively on Enriqueta Longeaux y Vásquez, expressed to me in a personal conversation that it would not be inaccurate to trace Longeaux y Vásquez's development from a cultural nationalist *womanist* to a cultural nationalist *feminist* given how her thought radically shifts in the course of her activist career. That is to say, she would later embrace the term "feminism" that earlier conjured up images of the "liberal *gabacha*" from whom many Chicanas attempted to distance themselves. In Pesquera and Segura (1993, 98), the authors note how Longeaux y Vásquez's essay (1970) "The Mexican American Woman," "albeit unintentionally, . . . reinforces stereotypes of Chicanas as submissive and passive and uninterested in feminism." Pesquera and Segura (1993, 98) also mention how, in an interview with Marta Cotera, Cotera recounted to them the time Longeaux y Vásquez phoned her "extremely upset—to the point of tears—that the Chicana caucus at [The Chicano Youth Liberation Conference] had adopted the position that 'the Chicana woman does not want to be liberated.'" It should go without saying that considering the conflicted positioning of Chicano identity at that historical moment, the double bind of being raced *and* sexed must be kept in mind. Also, as Dionne Espinoza (1995, 63) points out in her dissertation "Pedagogies of Nationalism and Gender: Cultural Resistance in Selected Representational Practices of Chicana/o Movement Activists, 1967–1972," "the popular slogan, 'I want to walk side by side with el hombre' was easily recuperated within the terms dictated by patriarchal nationalism.' Perhaps I am taking the passage cited in the text to the other extreme to critique this patriarchal nationalism that recruited women in its ranks. Yet for an early and pointed critique of Longeaux y Vásquez in relation to gender issues largely ignored by Chicanos at this historical moment, see Beverly Padilla's "Chicanas and Abortion" (1972; reprinted in A. García 1997).

18. In her introduction to the 1980 anthology *Twice a Minority: Mexican American Women*, anthropologist Margarita B. Melville advances this very dynamic when she argues that "the moral strength of Mexican American women lies in their self-identification as members of the Family of la Raza. Within that Family, they believe they have a uniquely female role to fill. It is the role of the mother who nurtures and sustains her children, a role of power based on love." Appropriate to the logic at hand, women are to blame for patriarchal oppression if they simply accept it by straying from their nature to nurture. According to Melville, "It is for Mexican American women to show Mexican American men and Anglo American society that female power can never mean the rejection of motherhood and the capacity to nurture but rather is its fulfillment in all aspects of life" (Melville 1980, 8). For a pointed critique of Melville and scholarship operating in a similar vein, see Maxine Baca Zinn's excellent review

essay "Mexican American Women in the Social Sciences" (1982b). I am grateful to Aidé Acosta for alerting me to these two texts.

19. In a personal conversation, Professor Robert Dale Parker questioned an easy categorization of the child as a boy given its arguably androgynous features. As compelling as his reading might be, I would insist that given the ideological forces propelling the image's circulation, the figure—with short hair and lack of precise "feminine" features—must inevitably be rendered male.

20. In *The Decolonial Imaginary*, Emma Pérez (1999, 57) insightfully discusses the gender politics of the Partido Liberal Mexicano (PLM), the "anarchist organization that carried slogans back and forth from Mexico City to Laredo and Los Angeles, as well as along the Baja California coast and the U.S.-Mexico border" during the Mexican Revolution. Fittingly, as Pérez notes, "PLM rhetoric . . . has served as a foundation for contemporary Chicano nationalist discourse."

21. According to her husband Roberto Perezdíaz, the family was always a leitmotif of Osuña's work. In an e-mail communication, Perezdíaz further explains: "She not only painted her own family members, she painted our family, and other families." Osuña died of ovarian cancer on June 25, 1999. For their help I am grateful to Mr. Perezdíaz and his and Osuña's daughter Lucia Angela Pérez.

22. For background information on this mural among others, see Cockcroft and Barnet-Sánchez's *Signs from the Heart: California Chicano Murals* (1990). It is worth mentioning the counteractivism of Harry Gamboa Jr. and Asco that railed against the paternal nationalist iconography of the mural movement by creating "instant murals" (the act of taping individuals to random walls in Los Angeles) and "walking murals" (murals dissatisfied with their topographical placement). See Gamboa's *Urban Exile: Collected Writings of Harry Gamboa Jr.* (1998). Gamboa's work has been especially insightful in challenging "conventional" Chicano thought, especially that pertaining to the family. The next chapter will discuss his video work within these terms.

23. In an interview, Silva—after commenting on the rarity of sensitive father-son images in Chicano culture—confesses: "I don't have a good relationship with my father. I never had, and I don't think I ever will. Many of my friends don't have close relationships with their fathers, either" (P. Pérez 2000, 50). If we can understand Silva to be substituting an "imaginary nostalgic" father-son relationship for the actual relationship he has with his own father (and I would argue that this imaginary nostalgic impulse is what makes Silva's work so appealing to many, for imaginary nostalgia is not necessarily the desire for what one has never had but what one wants or what one is told he or she needs), one could compare Silva to the young boy in Freud's "Family Romances," given how both wish to replace "the real father by a superior one" (Freud 1989, 300). Arjun Appadurai also elaborates on "imaginary nostalgia" (the creation of "experiences of losses that never took place") with regard to mass merchandised

images such as Norman Rockwell paintings (which beg a comparison to Silva's work). Appadurai (1996, 77) significantly notes that such images assist in creating "experiences of duration, passage, and loss that rewrite the lived histories of individuals, families, ethnic groups, and classes."

24. For a prime example of how family images have provoked dissent within Chicano/a communities, see Ruben Navarrette Jr.'s autobiographical memoir *A Darker Shade of Crimson: Odyssey of a Harvard Chicano* where he recalls a moment of "ethnic infighting" in a Chicano university organization around the issue of sexuality. Navarrette (1993, 221) explains: "During a group meeting, a member had hung a picture on the wall. A portrait of the typical Mexican family, he had said. Man, woman, and child. When one of the group's openly gay members had bravely objected to the characterization as not being 'typical' to the life that he would lead, the mood got ugly. Fueled by defensiveness, the proceedings had fallen into a frenzy of division, intolerance, and outright bigotry." I'm assuming that the image that caused controversy was Joaquín Chiñas's *La Familia*. I would also like to mention a pamphlet written by Roberto Vargas entitled *The Spirit of Cinco de Mayo: Reflections and Challenges for 1999* that I purchased during a Cinco de Mayo celebration in the Bay Area. In the section "Our Strategy for Shared Success," caring for familia is listed as "our" first responsibility. There is also a drawing of a family that shares shades of the images I have been discussing: father, mother, son, and daughter. Interestingly, one of the opportunities offered by Cinco de Mayo, Vargas writes, is being able to "celebrate our culture and achievements with friends from different cultures." Along with racial and ethnic groups like African Americans and Asian Americans, gays and lesbians are also potential friends. While this inclusion is admirable, it renders gays and lesbians a mutually exclusive group, and thus sexual minorities are not seen as a potential segment of "our" culture. Doing so would most likely contradict the image of the family offered in the text.

25. See, for example, Alfredo Mirandé's "A Reinterpretation of Male Dominance in the Chicano Family" (1979) and *Hombres y Machos: Masculinity and Latino Culture* (1997); and Baca Zinn's "Political Familism: Toward Sex Role Equality in Chicano Families" (1975) and "Chicano Men and Masculinity" (1982a).

26. Or, consider Rodolfo "Corky" Gonzales's comments on Chicana leadership: "I hope that our Chicana sisters can understand that they can be in the leadership of any social movement, but I pray to God that they do not lose their Chicanisma or their womanhood and become a frigid gringa. So I'm for equality, but still want to see some sex in our women" (1973, 425).

27. For example, see Lionila López Saenz's "Machismo, No! Igualdad, Si!" (1972); Adaljiza Sosa Riddell's "Chicanas in El Movimiento" (1974); Rosalie Flores's "The New Chicana and Machismo" (1975); Marcela Lucero Trujillo's "The Ter-

minology of Machismo" (1978) as well as many of the essays collected in *Chicana Feminist Thought: The Basic Historical Writings* (A. García, 1997).

28. For further elaboration on these terms and their implications, see Norma Alarcón's "Chicana's Feminist Literature: A Re-vision through Malintzin/or Malintzin: Putting Flesh Back on the Object" (1983) and "Chicana Feminism: In the Tracks of 'the' Native Woman" (1990); Cherríe Moraga's *Loving in the War Years: Lo que nunca pasó por sus labios* (1983); Carmen Tafolla's *To Split a Human: Mitos, Machos y La Mujer Chicana* (1985); and Ana Castillo's *The Massacre of the Dreamers: Essays on Xicanisma* (1994).

29. Aída Hurtado (1996, 49) argues that Delgado's "femme-macho" [sic] symbolizes "the neuter woman . . . a woman who is attractive to men because she is strong and powerful but not like a whore or meek like a wife." Yet the feme-macho is anything but neutered. Rather, because her allegiance and, hence, her sexuality are unavailable to men, she is simultaneously masculinized and marginalized as an improper (read lesbian) subject who interrupts an otherwise smooth sex-gender system.

30. For Ana Castillo (1994, 82), "Machismo has divided society in half. It divides the world into the haves and have-nots, those with material power and those who are rendered powerless. It has divided our behavior into oppositions, our spirituality regards Catholicism in dualistic terms of good and evil, and an economic world politic based on brute might. The feminine principle is not the opposite of machismo. 'The feminine' may be generally termed as the absence of machismo—all the qualities that have been negated, denied, denigrated, and made to be essentially valueless by our society. Machismo has served to distort our perceptions of humanity, which includes the feminine."

31. I thank Cindy Ingold from the Women and Gender Studies Resource Library at University of Illinois, Urbana-Champaign for her help in locating this essay.

32. Professor María Cotera of the University of Michigan alerted me to this important comparison.

33. Miguel Montiel (1970, 62) forecasts Mirandé's position eight years earlier when he writes: "Terms like *machismo* are abstract, value-laden concepts that lack the empirical referents necessary for the construction of sound explanations."

SHOOTING THE PATRIARCH

1. I include "Latino" when speaking of filmmakers and video artists who focus on the Chicano family given how, for example, the work of Miguel Arteta (a Puerto Rican), Patricia Cardoso (a Colombian) and Carlos Avila (a Peruvian who grew up in Los Angeles's Echo Park neighborhood) necessarily contributes to the genealogy I attempt to map.

2. In her chapter "The Chicano Familia Romance," Rosa Linda Fregoso attempts to read Nava's film in conjunction with Chicano movement discourses on the

family. While Fregoso is right to suggest that the film "conform[s] so closely to the mainstream ideology of family values," her claim that the film "mimic[s] the Western concept of the family system" because "this paradox rests squarely in *My Family*'s cultural nationalist orientation" (2003, 72) is symptomatic of her rush to collapse distinct articulations of nationalism without ascertaining their specific historical, cultural, and political modalities. In an earlier reading of the film I made an argument that shared a striking family resemblance with Fregoso's from which I now part ways in this chapter ("Reimagined Communities" 2000).

3. For an insightful investigation of Morales and her work, see Teresa "Osa" Hidalgo-de la Riva's "Mujerista Moviemaking: Chicana Filmmakers Sylvia Morales and Lourdes Portillo" (2004). Hidalgo-de la Riva's efforts to foreground the contributions of Chicana filmmakers has also been crucial, represented most recently in her edited special issue of *Spectator: The University of Southern California Journal of Film and Television Criticism*, "Chicana Spectators and Mediamakers: Imagining TransCultural Diversity" (2006).

4. While Valdez did indeed serve as the film's director, the end credits do not make this clear.

5. Chon Noriega has noted that although Treviño assigns *Joaquín* a 1967 completion date, the same year the poem was written, the film actually carries a 1969 copyright. This "may indicate that the film was shown before it was copyrighted, or that it took over a year to edit the film" (Noriega 2000b, 207). Like David James (2005, 504), I have elected to date it 1968, the year in between its year of completion and its copyright.

6. According to Noriega (1996a, 17), "Indeed, *I Am Joaquín* is not the 'first' Chicano film in the strict sense of the word, since there are at least two earlier avant-garde films: Ernie Palomino's *My Trip in a '52 Ford* (1966), also a film poem, but one that follows in the tradition of Beat counterculture rather than the neo-indigenist floricanto (Chicano poetry); and Severo Pérez's *Mozo: An Introduction into the Duality of Orbital Indecision* (1968), a pot-induced send-up of the trance film that circulated as part of the Texas Underground National Tour."

7. For comparative analyses of "Joaquín" as both poem and film, see Eliud Martínez's "*I Am Joaquín* as Poem and Film: Two Modes of Chicano Expression" (1980) and Rolando Hinojosa's "*I Am Joaquín*: Relationships between the Text and the Film" (1985). A 1977 issue (number 91/92) of the Cuban film journal *Cine Cubano* includes the entire poem in Spanish while the film is discussed in relation to the cultural and political struggles of Chicanos in the United States.

8. Sarabia works with film and video and her productions include *What is Art?* (1989), broadcast on public television in cities such as Los Angeles, San Fran-

cisco, and Chicago. Her most recent work includes *Chismosa y Manteca en Jealousy* (2003), a short black and white film that has screened at national and international film festivals.

9. While Valdez's film may sidestep issues of mestizaje by glorifying the "'Indian side" over the Spanish side, this does not necessarily make the film problematic with regards to its patriarchal tenets. Chicano cultural production that draws its signifying force from pre-Columbian iconography and history isn't always fueled by masculinist energies. For instance, one might consider the significance of Osa Hidalgo de la Riva's work, especially the experimental videos *Mujería: Primitive and Proud* (1992) and *The Olmeca Rap* (1992). As Chon Noriega writes in a blurb for the video in the *1998 Women Make Movies Film and Video Catalogue*, "*Mujería* obliges us to 'focus' on our historical genealogy." Carrying this proposition further, I would suggest that it actually obliges us to "refocus," or reconfigure, women's historical genealogy in light of pre-Columbian iconography.

10. In her paper, "Making It Public: A Visual Archive of Chicana/o Activism," presented at the American Studies Association, Washington, D.C., November 1, 1997, Dionne Espinoza argues that Huerta denaturalized motherhood by contextualizing reproductive labor within the labor movement.

11. See Sylvia Morales, "Filming a Chicana Documentary" (1979) on the making of *Chicana*. Osa Hidalgo-de la Riva's *Marginal Eyes* (1999) also stands as an example of the potential matriarchal impulse behind indigenista cultural production and is insightfully discussed in José Esteban Muñoz's *Disidentifications* (1999).

12. Another film commonly considered alongside those discussed here is Esperanza Vásquez's *Agueda Martínez: Our People, Our Country* (1977) which, Fregoso (1993a, 13) argues, rescues the association of woman to Mother Earth and land from a strictly "masculine enterprise among Chicano filmmakers of this early period." Fregoso maintains that Vásquez's film "portrays a woman who is passionately linked to the earth. Yet, in contrast to the totalizing abstraction of women in *I Am Joaquín* or to the discrepancy between the symbiotic depiction of the woman activist and men activists in *Yo Soy Chicano, Agueda Martínez* depicts a woman who simultaneously figures as historical subject and metaphor" (13). This does not mean, however, that the film is not devoid of nationalist attachments. For certain, the film's subtitle, *Our People, Our Country*, turns the nominal subject of the film—Agueda Martínez, the elderly, self-sufficient woman who has raised eight children and claims sixty-seven grandchildren and forty-five great-grandchildren—into a figure of the nation.

13. Treviño was also an active participant in La Raza Unida Party, both filming the Party's convention and serving as the event's national media coordinator (Zheutlin and Talbot 1978).

14. Recordings of *¡Ahora!* are available at Stanford University's Special Collections Library, which houses the Jesús Salvador Treviño Papers. See Treviño's *Eyewitness* (2001) for a comprehensive, personal account of this historical moment.

15. Valdez directed the well-known feature films *Zoot Suit* (1981) and *La Bamba* (1987). *La Bamba* is frequently considered the first successful (i.e., mainstream) Chicano film. Treviño, aside from directing and writing the short narrative *Seguín* (1982) and directing the documentary *Yo Soy* (1985), went on to direct commercial episodic television programs for the follow series: *Star Trek: Voyager* and *Babylon Five*, *The Practice*, *New York Undercover*, NYPD *Blue*, *Resurrection Blvd.*, *The O.C.*, and *Prison Break*.

16. The plan was for Nava to develop, produce, and direct at least one of three films made within a two-year time period with an average budget of around ten million dollars. Fittingly, one film initially lined-up for development was an adaptation of Victor Villaseñor's epic family memoir, *Rain of Gold*.

17. For an extensive account of *El Norte* regarding its production, distribution, and reception, see David Rosen and Peter Hamilton's *Off-Hollywood: The Making and Marketing of Independent Films* (1990). Nava's production company, El Norte Films, recently signed a distribution deal with Artisan Entertainment for all domestic rights to *El Norte*. The film is scheduled for rerelease in the near future. I am thankful to El Norte Films for making much of this information available to me.

18. Although I have chosen to highlight the aforementioned films, Nava has also directed *The Journal of Diego Rodríguez Silva*, a film made while at UCLA in the early 1970s, based on the life of poet Federico García Lorca, as well as *The Confessions of Aman* (1973) and *A Time of Destiny* (1987).

19. *Mi Familia/My Family*'s first week gross was $2,164,840 with receipts for the film's run totaling $11,079,373. The film's budget is estimated at $5,500,000. Figures accessed from the web site of The Numbers. Although the film received mixed reviews, it has become a classic for many Chicanos and Latinos starved for "positive" representations. Employees at various video stores in California have informed me that, since its release on both VHS and DVD, it is at times difficult to keep in stock copies of *Mi Familia/My Family* as it is a constant best-selling title. Prior to its closure in late 2006, Tower Records in Monterey Park, California—bordering the community of East Los Angeles—had the DVD listed as one of its top twenty-five titles. To be sure, *Mi Familia/My Family* is one of the few feature films that hold significant cultural currency in the Latino public sphere in the United States.

20. Coexistent with the pre-Columbian dimension of the film are aspects of Catholicism. Nava reveals that "Ometeotl and the Tezcatlipocas become at the same moment José and María, which is Joseph and Mary, and Chucho is Jesus; and so there's the Catholic sacrifice of the Jesus character in the film, which

forms the central traumatic moment of the family. So there is a syncretic, mythic, logical structure to the movie that is at once pre-Columbian and Catholic" (West 1995, 27).

21. See "The Erotic Zone: Sexual Transgression on the U.S.-Mexican Border" in which Ramón Gutiérrez (1996, 260) notes that the migrant "Mexican workforce" in "Encinitas [California] was large, single, and male—men who did not duplicate the American ideal of compulsory heterosexuality." Gutiérrez informs us that social worker Nina LeShan crystallizes the "illegal's" threat to "Anglo-American middle-class . . . marital sexual intercourse . . . rooted in nature and law" when she observes "Most of the time, men come up here, and without their family or without any women" (260).

22. Laura Angélica Simón's excellent documentary *Fear and Learning at Hoover Elementary* (1997) provides a pointed critique of Proposition 187 and records some of these commercials to juxtapose rampant immigrant hatred with the life-struggles of Latino immigrants working for menial wages in Los Angeles and their children who must maneuver within a racist educational system. For an insightful collection of essays on anti-immigration policy and sentiment, see Juan F. Perea's edited book *Immigrants Out! The New Nativism and the Anti-Immigrant Impulse in the United States* (1997).

23. These issues are taken up in a more contemporary context in Richard "Cheech" Marín's 1985 music video "Born in East L.A." and the 1987 feature film he directed of the same name.

24. It should be clear that "America" here refers to the United States despite challenges from José Martí and numerous commentators after him to geopolitically map "America" within a hemispheric trajectory.

25. Karen Voss (1998, 164–65) argues that the film's "central narrative and spatial goal" functioned in pedagogical terms "for a mainstream (presumably white) audience," drawing her evidence from "the bulk of press reviews accompanying the film's release, one going so far as to claim that the film was useful to teach your kids about how similar East Los Angeles is to Mexico, conflating differences between Mexicans and Mexican-Americans, and relegating both to the realm of spatial spectacle." See also Lynn Smith, "*My Family* Offers Different Perspective" (1995). While I find her argument convincing, it does not address the significance of the film for Chicano and Latino spectators.

26. For a compelling argument to the contrary, see John Ramírez's "Joto Theory and Chicana/o Cinema: The Closet of Gregory Nava's *Mi Familia*." Paper presented at the National Association for Chicana/Chicano Studies, Los Angeles, California, April 4, 2003.

27. See, for example, the introductions to Roy Armes's *On Video* (1988), Doug Hall and Sally Jo Fifer's *Illuminating Video: An Essential Guide to Video Art* (1990), and Sean Cubitt's *Videography: Video Media as Art and Culture* (1993).

28. The paucity of critical analyses of Gamboa's video production may have to do with the difficulty of obtaining it other than from the artist himself. This may soon change given that in 2004 the UCLA Chicano Studies Research Center released two DVDs containing Gamboa's videos from the 1980s and 1990s.

29. See C. Ondine Chavoya's "Pseudographic Cinema: Asco's No-Movies" (1998), the exhibition catalog *Patssi Valdez: A Precarious Comfort/Una comodidad precaria*, The Mexican Museum, San Francisco, Calif., January 22–March 28, 1999, and Max Benavidez's *Gronk* (2007).

30. Recent scholarship has insightfully "queered" the history of Asco. For example, Max Benavidez has detailed how Gronk's gay identity has informed his work as well as his collaborations and relationships in various Los Angeles–based circles. Although not officially a member of Asco, self-identified homosexual artist Cyclona influenced and worked alongside Gronk, Valdez, and Gamboa while playing an early, formative role in shaping Asco's sense of counteraesthetics. See Jennifer Flores Sternad, "Cyclona and Early Chicano Performance Art: An Interview with Robert Legorreta" (2006) and Robb Hernández, "Performing the Archival Body in the Robert 'Cyclona' Legorreta Fire of Life / El Fuego de la Vida Collection" (2006).

31. In *Shot in America*, Chon Noriega observes that the No-Movies satirized the Chicano filmmakers and films associated with KCET-TV in Los Angeles, undoubtedly showcased on programs like *¡Ahora!* and *Acción Chicano.*

32. David E. James (2005, 66) notes that Asco practices "also fed back into mainstream cinema. Gronk and Gamboa were featured in Agnes Varda's film *Murs Murs.* Many of Patssi Valdez's later paintings resemble set designs, and after making installation environments based on them, she eventually became a theatrical set-designer, and artistic consultant for feature films such as *Mi Familia*, and also designer of the 1995 and 1996 awards for the Latino Oscars, the Bravo Awards given by the National Council of La Raza." While these points are accurate, it is difficult to suggest that Gamboa's video work feeds back into the mainstream given its decidedly alternative content and form and the spaces within and means by which it circulates.

33. Prior to his use of video, Gamboa utilized Super-8 to create *Cruel Profit* (1973), an experimental film which forcefully critiqued Chicano nationalist rhetoric. The film was screened at the *Chicanismo en el Arte* exhibition at the Los Angeles County Museum of Art in 1975. It was, however, subsequently destroyed.

34. I am reminded here of Clara Gloria Castrellón (1977, 7) who wrote children are "the most insidious group of counter-revolutionary agents" because of the demands they impose upon women. Such a position counters characterizations of Chicanas as natural-born, nurturing mothers.

35. *L.A. Familia* has screened at numerous festivals and exhibitions, including "Family Album" at the California State University at Fullerton and "Identity

and Home" at the New York Museum of Modern Art, and was also broadcast in twenty-three states on fifty-six cable TV stations across the United States on Free Speech TV (via satellite distribution).

36. While Gamboa was born and raised in East Los Angeles, he also cut his artistic teeth on the streets of downtown Los Angeles.

37. The point about positive portrayals is important to highlight given how the 1999 season premier episode of NBC's popular "queer" comedy *Will and Grace* generated controversy over the Latina maid from El Salvador, Rosario (played by Shelley Morrison), who was referred to by one of the characters as a "hot tamale."

38. This was made clear in the messages posted on the now-defunct Chicano/Latino list-server, CHICLE, based at the University of New Mexico. See the report, *Prime Time for Latinos*, available from the web site of the National Hispanic Foundation for the Arts. In a piece also titled "Prime Time for Latinos," available from the web site of UCLA Today Online, Chon Noriega argues that the 1999 "brownout" gave rise to shows like *The George Lopez Show, Resurrection Blvd., American Family*, and *The Brothers Garcia* (all family shows, one must note.) See also Noriega's "Ready for Prime Time: Minorities on Network Entertainment Television" (2002b) for a broader context in which to situate the terms of debate.

39. The boxing ring is indeed one place where one can easily trace a genealogy of Latino media images. Stemming from early films like John Sturges's *Right Cross* (1950), Kurt Neumann's *The Ring* (1952), and Ralph Nelson's *Requiem for a Heavyweight* (1962), one could also point to Oscar de la Hoya's and Julio Cesar Chávez's pay-per-view fights and even gay porn titles like *Latin Knockout*. Unquestionably the Latino boxer has also become a popular image in American culture. Leoni's inspiration in crafting *Resurrection Blvd.* came from watching a boxing match on Showtime. As he explains, "I just put it together: boxing, Latinos, and Showtime," quoted in Kristal Brent Zook (2001, C1). For a discussion of early, Anglo, representations of the Latino boxer in fiction and film, see Arthur G. Pettit's *Images of the Mexican American in Fiction and Film* (1980).

40. Part of the importance of Wible's article is its discussion of the limits placed on *Resurrection Blvd.* that fell under Showtime's "No Limits" programming campaign. Hence the article records Treviño's beliefs that one can't "do 'universals' in the abstract" and that the series "should be doing more" despite the conservative opinion that the show "goes too far" (2004, 51). In a personal communication, Treviño conveyed to me that his decision to leave the show had in part to do with a reduced budget and a gradual drifting away from the community-based production values of its early stages.

41. Nava initially developed the pilot of *American Family* for CBS, which would end up rejecting it. PBS ultimately signed the show for initially one season but also

took it on for a second. In a media culture where firsts for people of color matter, *American Family* holds the title for being "the first Latino-themed, Latino-produced drama series on broadcast television" (Noriega 2002b, B15).

42. The episode itself might be read as critiquing Tommy's willingness to use his hands to fight back when Bibi sarcastically refers to him and his father as "a couple of machos." *Resurrection Blvd.* received an award in 2002 from the Gay and Lesbian Alliance Against Defamation for its positive portrayal of Tommy's homosexuality.

THE VERSE OF THE GODFATHER

1. For a comprehensive overview, see Jeff Chang's *Can't Stop Won't Stop: A History of the Hip-Hop Generation* (2005).

2. Two important studies on Puerto Ricans in hip-hop culture include Juan Flores, *From Bomba to Hip-Hop: Puerto Rican Culture and Latino Identity* (2000) and Raquel Z. Rivera, *New York Ricans from the Hip Hop Zone* (2003).

3. Throughout the chapter I bracket the "off-stage" names of selected performers I wish to highlight; this endeavor was also dependent on my ability to acquire these names in the first place.

4. Certainly this is in stark contrast to *Time Magazine*'s February 8, 1999 issue that outlines hip hop's impact on America after twenty years (coinciding with the Grammy success of Lauryn Hill, whose face graces the magazine's cover) and fails to mention Chicanos or Latinos all together. *Time*'s need to include white rappers Vanilla Ice and the Beastie Boys (a group that has made rap palatable for an extensive, white audience) should also come as no surprise. One might also note that white rappers are often afforded more privileges than rappers of color as evidenced by "alternative rock" stations that play only white rappers such as the Beastie Boys and Eminem. The November/December 1999 issue of the magazine *Latin Style* offers a nice contrast to the *Time Magazine* issue given that its cover displays "The Latin Rappers," namely The Beatnuts, B-Real of Cypress Hill, Sinful, Fat Joe, and Cuban Link. Aside from *Latin Style*, other periodicals—both currently in print and now defunct—which have prominently featured Chicano and Latino rap artists include *Boca, Frontera, Hoodtimes Magazine, Hispanic Magazine, Murder Dog, Lowrider Magazine, Urban Latino, Mia, Street Low, Teen Angel's, The Illtip, Blu, QV Magazine, Q-Vo, Street Beat*, and, of course, *Chicano Rap Magazine* and *Latin Rap Magazine*.

5. The ethnographic impulse in the study of rap and hip-hop need not consist of only examining rappers themselves but also their audiences. See William Shaw's *West Side: Young Men and Hip Hop in L.A.* (2000) and Greg Dimitriadis's *Performing Identity/Performing Culture: Hip-Hop as Text, Pedagogy, and Lived Practice* (2001), which adopt an audience-reception approach.

6. Yet this cannot be reduced to a Chicano "nationalist" response. As Yoatl explains: "I showed him my Aztec medallion, and he pulled it and threw it and said, 'Fuck this nigger shit', and I said, 'Man, that was an Aztec calendar', and he said, 'It was the niggers who gave you that fucking idea'. I'm like fuck, you know, I shoulda told him what do you think oldies are, right? How can we begin to talk about coalitions when the average Chicano doesn't even understand about chicanismo or Aztlán?" Kelly 1993a, 267.

7. This claim is not meant, however, to dismiss Chicano rap's development in, and impression on, the greater Southwest United States and other locations where it may emerge.

8. See Fred Álvarez's insightful article "The Latino Rap Scene: Chicanos' Time for Rhythm 'n' Rhyme" (2000) for a related discussion.

9. Brown Pride, Mr. Shadow, Monte Loco, Conejo, Dark Room Familia, JV, Pure Chicano Poetry, Homebase Aztlán, Lil Rob, The Young Pachukos, Cisco, Aztec Tribe, J-Loc, Young Ant, Slow Pain, Sir Dyno, MC Magic, DJ MT, Krazy Race, El Demonio, Central Coast Clique, Psycho Realm, SalviMex, Royal T, Delinquent Habits, Cali Life Style, Kinto Sol, Hogg Boss, Ese Daz aka Lil Blu, Ese Rich Roc, The Brown Intentions, Capone, The Funky Aztecs, Baby Bash, Trava, Rhyme Poetic Mafia, N'Land Clique, Spanish Fly, Aztlán Nation, Street Mentality, Immortal Technique, Knight Owl, 2Mex, Brown Skin Artists, Santa Ana Posse, Norwalk's Most Wanted, Los Nativos, Brown Town Looters, Sol, ES Clique, Funky Minoriteez, MC Man, Nenna, ALG, Brown Town, Mr. Sancho, Ethnic Playground, Phame, The Young Bucks, Paisas, G' Fellas, Cuete, Tommy Gun, His-panic, Jonny "Z," Wicked Minds, Lil Bandit, Hispanic MC's, Latino Velvet Clique, Mr. Capone-E, Jerry G, Chicano Brotherhood/Thee Suspect, Payaso and the Dukes Click, The Unit, Chulo, Princess, Lethal Assassins Clique, Brown Boy, Of Mexican Descent, Low Down, Duke, MC Fernie and Primo, Lil Chico, Mr. Criminal, Los Marijuanos, Chicano Soul & Power, Xica, MC Magic, South Park Mexican, MC Raza, Tre Vásquez, Gambino All Stars, Lone Star Ridaz, Green Side Ridaz, Junebug Slim, and Never. This is by no means a comprehensive list and, furthermore, a good number of these acts have ceased to exist. Yet for the sake of archiving their contributions to Chicano/a rap history I attempt to name all the performers to which I've been exposed over the past fifteen years.

10. The impulse of "latinidad" is clearly articulated by Alberto Sandoval-Sánchez (1999, 15) as that which results "from Latino/a agency and intervention when U.S. Latinos/as articulate and construct cultural expressions and identity formations that come from a conscious political act of self-affirmation."

11. Jae-P's song "Pa Mi Raza," and the eponymously titled CD, clearly resonate with Kid Frost's "La Raza."

12. An excellent example of this necessary practice is the ethnographic work of Brenda Jo Bright, which analyzes Chicano low rider cultures in Houston, Los Angeles, and northern New Mexico. See her Ph.D. dissertation "Mexican American Low Riders: An Anthropological Approach to Popular Culture" (1994) and her essays "Remappings: Los Angeles Low Riders" (1995) and "Nightmares in the New Metropolis: The Cinematic Poetics of Low Riders" (1998), especially the former, which notes the influence of rap and hip-hop on Chicano low riders.

13. See Rafael Pérez-Torres, "Popular Music and Postmodern Mestizaje" (2006b) in his *Mestizaje: Critical Uses of Race in Chicano Culture* (2006a) for a critical analysis of mestizaje in Chicano rap that assists in challenging an easy embrace of hybridity.

14. See Yvette C. Doss's appropriately titled essay "Choosing Chicano in the 1990s: The Underground Music Scene of Los(t) Angeles" (1998). Masterfully detailing the emergence of alternative Chicano music in contemporary Los Angeles, "choosing Chicano" for Doss refers to the reclamation and resignification of the term "Chicano" for young, politically driven musicians and their audiences. Victor Hugo Viesca advances Doss's theme and importantly grounds it within a wider geopolitical context in "The Battle of Los Angeles: The Cultural Politics of Chicana/o Music in the Greater Eastside" (2004).

15. For John M. González (1996, 36), "even when Chicano nationalism celebrates the flux of mestizaje, hybridity, and creolization, it makes these qualities the mark of authenticity in judging cultural production as expressive of some imagined totality. For Chicano nationalism, mestizaje metaphorically resolves the differences of class, gender, sexuality, etc., in constructing community." It is interesting, however, that Saldívar and Kun, who separate nationalism from hybridity, neatly return us to a position that moves beyond the sociopolitical "differences of class, gender, sexuality, etc." without asking why nationalism is always already present in Chicano cultural productions such as rap and what is at stake for feminist, gay, lesbian, and working-class Chicanos and Chicanas.

16. See Michael Coyle's article "Cypress Hill" (2000) for more on this point. Mc-Farland's take is also somewhat ironic considering how Cypress Hill has been accused of cultural opportunism, such as releasing the CD *Los Grandes Éxitos en Español* (1999), a collection of their well-known tracks recorded in Spanish, at the height of the recent Latin music craze, as epitomized by the commercial success of Ricky Martin and Jennifer López, as well as Carlos Santana's ten Grammy nominations that same year. Raquel Z. Rivera (2003, 156–57) confirms this point in *New York Ricans from the Hip Hop Zone*.

17. For a brief yet excellent example of work that takes seriously these exchanges, see Todd Boyd's *Am I Black Enough for You? Popular Culture from the 'Hood*

and Beyond (1997), especially the section "Hispanics Causin' Panic," 92–95. Boyd elaborates on the cultural exchanges between African Americans and Chicanos and Latinos through an analysis of rap, low riders, and film, concluding the section with a revealing reading of how Edward James Olmos's *American Me* influenced Albert and Allen Hughes's *Menace II Society* (1993), a film that "underscores the attempt at dialogue between distinct sets of marginal voices, as opposed to the perpetuation of racial hostility between African Americans and Latinos" (95). Boyd's more recent *The New H.N.I.C.: The Death of Civil Rights and the Reign of Hip Hop* (2003) offers an illuminating critique of African Americans in Los Angeles who supported James Hahn over Antonio Villaraigosa in the 2001 mayoral race, a critique that I see as extending the debate I present here into the realm of electoral politics.

18. For more on Kid Frost, and his rise to prominence, see the interview conducted by Brian Cross (1993, 190–95), "Kid Frost," in *It's Not about a Salary: Rap, Race and Resistance in Los Angeles*.

19. Or, as Alfonso Ruíz (1996, 28) puts it in his article "No Longer a Kid" in *Frontera Magazine*, "the godfather of Latino hip hop." The idea of Frost as "godfather" is also clear by the titles of articles on Chicano rap, such as Lorraine Ali's in *Option*: "Latin Class: Kid Frost and the Chicano Rap School" (1993). Also see the recent ads in *Lowrider Magazine* for his *That Was Then, This Is Now, Vol. 1* and the CD cover itself that declare: "The Godfather of the Latin Rap Game Returns!"

20. Frost is featured, albeit under a different name, on the controversial 2004 home entertainment video game *Grand Theft Auto: San Andreas*, an homage of sorts to early 1990s gangsta-inflected California culture. His "La Raza" is also on the eight-CD box set soundtrack.

21. Drawing from Barbara Harlow (1987) who suggests that "poetry is the genre par excellence of resistance literature" and "poetry may act as a kind of cultural manifesto of a given movement," Carla Frecerro (1999, 89) argues that "rap too is a form of poetry: it is recitative, it rhymes, and it has a distinct meter and rhythm. In many ways, we might regard the rap explosion as a kind of manifesto of what [bell] hooks calls the neonationalism among African Americans, Chicanos, and occasionally other groups in the United States today." One could also highlight the shared strands between rap and poetry as both function as popular cultural practices. In "Chicano Poetry: A Popular Manifesto," Frank Pino (1973, 729) writes: "As most popular cultural manifestations, the Chicano poetry, literature and cultural arts reflect the daily contacts and references experienced by the masses."

22. More recently, Bay Area rapper Sir Dyno entered the Chicano literary scene with the publication of his novel *Midst of My Confusion* (1999).

23. In *Hombres y Machos: Masculinity and Latino Culture*, Alfredo Mirandé (1997, 134) argues the pachuco "is a positive symbol of cultural identity, heterosexuality, and machismo." Such an argument forecloses any consideration of the pachuco's "negative" impact on cultural identity, exempting him from possibly advocating sexist and homophobic attitudes or behavior. Furthermore, Mirandé sharply distinguishes between pachucos and homosexuals—despite comparing the pachuco with the dandy—thus eliminating the possible existence of queer pachucos.

24. Although gangsters and pachucos are often conflated, the pachuco is more precisely the forefather of the contemporary gangster. However, each must also be understood within their particular historical moment so as not to blur their differences.

25. See relevant discussions and interviews with Chicano rap artists in David Toop's *Rap Attack 2: African Rap to Global Hip Hop* (1991), Michael Small's *Break It Down: The Inside Story from the New Leaders of Rap* (1992), Brian Cross's *It's Not about a Salary: Rap, Race and Resistance in Los Angeles* (1993), and Steven Stancell's *Rap Whoz Who: The World of Rap Music* (1996). Also, in William Eric Perkins's *Droppin' Science: Critical Essays on Rap Music and Hip Hop Culture* (1996), a book that largely focuses on African American hip-hop culture, it is the essays by Guevara, Flores, and del Barco, which are Latina/o written and Latina/o concentrated, that compose the first section of the book, "Roots."

26. In 1990, La Clinica de la Raza, located in the largely Latino community of the Fruitvale District in Oakland, California, sponsored a community health fair entitled "This Is for La Raza!" The title was a direct response to Frost's exclusionary practices of who counted as raza to his mind. Also, in an article "An East Side Story: Kid Frost" in *Lowrider Magazine*, Savage (1992, 20) changes his earlier position on Frost whom he has "grown to respect" given that both find themselves on the same road: "The road for better education, and unity for our people, la Raza of Aztlán."

27. That Frost occasionally wavers in his position of leadership does indeed separate him from Corky Gonzales. However, working-class Chicano youths, especially young men, absorb nationalist sentiment through music such as Frost's, thus igniting their claims to political consciousness. If this sentiment isn't inspired by music, it is often times by interrelated forces of, for example, family, community, and an assortment of cultural iconography (Aztec imagery and barrio symbolism on tee shirts and as tattoos) in working-class Chicano locations.

28. See David Lloyd's essay "Adulteration and the Nation" in which he argues, "Irish cultural nationalism has been preoccupied throughout its history with the pos-

sibility of producing a national genius who would at once speak for and forge a national identity" (1993, 88).

29. Chicano movement poet Abelardo Delgado could be seen as a precursor to Wino given how his poems are frequently addressed to "hermanos" and "compadres." See especially Delgado's "La Causa" and "El Compadre" in *Chicano: 25 Pieces of a Chicano Mind* (1969). Wino has since taken up the name Thee Suspect and has released music under this name.

30. Fittingly, Frost makes a cameo appearance in Anders's film as the father of one of the female protagonists. I am indebted to Angel Carrillo for this observation.

31. This is Frost's first LP on the late African American rapper Eazy-E's label Ruthless Records. Eazy, one of the founding members of the group N.W.A. (Niggas With Attitude), took a strong interest in Chicano rappers and signed performers like Frost, ALT, and the Brownside to his label before his AIDS-related death in 1995. Here I would like to acknowledge ALT for his help with this information and introducing me to Frost and A Lighter Shade of Brown when I began this project.

32. In a movement context (and instructive here), Ramón Gutiérrez (1993, 45–46) notes, "Chicanos faced what was undoubtedly a rather similar [to black men] experience—social emasculation and cultural negation—by seeking strength and inspiration in a heroic Aztec past. The Aztec past they chose emphasized the virility of warriors and the exercise of brute force. Young Chicano men, a largely powerless group, invested themselves with images of power—a symbolic inversion commonly found in the fantasies of powerless men worldwide, a gendered vision that rarely extends to women." Frost notes: "Chicanos don't have a lot of positive role models in the first place. We don't have Michael Jordan, we don't have Magic Johnson. Our heroes are gladiators, thumpers—Julio Cesar Chávez, Salvador Sánchez. We look up to people who get it on and mix it up. The Aztecs were straight-up warriors. People nowadays still have that mentality. That's why you see different Chicanos from different areas clash, because of that pride and honor" (Ali 1993, 68).

33. Bandit from Street Mentality echoes this sentiment, and takes it to another level, when he claims: "A gang supplies love; they're filled with surrogate father figures for youth from mother-centered households; they teach you about the streets and help you earn money through drug trafficking" (Ro 1996, 46).

34. A case in point is the influence of Brian De Palma's film *Scarface* (1983). In *Def Jam Presents: Origins of a Hip Hop Classic* (Benny Boom, 2003), a documentary featured on a bonus DVD to commemorate the twentieth anniversary of the film—a "ghetto classic" we're told—Los Angeles Chicano tattoo artist Mr. Cartoon discusses the impact *Scarface* has had on Latinos, but the documentary itself fails to include any Chicano rappers whose lyrics reflect the

film's influence in the same way as black rappers like Scarface from the Ghetto Boys, Notorious B.I.G., Sean "P-Diddy" Combs, and Eve, who testify to this fact in their role as talking heads.

35. For varied, yet insightful, examinations of the gangsta rap phenomenon, see Robin D. G. Kelley's "Kickin' Reality, Kickin' Ballistics: 'Gangsta Rap' and Postindustrial Los Angeles" (1994), Bakari Kitwana's *The Rap on Gangsta Rap* (1994), Peter McLaren's "Gangsta Pedagogy and Ghettoethnicity: The Hip-Hop Nation as Counterpublic Sphere" (1995), Nick De Genova's "Gangsta Rap and Nihilism in Black America: Some Questions of Life and Death" (1995), Todd Boyd's "A Small Introduction to the 'G' Funk Era: Gangsta Rap and Black Masculinity in Contemporary Los Angeles" (1996), and Eithne Quinn's *Nuthin' but a "G" Thang: The Culture and Commerce of Gangsta Rap* (2005). Also, Ronin Ro's books, the aforementioned *Gangsta: Merchandising Rhymes of Violence* (1996) and *Have Gun Will Travel: The Spectacular Rise and Violent Fall of Death Row Records* (1998), expose the multi-layered connections between organized gangs and gangsta rap.

36. The controversy over San Diego rapper Lil Rob's shift from a self-declared "Southsider" to a rapper who wears "a brown bandana for brownpride" is addressed in the third issue of *Latin Rap Magazine* (2005). Resentful former fans, we are told, use Snoop Dog as an example of an artist who has not denounced his "colors" but continues to embrace his Crip affiliation even as he moves in mainstream circles.

37. On the sleeve of his 1999 single "Hustling Ain't Dead" with rapper Cisco, Slow Pain lists his nationality as "Gangster" on a description list fashioned after one on an FBI wanted poster. Important to note here is that in an early interview with (Kid) Frost (see Michael Small's *Break It Down* [1992]) he lists the following locations as his "Hometown": L.A., Panama, Guam, Costa Rica, Ecuador, and Bolivia. Although he may be gesturing toward the pan-Latino identification articulated on the Latin Alliance LP by claiming various South American locations as home, Frost's more recent claims are in synch with Slow Pain's as he consistently declares himself an O.G. (original gangster) from Los Angeles.

38. This is the cover for *I Remember You Homie* rereleased in 1997 that differs from the cover of the original 1994 release.

39. Alternatively, the valorization of mothers in Chicano rap is also evident, for example, in the 2004 compilation *Tributo a las Madres* (a project orchestrated by Mr. Pelón) and Lil Bandit's "Dedication to My Family" from his CD *Let It Be Known* (2005).

40. This position also undermines the Sister Sledge song in which the family in "We Are Family" is a sisterhood ("We are family/I've got all my sisters with me"). Also worth noting is how Blvd.'s use of the song stands in stark contrast to the way the song has been claimed by queer communities. Brian Currid (1995,

165) argues in "'We Are Family': House Music and Queer Performativity" that the song is "recognized as something of a queer national anthem" and "has served and continues to serve as an important site for the performance of gay and lesbian/queer community identity."

41. The previously mentioned films *American Me* and *Bound by Honor/Blood In, Blood Out* highlight the situations of prison gangs such as La Nuestra Familia and La Eme (the Mexican Mafia). In 1993, the Mexican Mafia targeted for death lead actor and director of *American Me* Edward James Olmos for what they saw as a skewed portrayal of the organization in the film. Many have suggested that La Eme objected to the explicit homosexual rape scenes attributed to them in the prison context. See Nina Fuentes's *The Rise and Fall of the Nuestra Familia* (2006) for an account of La Nuestra Familia. For an extended commentary on street and prison gangs, see Tom Hayden (2004).

42. See Kelly (1993b) for a discussion on carnalismo in rap.

43. Tricia Rose's "Black Texts/Black Contexts" importantly argues for a critical understanding "that male rappers did not invent sexism. Black practices have been openly sexist for a long time, and in this regard they keep solid company with many other highly revered dominant Western practices. Today's rappers are not alone in their symbolic objectification of Black women. They have lots of real live, and substantially more powerful, company, none of whom rap or make records" (Rose 1992, 226). Yet it is also critical to consider the power of rap on youth of color and the repercussions of its influence on numerous fronts.

44. Another example that immediately comes to mind is Brown Pride's "I Don't Wanna Be the One" from *Livin' in the Barrio* (1993), which begins with a conversation between women, one of whom "messed with" one member of the crew and plans on cashing in on his success. In a related vein, Kimberlè Williams Crenshaw (1993, 132) has argued that black women are always at the heart of both racial and sexual subordination in both legal and rap discourses, rendering them "virtually voiceless." However, Chicana rappers, such as JV, Laura "La Nenna," Teardrop, and Xica contested such representations, struggling to make their voices heard. Princess, a rapper based in San Diego, is a recent artist whose female-centered narratives defy Chicano rap's masculinist stance toward women. Although recordings by Princess and JV are exceptions to the rule, Chicana rap CDs and tapes are few and far between. For informing me about Princess, I am indebted to Professor Gail Pérez of the University of San Diego, and Norma Chávez, then an undergraduate at San Diego State University, and their illuminating paper "Shaking It Up: De-mythologizing the Mex-Generation" presented at the 1999 National Association of Chicana/Chicano Studies Annual Conference, in San Antonio, Texas, on the panel "Narratives of/from the Chicana/o Popular: Orality, Working Class Culture, and

Gender." Mention of the contributions made by Angie Martínez in the name of Latinas in rap and hip-hop is imperative. A prominent DJ and rapper who has worked with KRS-1, Lil Kim, Red Man, and the Beatnuts, Martínez has made it virtually impossible to discuss Latino hip-hop culture without paying attention to women. For an insightful interview with Martínez, see Rivera (2003, 229–32).

45. In an interview with Sylvia Patterson for the British music weekly *NME: New Musical Express*, Sen Dog of Cypress Hill declares: "I can't understand how there's fags. I can't. 'Cos once you've had poooh-see [pussy]'?!" (Patterson 2000, 27). Patterson rightly recognizes Sen Dog to be "flailing in the bigotry quagmire, a different kind of old-fashioned Family Value that's of no benefit to anyone, merely a screen for the general ignorance and bile that continues to ruin the world" (27). After Patterson challenges his homophobia, Sen Dog waxes apologetic, confessing that he had an uncle who passed away who was "like that." He also realizes he "can't disrespect anybody for their preference" and if "anybody that's gay . . . digs Cypress Hill, keep diggin' it man, I'll shake your hand, just like anybody else's" (27). In addition, Cypress Hill was banned in the late 1990s by San Francisco radio station KMEL for making derogatory remarks about gay people. Ironically, the now-defunct, gay Latino publication that was based in Los Angeles, *QV Magazine*, interviewed Cypress Hill, but the interviewer failed to foreground the topic of homosexuality. San Francisco native and bisexual MC and producer Judge Muscat (a.k.a. Dutchboy) has established a web site of antigay rap lyrics. Entitled Da.Dis.List, it contains numerous entries from a variety of artists. See Chris Nutter's "Ill Communication" (2000). Alternatively, for an important challenge to the idea of hip-hop as an unbreakable pillar of homophobia, see R. K. Byers's "The Other Side of the Game: A B-Boy Adventure into Hip Hop's Gay Underworld" (1997).

46. Aside from Montes's *Pass the Mic*, Dave O'Brien's *Hip Hop Homos* (2004) addresses the participation of queers in hip-hop and the homo-hop movement.

47. Along the lines of defying heteronormativity in the rap context, Judith Halberstam discusses women of color "drag kings" Shon and Dred who adopt an on-stage hip-hop style, especially when they perform as Run-DMC. See "Mackdaddy, Superfly, Rapper: Gender, Race, and Masculinity in the Drag King Scene" (1997).

48. See my essay "Queering the Homeboy Aesthetic" (2006), which examines the work of Silva as short-circuiting while reconfiguring the masculinist impulse of the Latino homeboy image. Rap acts like cross-ethnic trio SalviMex have also declared their support of Homo-Hop, thus creating alliances across sexual identity. Thanks here are due to Drastiko of SalviMex for his e-mail communication.

49. For an important intervention, see Tomás Ybarra-Frausto (1992).

50. Genaro Padilla, who cites the same Fanon passage for a discussion of the concept of Aztlán, writes: "Even when the romanticizing of the past, as well as the present cultural identity, is exposed as a self-serving illusion and corrected by those social critics, historians or political theorists whose view of social relations remains dispassionately fixed upon material forces in society, the mythic element that permeates the popular consciousness may not easily be exorcised as useless trivia since it has come to assume a life of its own in the group's imagination." Furthermore, "the role of the artist, then, proves to be a significant and often more continuous one than that of the political nationalist" (1989, 114). In his essay "Frantz Fanon and the National Culture of Aztlán," Alfred Arteaga (1975) insightfully elaborates on the use-value of Fanon's work in comprehending the political ramifications of Chicano cultural nationalism. Of particular import here, Arteaga reminds us, after Fanon, that "it is not enough to build a national culture only on past triumphs to counteract colonialism's cultural genocide" but Chicano cultural producers "should use the past to inspire work towards a future and provide basis for hope in that future" (1975, 17).

CARNAL KNOWLEDGE

1. My understanding of "reproductive futurism" is indebted to Lee Edelman's groundbreaking work on futurity and heteronormativity. See his book *No Future: Queer Theory and the Death Drive* (2004).
2. Here I take a cue from José Esteban Muñoz's critical engagement with "world-making" queer cultural productions to tease out oppositional modes of "being in the world." See his *Disidentifications: Queers of Color and the Performance of Politics* (1999) and "Feeling Brown: Ethnicity and Affect in Ricardo Bracho's *The Sweetest Hangover (and Other STDs)*" (2000).
3. "Recovery projects" to unearth Chicano gay male narratives would not be unlike the Recovering the U.S. Hispanic Literary Heritage project based at the University of Houston in Texas, an attempt at restoring the narrative voices in literature and personal memoirs by Chicanos and Latinos in the United States from the nineteenth century to the 1950s. Recently, a significant number of Chicano and Latino gay male-focused publications have appeared. See, for example, Bernardo García's qualitative study *The Development of a Latino Gay Identity* (1998); Rafael M. Díaz's *Latino Gay Men and HIV: Culture, Sexuality, and Risk Behavior* (1998); Jaime Cortez's literary anthology, *Virgins, Guerillas, and Locas: Gay Latinos Writing about Love* (1999); Frankie Barrera's collection of poems and diary entries entitled *The Diary of Baby Chulo* (1999); Manuel Muñoz's compelling short story collections, *Zigzagger* (2003) and *The Faith Healer of Olive Avenue* (2007); and Rigoberto González's moving *Butterfly Boy: Memories of a Chicano Mariposa* (2006).

4. The groundbreaking work of Chicana feminists has certainly made this clear. See, e.g., Cherríe Moraga, *Loving in the War Years: Lo que nunca pasó por sus labios* (1983); Emma Pérez, "Sexuality and Discourse: Notes from a Chicana Survivor" (1991); Deena J. González, "Malinche as Lesbian: A Reconfiguration of 500 Years of Resistance" (1991); Alma M. García, ed., *Chicana Feminist Thought: The Basic Historical Writings* (1997); and Dionne Espinoza, *Revolutionary Sisters: Chicana Activism and the Cultural Politics of Chicano Power* (forthcoming). In a personal communication, artist Barbara Carrasco pointed out to me that members of the United Farm Workers, at the request of César Chávez, often marched in gay pride parades as a show of support for a community historically in solidarity with farm workers' struggles. Yet participation, according to Carrasco, often rendered marchers suspect by some U F W members as well as by blood relatives.

5. One might ponder how therefore to situate Dan Guerrero's solo performance *¡Gaytino!* that first debuted in 2005, which chronicles the life history of a Chicano gay man (the son of legendary musician Lalo Guerrero) who grew up in East Los Angeles in the 1950s. See my review (2007) that details the cultural and historical stakes of *¡Gaytino!*

6. Often used is the word *"floricanto"*—the term in which the words *"flor"* and *"canto"* are condensed. Flor y canto, or floricanto, symbolizes a neoindigenous aesthetics grounded in Aztec and Nahuatl cultural expression and represented by writers like Alurista and Luis Valdez. See, for example, Alurista's *Floricanto en Aztlán* (1971). For the Aztec significance of flor y canto, see Miguel León-Portilla's *Aztec Thought and Culture: A Study of the Ancient Nahuatl Mind* (1963).

7. In contemporary popular culture, evidence of gay men being reduced—both literally and figuratively—to "assholes" is exemplified by the white rapper Eminem, also known as "Slim Shady," in his response to his use of the word "faggot" ("'Faggot' to me doesn't necessarily mean gay people. 'Faggot' to me just means . . . taking away your manhood. You're a sissy. You're a coward. This does not necessarily mean you're being a gay person. It means you're being a fag. You're being an asshole.") and in his song lyrics ("Slim Anus?/You're damn right, slim anus/I don't get fucked in mine/Like you two little flaming faggots"). See Anthony DeCurtis, "Eminem's Hate Rhymes" (2000).

8. For a related discussion, see John Ramírez's "The Chicano Homosocial Film: Mapping the Discourses of Sex and Gender in *American Me*" (1995). Ramírez (1995, 262) insightfully reads the family "as a fundamental social technology for the construction and management of gender and sexuality" in the rocky relationship between Chicanos and Hollywood.

9. See also, however, Lionel Cantú's, "Entre Hombres/Between Men: Latino Masculinities and Homosexualities" (2000), which rightly problematizes Alma-

guer's reification of culture, which in turn allows him to make sweeping claims about Latino and Latin American male sexual practices. Even in contemporary western gay culture, for example, these roles continue to be played out as men may identify, or are identified, as "tops" or "bottoms."

10. On these issues I have also benefited from Lee Edelman's *Homographesis: Essays in Gay Literary and Cultural Theory* (1994).

11. Chicano machismo's codes of behavior are said to be "not unlike [those] which Hemingway tried to live by. Much of Hemingway's fondness for the Raza, for Latino values, is closely tied to the values and attitudes toward life and death that he found in these communities and that he shared" (Armas 1975, 54). Hemingway's devotion to the bullfight is also said to closely link him to Chicanos. Armas (1975) argues in "Machismo," as well as in *La Familia de la Raza* (1971, 24–25), that the bullfight is an exemplary metaphor for how to exercise one's machismo not because it is a "manly" act, but because it "is a ceremony and a ritual in which an individual is pitted with the dark forces of the world" (1975, 54). In *La Familia de la Raza*, however, the bullfight scene is *very* manly in Armas's description of the male torero doing battle with the forces of evil symbolized by the bull. In 1971, noted folklore scholar and one of Chicano studies' "founding fathers," Américo Paredes published "The United States, Mexico, and *Machismo*" in which Hemingway is figured as "the most hallowed interpreter of the macho" (1993b, 226). According to Paredes: "The popularity of Hemingway's works in the period between the two world wars—as much among the critics as with the general public—shows the attraction the *macho* still had for the North American, although in real life the man of the United States made less and less of a show over his masculinity. Hemingway himself understood this, and almost all his novels and short stories develop the theme of *machismo* in Spain, Mexico, or Cuba. Today Hemingway is scorned by the critics. This is not surprising, since the protagonist of the novels now acclaimed by the critics no longer is the macho but the homosexual—the other extreme, or perhaps the same thing seen from another point of view" (226). Although John Cunningham (2002, 69) reads Paredes as offering "a radical challenge to an understanding of male homosexuality as antithetical to masculinity," I am not sure situating homosexuals and heterosexuals on opposite sides of a continuum—thus making them "the same thing," depending on mere point of view—is all that radical. For an excellent study that challenges the rigidity of Hemingway's macho image in light of homosexuality, see Debra Moddelmog's *Reading Desire: In Pursuit of Ernest Hemingway* (1999).

12. Even in the early 1970s, heterosexual men of color involved in radical movements were challenging homophobia. Indeed, Armas's position stands in stark contrast to Huey Newton's essay "The Women's Liberation and Gay Liberation Movements" (1970), which argues that the Black Panther Party would be wise

to "form a working coalition with the gay liberation and women's liberation groups." Confessing his own "hang-ups" with (male) homosexuality, Newton insists that homophobia is ultimately the result of one's own sexual insecurities ("We want to hit a homosexual in the mouth because we are afraid we might be homosexual"). Although there is a question about whether the homosexuals he is talking about are exclusively white (can there be black gay men in the Black Panthers?), it is exhilarating to read Newton (1995, 153) declare: "there is nothing to say that a homosexual cannot also be a revolutionary. And maybe I'm now injecting some of my prejudice by saying that even a homosexual can be a revolutionary. Quite the contrary, maybe a homosexual could be the most revolutionary."

13. That Armas's understanding of machismo sharply resonates with the basic tenets of cultural nationalism is evident when he writes, "Machismo is [an] element which shields the individual from outside forces." Furthermore, "there is, then, the aggressivity of Machismo that says that one cannot be static within the world in which the individual lives. That aggressivity demands that positive interaction must take place if one is to live successfully. The individual must interact, passivity is not permitted" (Armas 1975, 59).

14. For the history and cultural politics of lowriding, see Calvin Trillin and Ed Koren's "Low and Slow, Mean and Clean" (1978); Wayne King's "Low Riders Are Becoming Legion among Chicanos" (1981); Luis F. B. Plascencia's "Low Riding in the Southwest: Cultural Symbols in the Mexican Community" (1983); Michael Cutler Stone's "'Bajito y Suavecito': Low Riding and the 'Class' of Class" (1990); James Diego Vigil's "Car Charros: Cruising and Lowriding in the Barrios of East Los Angeles" (1991); Brenda Jo Bright's "Mexican American Low Riders: An Anthropological approach to Popular Culture" (1994) and "Nightmares in the New Metropolis: The Cinematic Poetics of Low Riders" (1998); and Denise Michelle Sandoval's "Cruising through Low Rider Culture: Chicano/a Identity in the Marketing of Low Rider Magazine" (2003).

15. The word "firme" is Chicano Spanish for "fine" or "cool."

16. The interview in Firme forces us to rethink the historical genealogy of queer Chicana/o discourse that has traditionally been said to begin with Chicana lesbians who then enabled Chicano gay men to speak. It should also compel us to examine how such discourses have been authorized within institutional settings, discourses that ignore or overlook how Chicana/o lesbian and gay communities and identities were being established well before the published works of creative writers or academics. In an interview with Dorothy Allison, Tomás Almaguer, and Jackie Goldsby for Out/Look: National Lesbian and Gay Quarterly, Cherríe Moraga (1989, 54) acknowledges that "in 1983, when Loving in the War Years came out, I left the country because I was very frightened of bringing up the issue of being lesbian and Chicana together within the covers

of a book." Although the *Firme* interview lacks the Chicana feminist agendas of writers like Moraga, it is important to note that two years earlier the issue of being gay and Chicano together was raised in a popular magazine (and not a book to which mostly middle-class readers, particularly academics, had access). The article also contradicts the argument Moraga (1993, 160) has made about the historical silence of Chicano gay men as compared to the audibility of Chicana lesbian voices: "In the last few years, Chicano gay men have also begun to openly examine Chicano sexuality." (Interesting to note is that both Moraga and *Firme* are from San Gabriel, California.) An even earlier conjoining of "Chicano" and "gay" is reflected in the heading of Rodrigo Reyes's classified ad in the October 30, 1975 issue of the gay San Francisco newspaper *Bay Area Reporter:* CHICANO AND GAY? The ad reads: "An organization [which would become GALA; see the afterword] is now forming in San Francisco to explore and attempt to fill the social, cultural and political needs of the Gay Chicano. Being a Gay Chicano is a unique experience only other Chicano Gays can truly understand." Cited in Horacio Roque Ramírez (2003, 356).

17. *Lowrider's* founders were involved in Chicano movement activities. See Denise Sandoval's "Cruising through Low Rider Culture: Chicana/o Identity in the Marketing of *Low Rider Magazine*" (2003).

18. *Lowrider* also requested photos of their readers' families, especially families from the 1940s who adopted "pachuco" aesthetics, which they would in turn publish in the pages of the magazine.

19. Denise Sandoval (2003) offers an interesting reading regarding the significance of such letters in *Lowrider.*

20. Over the years, provocative representations of women in *Lowrider* have increased, and they are certainly more risque today than they were in the late 1970s. Furthermore, while many women were protesting these images, they were also noting the disparity of male models, thus crystallizing the magazine's general heterosexual inclination. Again, I would like to emphasize the importance of purusing the letters sections of these magazines given how they are excellent sources for tracking the sentiments of readers—both male and female—about gender issues affecting working-class Chicano and Latino communities in which these magazines circulated.

21. These "images of men aimed at women," as Richard Dyer (1992, 104) has described the "male pin-up" in the UK tabloid *The Mirror*, are nevertheless images informed by *Firme's* chauvinistic assumptions of knowing what women want and the presumption that these men are indeed straight. Ironically, in *Firme's* fourth issue, "*Firme's* Finest" David Valdez, "a business major at UCLA, who is known to frequent Club Juárez and the Red Onion," also "occasionally goes to . . . Circus Disco." It is a well-known fact that Circus Disco in Los Angeles was a *gay* disco throughout the 1970s and 1980s. See Luis Alfaro's poem "Heroes & Saints"

from his spoken-word CD *Down Town* (1993) about Chicano gay men, the rise of AIDS, and "the great Latino watering hole, Circus Disco." Indeed, it seems *Firme* is aware of this given the ellipsis before mentioning Circus Disco. One might assume that David is in fact Victor in the next issue, but the magazine cannot reveal this information given the heterosexual tendencies of the magazine and the heterosexual female gaze for which "*Firme*'s Finest" was created.

22. See Peter Barbosa's and Garrett Lenoir's *De Colores* (2001), a documentary video that carries out a similar project.

23. And yet not all "straight" men disavow homosexual desire and practices. This is evident when Victor reveals that the men he has "picked up on" are not only gay but also straight. One must bear in mind, though, that although these men may not be straight in terms of sexual practices, they are with regard to self-identification. In fact, even when naming those Chicano and Latino married or straight men as "MSMs," or "men who have sex with men," it is still important to point to the homophobia pervasive in the community, sometimes perpetuated by these men. For a compelling ethnographic analysis of MSMs—particularly Mexican immigrant men—in relation to the family, see Lionel Cantú's "A Place Called Home: A Queer Political Economy of Mexican Immigrant Men's Family Experiences" (2001).

24. Rosemary Hennessy (2000, 206) critiques Muñoz on the grounds that he fails to foreground Aguirre's transformation of self-shame into a "love for his community," opting instead for what she understands as a queer reading of Ché Guevara that comprehends "El Ché" as nothing more than an eroticized figure. This might have been a valid critique had Muñoz not written the sentence I have cited. Overall, Hennessy miscalculates the crucial politics of cultural nationalism of which Muñoz is cognizant.

25. This quote is taken from the exhibition statement displayed at Encantada Gallery of Fine Arts in San Francisco that ran from July 8 to August 25, 2000. "Interruptions" was subsequently exhibited at the Sánchez Art Center of San Francisco from September 8 to October 15, 2000.

26. Appropriately, Rodríguez admits to feeling a stronger affinity with his father's sense of style: "In many ways I also had the look of my father which was of the 1940s, an era in which style and aesthetics were important. It was weird that I felt closer to being Latino in some senses in carrying on traditional style in terms of male dress" (E. Rodríguez 1998). Even though many in the Chicano movement reified the pachucos of the 1940s for their resistance stance to the state, it is curious that their flashy sense of style, which could very well be considered a precursor to glam, was not embraced by a movement that instead relied upon traditional codes of masculinity. See José Antonio Villarreal's classic novel *Pocho* (1959) in which pachucos are seen as "dandy" figures.

27. In his artist's statement, Rodríguez insists that his work "comes out of personal frustration of not having role models for Latino gay men trying to create their own family" (1999).

AFTERWORD: MAKING QUEER *FAMILIA*

1. This description of the film is Aguirre's and Robles's from a synopsis submitted to Frameline for inclusion in the annual San Francisco International Lesbian and Gay Film Festival. *¡Viva 16!* screened at the festival in 1994.

2. Significant to note is that while Esta Noche still exists at the time of this writing, La India Bonita does not as a result of the drastic gentrification in the area since the tape's release. In *Queer Latinidad: Identity Practices, Discursive Spaces* (2003), Juana María Rodríguez discusses how the Mission District "has become a more desirable and chic neighborhood as the quality of life for its Latina/o residents worsens." Furthermore, according to Rodríguez, "La India Bonita . . . is now a yuppie bar called Skylark" (175).

3. Importantly, the term "Queer Raza" has been used to crystallize a transnational Latino alliance. See the essay by Bustamante and Rodríguez (1995) in the exhibition catalog *Queer Raza*.

4. That *¡Viva 16!* retains its Chicano specificity is important given how, in many discussions of Latino gay male cultural production (including that which is U.S. Latino), Chicano identity is often subsumed under a banner that may tout itself as "all encompassing," yet this banner may also gloss over differences within that category, thus eliminating differences of race and class among Latinos and treating privileged Latin Americans and working-class Mexicans and Chicanos as one and the same. It must also be noted that diaspora and nationalism are never mutually exclusive categories. For more on this point, see James Clifford's "Diasporas" (1997).

5. This is taken from a letter GALA wrote in protest of a gay white man who criticized the organization's politics and Latino culture in general. See GALA, "GALA: In the Community," *Coming Up!* February 1982, 4, cited in Horacio Roque-Ramírez, "'That's *My* Place!': Negotiating Racial, Sexual, and Gender Politics in San Francisco's Gay Latino Alliance, 1975–1983," 250–51. Roque Ramírez's essay also perceptively reveals the complexity and pervasiveness of kinship dynamics in and around the organization.

6. See Rodrigo Reyes's "Latino Gays: Coming Out and Coming Home" (1981) for a first-person account of GALA's formation in the late 1970s and early 1980s. Horacio N. Roque Ramírez (2003) provides an excellent account of GALA in the context of Latino/a queer history and further elaborates on the gendered tensions between gay men and lesbians raised in *¡Viva 16!*

7. Spaces that foster racial or ethnic specificity are pivotal within a larger queer cultural economy. Two young men in ¡Viva 16! confess that, unlike in the predominantly white Castro District, they felt a sense of belonging at Esta Noche. The work of Marlon Riggs and Luis Alfaro, for example, has shown that predominantly white gay bars have been known to adopt exclusionary practices toward people of color by asking for three pieces of identification for entrance or simply turning them away at the door. In a similar vein, the largely white San Francisco gay bar The Stud held an event in 1999 called "Wet Back Night." Needless to say, protests were staged by members off the local queer Latino community. Furthermore, the San Francisco Human Rights Commission received formal complaints of discrimination regarding the event.

8. Mark Doty (1993, 18–20) similarly pays homage to a drag performer (identified as "la fabulosa Lola") at Esta Noche in his poem named after the bar in My Alexandria. Fittingly, Doty contrasts "Esta Noche, a Latin drag bar in the Mission" with "neighborhood storefront windows" displaying items such as "wedding dresses, First Communion's frothing lace," thus highlighting how Lola's extravagant presence in the neighborhood jostles with signifiers of Catholicism and heteronormativity.

9. In an argumentative vein similar to Butler's, Manuel Guzmán (1993, 18–20) extends Pierre Bourdieu's formulation of the dialectical body/space "mythico-ritual oppositions" to account for the Latino gay patrons of La Escuelita who "find their bodies engaged not with homologous, mythico-ritual oppositions, but their inversion."

10. In Homos, Leo Bersani (1995, 49) takes issue with Judith Butler, arguing that the families formed by the "drag queens" in the film "remain tributes to the heterosexual ideal of the family itself." Bersani is correct to the extent that the queens in the film aspire to "get out of the drag family and become a success in the real (straight) fashion and entertainment world" (49), yet his contention is also largely anchored by his belief that attempts to "'resignify' the family for communities that defy the usual assumptions about what constitutes a family" "have assimilative rather than subversive consequences" (5). Although Bersani's version of gay community may reject family tropes, it is, however, almost exclusively—and unapologetically—homogeneous (read white and middle-class). We must therefore question his community's ideological trappings in relation to queer people of color.

Bibliography

Acuña, Rodolfo. 1988. *Occupied America: A History of Chicanos.* 3rd ed. New York: Harper and Row.

Ada, Alma Flor. 1997. *Gathering the Sun: An Alphabet in Spanish and English.* Illustrations by Simón Silva. New York: HarperCollins.

Alarcón, Francisco X. 1985. "Dialectics of Love." In *Ya Vas, Carnal,* 48. San Francisco: Humanizarte Publications.

Alarcón, Norma. 1983. "Chicana's Feminist Literature: A Re-vision through Malintzin/or Malintzin: Putting Flesh Back on the Object." In *This Bridge Called My Back: Writings by Radical Women of Color,* Cherríe Moraga and Gloria Anzaldúa, eds., 147–59. New York: Kitchen Table Press.

———. 1990. "Chicana Feminism: In the Tracks of 'the' Native Woman." *Cultural Studies* (October): 248–56.

Albino, José. 1999. "Selective Amnesia or Arrested Development? Latinos and Hip Hop." *Mía* (winter): 50–55.

Aldama, Arturo J., and Naomi H. Quiñonez, eds. 2002. *Decolonial Voices: Chicana and Chicano Cultural Studies in the 21st Century.* Bloomington: Indiana University Press.

Ali, Lorraine. 1993. "Latin Class: Kid Frost and the Chicano Rap School." *Option: Music Alternatives* 53 (November–December): 66–72.

Almaguer, Tomás. 1991. "Chicano Men: A Cartography of Homosexual Identity and Behavior." *differences* 3 (summer): 75–100.

Alurista. 1971. *Floricanto en Aztlán.* Los Angeles: UCLA Chicano Studies Center.

———. 1972. *Nationchild Plumaroja.* San Diego: Toltecas en Aztlán.

———. 1981. "Cultural Nationalism and Xicano Literature during the Decade of 1965–1975." *MELUS* 8 (summer): 22–34.

Álvarez, Fred. 2000. "The Latino Rap Scene: Chicanos' Time for Rhythm 'n' Rhyme." *Los Angeles Times,* June 11, B1.

Anaya, Rudolfo, and Francisco Lomelí, eds. 1989. *Aztlán: Essays on the Chicano Homeland.* Albuquerque: University of New Mexico Press.

Anderson, Benedict. 1983. *Imagined Communities: Reflections on the Origin and Spread of Nationalism.* New York: Verso.

Anzaldúa, Gloria. 1987. *Borderlands/La Frontera: The New Mestiza.* San Francisco: Spinsters/Aunt Lute.

Appadurai, Arjun. 1996. *Modernity at Large: Cultural Dimensions of Globalization.* Minneapolis: University of Minnesota Press.

Armas, José. 1972. *La Familia de La Raza.* Self-published.

———. 1975. "Machismo." *De Colores: Journal of Emerging Raza Philosophies* 2 (2): 52–64.

———. 1976. "Preface to the Third Edition." *La Familia de la Raza. De Colores: Journal of Emerging Raza Philosophies* 3 (2): 4–10.

———. 1986. "Chicano Writing: The New Mexico Narrative." In *Contemporary Chicano Fiction: A Critical Survey*, ed. Vernon E. Lattin, 32–45. Binghamton, N.Y.: Bilingual Press/Editorial Bilingüe.

Armas, José, and Bernice Zamora, eds. 1980. *Flor y Canto IV and V: An Anthology of Chicano Literature.* n.p.: Pajarito Publications/Flor y Canto Committee.

Armes, Roy. 1988. *On Video.* New York: Routledge.

Arteaga, Alfred. 1975. "Frantz Fanon and the National Culture of Aztlán." *La Raza* 2 (4): 16–17.

———. 1997. *Chicano Poetics: Heterotexts and Hybridity.* New York: Cambridge University Press.

Austin, Joe, and Michael Nevin Willard, eds. 1998. *Generations of Youth: Youth Cultures and History in Twentieth-Century America.* New York: New York University Press.

Avila, Ricardo. 1993. "Homo/Latino." *Changing Men: Issues in Gender, Sex, and Politics* 26 (summer/fall): 23.

Baca Zinn, Maxine. 1975. "Political Familism: Toward Sex Role Equality in Chicano Families." *Aztlán* (spring): 13–26.

———. 1979. "Chicano Family Research: Conceptual Distortions and Alternative Directions." *Journal of Ethnic Studies* 7 (spring): 59–71.

———. 1982a. "Chicano Men and Masculinity." *Journal of Ethnic Studies* 10 (summer): 29–44.

———. 1982b. "Mexican American Women in the Social Sciences." *Signs: Journal of Women in Culture and Society* 8 (winter): 259–72.

Balderrama, Francisco E., and Raymond Rodríguez. 2006. *Decade of Betrayal: Mexican Repatriation in the 1930s.* Rev. ed. Albuquerque: University of New Mexico Press.

Barrera, Frankie. 1999. *The Diary of Baby Chulo.* Sacramento, Calif.: Popul Vuh Press.

Beitiks, Edvins. 2000. "Smits in All His 'Glory.'" *San Francisco Examiner*, March 28, C1, C6.

Benavidez, Max. 2007. *Gronk.* Los Angeles: UCLA Chicano Studies Research Center Press.

Bersani, Leo. 1988. "Is the Rectum a Grave?" In *AIDS: Cultural Analysis, Cultural Activism*, ed. Douglas Crimp, 197–222. Cambridge, Mass.: MIT Press.

———. 1995. *Homos.* Cambridge, Mass.: Harvard University Press.

Blackwell, Maylei. 2003. "Contested Histories: *Las Hijas de Cuauhtémoc*, Chicana Feminisms, and Print Culture in the Chicano Movement, 1968–1973." In *Chicana Feminisms: A Critical Reader*, ed. Gabriela F. Arredondo, et al., 59–89. Durham, N.C.: Duke University Press.

Boyd, Todd. 1996. "A Small Introduction to the 'G' Funk Era: Gangsta Rap and Black Masculinity in Contemporary Los Angeles." In *Rethinking Los Angeles.* Michael J. Dear, H. Eric Schockman, and Greg Hise, eds., 127–46. Thousand Oaks, Calif.: Sage Publications.

———. 1997. *Am I Black Enough for You? Popular Culture from the 'Hood and Beyond.* Bloomington: Indiana University Press.

———. 2003. *The New H.N.I.C.: The Death of Civil Rights and the Reign of Hip Hop.* New York: New York University Press.

Brah, Avtar. 1996. *Cartographies of Diaspora: Contesting Identities.* London: Routledge.

Brandley, Kent. 1994. "Gay and Latin on the Sixteenth Street Corridor." *Bay Area Reporter* 24 (August 25): 13.

Bravmann, Scott. 1990. "Telling (Hi)stories." *Out/Look* 8 (spring): 68–74.

Breuilly, John. 1982. *Nationalism and the State.* Chicago: University of Chicago Press.

Bright, Brenda Jo. 1994. "Mexican American Low Riders: An Anthropological Approach to Popular Culture." Ph.D. diss., Rice University.

———. 1995. "Remappings: Los Angeles Low Riders." In *Looking High and Low: Art and Cultural Identity.* Brenda Jo Bright and Liza Bakewell, eds., 89–123. Tucson: University of Arizona Press.

———. 1998. "Nightmares in the New Metropolis: The Cinematic Poetics of Low Riders." In *Generations of Youth: Youth Cultures and History in Twentieth-Century America.* Joe Austin and Michael Nevin Willard, eds., 412–26. New York: New York University Press.

Bruce-Novoa. 1982. *Chicano Poetry: A Response to Chaos.* Austin: University of Texas Press.

———. 1986. "Homosexuality and the Chicano Novel." *Confluencia* 2 (fall): 69–77.

Buchanan, Patrick J. 2002. *The Death of the West: How Dying Populations and Immigrant Invasions Imperil Our Country and Civilization.* New York: St. Martin's Press.

———. 2006. *State of Emergency: The Third World Invasion and Conquest of America.* New York: St. Martin's Press.

Burnham, Linda. 1986. "Harry Gamboa Jr. and Asco." *High Performance* 9 (3): 51–53.

Bustamante, Nao, and Eugene Rodríguez. 1995. "El Corazón Me Dio Un Salto." *Queer Raza: El Corazón Me Dio Un Salto.* Exhibition catalog. San Francisco: Galería de la Raza.

Butler, Judith. 1993. *Bodies That Matter: On the Discursive Limits of 'Sex.'* New York: Routledge.

——. 2000a. *Antigone's Claim: Kinship between Life and Death.* New York: Columbia University Press.

——. 2000b. "Quandaries of the Incest Taboo." In *Whose Freud? The Place of Psychoanalysis in Contemporary Culture,* Peter Brooks and Alex Woloch, eds., 39–46. New Haven, Conn.: Yale University Press.

——. 2004. "Is Kinship Always Already Heterosexual?" In *Undoing Gender,* 102–30. New York: Routledge.

Byers, R. K. 1997. "The Other Side of the Game: A B-Boy Adventure into Hip Hop's Gay Underworld." *Source* 99 (December): 108.

Candelaria, Cordelia. 1986. *Chicano Poetry: A Critical Introduction.* Westport, Conn.: Greenwood Press.

Cantú, Lionel. 2000. "Entre Hombres/Between Men: Latino Masculinities and Homosexualities." In *Gay Masculinities,* ed. Peter Nardi, 224–46. Thousand Oaks, Calif.: Sage Publications, Inc.

——. 2001. "A Place Called Home: A Queer Political Economy of Mexican Immigrant Men's Family Experiences." In *Queer Families, Queer Politics: Challenging Culture and the State,* Mary Bernstein and Renate Reimann, eds., 112–36. New York: Columbia University Press.

Cárdenas de Dwyer, Carlota. 1981. "Cultural Nationalism and Chicano Literature in the Eighties." *MELUS* 8 (summer): 40–47.

Castañeda, Omar S. 1996. "Guatemalan Macho Oratory." In *Muy Macho: Latino Men Confront Their Manhood,* ed. Ray González, 37–56. New York: Doubleday.

Castillo, Ana. 1991. "La Macha: Toward a Beautiful Whole Self." In *Chicana Lesbians: The Girls Our Mothers Warned Us About,* ed. Carla Trujillo, 24–48. Berkeley: Third Woman Press.

——. 1994. *The Massacre of the Dreamers: Essays on Xicanisma.* Albuquerque: University of New Mexico Press.

Castrellón, Clara Gloria. 1977. "Love and Revolution." *Capirotada* (spring): 7.

Chabram, Angie, and Rosa Linda Fregoso. 1990. "Chicana/o Cultural Representations: Reframing Alternative Critical Discourses." *Cultural Studies* 4 (3): 203–12.

Chabram-Dernersesian, Angie. 1992. "I Throw Punches for My Race, but I Don't Want to Be a Man: Writing Us—Chica-nos (Girl, Us)/Chicanas—into the Movement Script." In *Cultural Studies,* Lawrence Grossberg, Cary Nelson, and Paula Treichler, eds., 81–95. New York: Routledge.

———. 1993. "And Yes . . . the Earth Did Part: On the Splitting of Chicana/o Subjectivity." In *Building with Our Hands: New Directions in Chicana Studies*, Adela de la Torre and Beatríz M. Pesquera, eds., 34–56. Berkeley: University of California Press.

———. 1999. "En-countering the Other Discourse of Chicano-Mexicano Difference." *Cultural Studies* 13 (2): 263–89.

———. 2000. "Critical Dialogues on Chicana/o Cultural Studies." In *Without Guarantees: In Honor of Stuart Hall*, Paul Gilroy, Lawrence Grossberg, and Angela McRobbie, eds., 53–66. London: Verso.

———, ed. 2006. *The Chicana/o Cultural Studies Reader.* New York: Routledge.

———, ed. 2007. *The Chicana/o Cultural Studies Forum: Critical and Ethnographic Practices.* New York: New York University Press.

Chang, Jeff. 2005. *Can't Stop Won't Stop: A History of the Hip-Hop Generation.* New York: St. Martin's Press.

Chatterjee, Partha. 1990. "The Nationalist Resolution of the Women's Question." In *Recasting Women: Essays in Indian Colonial History*, Kumkum Sangari and Sudesh Vaid, eds., 233–53. New Brunswick, N.J.: Rutgers University Press.

———. 1993. *The Nation and Its Fragments: Colonial and Postcolonial Histories.* Princeton, N.J.: Princeton University Press.

Chávez, César E. 2002. *The Words of César Chávez*, Richard J. Jensen and John C. Hammerback, eds. College Station: Texas A&M University Press.

Chávez, Ernesto. 1998. "'Birth of a New Symbol': The Brown Berets' Gendered Chicano National Imaginary." In *Generations of Youth: Youth Cultures and History in Twentieth-Century America*, Joe Austin and Michael Nevin Willard, eds., 205–22. New York: New York University Press.

———. 2002. *"¡Mi Raza Primero!": Nationalism, Identity, and Insurgency in the Chicano Movement in Los Angeles, 1966–1978.* Berkeley: University of California Press.

Chavoya, C. Ondine. 1998. "Pseudographic Cinema: Asco's No-Movies." *Performance Research* 3 (1): 1–14.

———. 2000a. "Orphans of Modernism: The Performance Art of Asco." In *Corpus Delecti: Performance Art of the Americas*, ed. Coco Fusco, 240–63. New York: Routledge.

———. 2000b. "Internal Exiles: The Interventionist Public and Performance Art of Asco." In *Space, Site, Intervention: Situating Installation Art*, ed. Erika Suderburg, 189–208. Minneapolis: University of Minnesota Press.

Chicano Liberation Youth Conference. 1972. "El Plan Espiritual de Aztlán." In *Aztlán: An Anthology of Mexican American Literature*, Luis Valdez and Stan Steiner, eds., 402–6. New York: Vintage.

Clifford, James. 1997. "Diasporas." *Routes: Travel and Translation in the Late Twentieth Century*, 244–77. Cambridge, Mass.: Harvard University Press.

———. 2000. "Taking Identity Politics Seriously: 'The Contradictory, Stony Ground.'" In *Without Guarantees: In Honor of Stuart Hall*, Paul Gilroy, Lawrence Grossberg, and Angela McRobbie, eds., 94–112. London: Verso.

Cockcroft, Eva Sperling, and Holly Barnet-Sánchez. 1990. *Signs from the Heart: California Chicano Murals.* Venice, Calif.: SPARC.

Coontz, Stephanie. 1992. *The Way We Never Were: American Families and the Nostalgia Trap.* New York: Basic Books.

———. 1997. *The Way We Really Are: Coming to Terms with America's Changing Families.* New York: Basic Books.

Cooper Alarcón, Daniel. 1988–90. "The Aztec Palimpsest: Toward a New Understanding of Aztlán, Cultural Identity and History." *Aztlán: A Journal of Chicano Studies* 19 (fall): 33–68.

Cortez, Jaime, ed. 1999. *Virgins, Guerillas, and Locas: Gay Latinos Writing on Love.* San Francisco: Cleis Press.

Cotera, Marta. 1977. "Our Feminist Heritage." *The Chicana Feminist*, ed. Marta Cotera, 1–7. Austin: Informational Systems Development.

Coyle, Michael. 2000. "Cypress Hill." *Mean Street Magazine* 10 (January): 23.

Crenshaw, Kimberlè Williams. 1993. "Beyond Racism and Misogyny: Black Feminism and 2 Live Crew." In *Words That Wound: Critical Race Theory, Assaultive Speech, and the First Amendment*, Mari J. Matsuda, Charles Lawrence III, Richard Delgado, and Kimberlè Williams Crenshaw, eds., 111–32. Boulder, Colo.: Westview Press.

Cross, Brian (with Raegan Kelly and T-Love). 1993. *It's Not about a Salary: Rap, Race, and Resistance in Los Angeles.* New York: Verso.

Cubitt, Sean. 1993. *Videography: Video Media as Art and Culture.* New York: St. Martin's Press.

Cunningham, John. 2002. "'Hey, Mr. Liberace, Will You Vote for Zeta?': Looking for the Joto in Chicano Men's Autobiographical Writing." In *Race-ing Masculinity: Identity in Contemporary U.S. Men's Writing*, 69–94. New York: Routledge.

Currid, Brian. 1995. "'We Are Family': House Music and Queer Performativity." In *Cruising the Performative: Interventions into the Representation of Ethnicity, Nationality, and Sexuality*, Sue-Ellen Case, Philip Brett, and Susan Leigh Foster, eds., 165–96. Bloomington: Indiana University Press.

Dávila, Arlene. 2001. "The American Dream Is Latino, for a Change." *Chronicle of Higher Education*, June 29, B16.

Davis, Mike. 2000. *Magical Urbanism: Latinos Reinvent the U.S. Big City.* New York: Verso.

Decker, Jeffrey Louis. 1993. "The State of Rap: Time and Place in Hip Hop Nationalism." *Social Text* 34 (spring): 53–84.

DeCurtis, Anthony. 2000. "Eminem's Hate Rhymes." *Rolling Stone*, August 3, 17–18, 21.

De Genova, Nick. 1995. "Gangsta Rap and Nihilism in Black America: Some Questions of Life and Death." *Social Text* 43 (fall): 89–132.

Del Barco, Mandalit. 1996. "Rap's Latino Sabor." In *Droppin' Science: Critical Essays on Rap Music and Hip Hop Culture*, ed. William Eric Perkins, 63–84. Philadelphia: Temple University Press.

Delgado, Abelardo. 1969. *Chicano: 25 Pieces of a Chicano Mind.* Denver: Barrio Publications.

———. 1978. "An Open Letter to Carolina . . . or Relations between Men and Women." *Revista Chicano-Riqueña* 6 (2): 33–41.

D'Emilio, John. 1983. "Capitalism and Gay Identity." In *Powers of Desire: The Politics of Sexuality*, Ann Snitow, Christine Stansell, and Sharon Thompson, eds., 100–113. New York: Monthly Review Press.

Dent, Gina, ed. 1992. *Black Popular Culture.* Seattle: Bay Press.

Diawara, Manthia. 1993. "Black American Cinema: The New Realism." In *Black American Cinema*, ed. Manthia Diawara, 1–23. New York: Routledge.

Díaz, Rafael M. 1998. *Latino Gay Men and HIV: Culture, Sexuality, and Risk Behavior.* New York: Routledge.

Dimitriadis, Greg. 2001. *Performing Identity/Performing Culture: Hip-Hop as Text, Pedagogy, and Lived Practice.* New York: Peter Lang.

Doss, Yvette C. 1998. "Choosing Chicano in the 1990s: The Underground Music Scene of Los(t) Angeles." *Aztlán: A Journal of Chicano Studies* 23 (fall): 191–202.

Doty, Mark. 1993. *My Alexandria.* Urbana: University of Illinois Press.

Dyer, Richard. 1992. *Only Entertainment.* New York: Routledge.

Ebron, Paulla. 1991. "Rapping between Men: Performing Gender." *Radical America* 23 (4): 23–27.

Edelman, Lee. 1994. *Homographesis: Essays in Gay Literary and Cultural Theory.* New York: Routledge.

———. 2004. *No Future: Queer Theory and the Death Drive.* Durham, N.C.: Duke University Press.

Eng, David L. 2003. "Transnational Adoption and Queer Diasporas." *Social Text* 76 (fall): 1–37.

Enloe, Cynthia. 1989. *Bananas, Beaches, and Bases: Making Feminist Sense of International Politics.* Berkeley: University of California Press.

Espinoza, Dionne. 1995. "Pedagogies of Nationalism and Gender: Cultural Resistance in Selected Representational Practices of Chicana/o Movement Activists, 1967–1972." Ph.D. diss., Cornell University.

———. 2001. "'Revolutionary Sisters': Women's Solidarity and Collective Identification among Chicana Brown Berets in East Los Angeles, 1967–1970." *Aztlán: A Journal of Chicano Studies* 26: (spring): 15–58.

———. Forthcoming. *Revolutionary Sisters: Chicana Activism and the Cultural Politics of Chicano Power.* Austin: University of Texas Press.

Fanon, Frantz. 1963. *The Wretched of the Earth.* Trans. Constance Farrington. New York: Grove Press.

Ferguson, Roderick A. 2004. *Aberrations in Black: Toward a Queer of Color Critique.* Minneapolis: University of Minnesota Press.

Fernández, Roberta. 1994. "Abriendo caminos in the Borderlands: Chicana Writers Respond to the Ideology of Literary Nationalism." *Frontiers* 14 (2): 23–50.

Flores, Juan. 1988. "Rappin', Writin', & Breakin'." *Buletin del Centro de Estudios Puertorriqueños* 2 (spring): 34–41.

———. 1997. "Latino Studies: New Contexts, New Concepts." *Harvard Educational Review* 67 (summer): 208–21.

———. 2000. *From Bomba to Hip-Hop: Puerto Rican Culture and Latino Identity.* New York: Columbia University Press.

Flores, Rosalie. 1975. "The New Chicana and Machismo." *Regeneración* 2: 55–56.

Flores, William V., and Rina Benmayor, eds. 1997. *Latino Cultural Citizenship: Claiming Identity, Space, and Rights.* Boston: Beacon.

Foucault, Michel. 1984. "Nietzsche, Genealogy, History." In *The Foucault Reader*, ed. Paul Rabinow, 76–100. New York: Pantheon Books.

Franklin, Sarah, and Susan McKinnon, eds. 2001. *Relative Values: Reconfiguring Kinship Studies.* Durham, N.C.: Duke University Press.

Freccero, Carla. 1999. *Popular Culture: An Introduction.* New York: New York University Press.

Fregoso, Rosa Linda. 1993a. *The Bronze Screen: Chicana and Chicano Film Culture.* Minneapolis: University of Minnesota Press.

———. 1993b. "Zoot Suit: The 'Return to the Beginning'." In *Mediating Two Worlds: Cinematic Encounters in the Americas*, John King, Ana M. López, and Manuel Alvarado, eds., 269–78. London: BFI Publishing.

———. 2003. *MeXicana Encounters: The Making of Social Identities on the Borderlands.* Berkeley: University of California Press.

Freud, Sigmund. [1908] 1989. "Family Romances." In *The Freud Reader*, ed. Peter Gay, 297–300. New York: Norton.

Fuentes, Nina. 2006. *The Rise and Fall of the Nuestra Familia.* Jefferson, Wisc.: Know Gangs Publishing.

Fusco, Coco. 1990. "Ethnicity, Politics, and Poetics: Latinos and Media Art." In *Illuminating Video: An Essential Guide to Video Art*, Doug Hall and Sally Jo Fifer, eds., 304–16. New York: Aperture/BAVC.

Gamboa Jr., Harry. 1977. "Film, Television, and Treviño." *La Luz*, October, 7–8.

———. 1978. "Silver Screening the Barrio." *Equal Opportunity Forum* 6 (November): 6–7.

———. 1998. *Urban Exile: Collected Writings of Harry Gamboa Jr.*, ed. Chon A. Noriega. Minneapolis: University of Minnesota Press.

Gangotena, Margarita. 1994. "The Rhetoric of *La Familia* among Mexican Americans." In *Our Voices: Essays in Culture, Ethnicity, and Communication: An Intercultural Anthology*, Alberto González, Marsha Houston, and Victoria Chen, eds., 69–80. Los Angeles: Roxbury Publishing Company.

García, Alma M. 1990. "Studying Chicanas: Bringing Women into the Frame of Chicano Studies." In *Chicana Voices: Intersections of Class, Race, and Gender*, Teresa Córdova, Norma Cantú, Gilberto Cardenas, Juan García, and Christine M. Sierra, eds. 19–29. Colorado Springs, Colo.: NACS Publications.

———, ed. 1997. *Chicana Feminist Thought: The Basic Historical Writings.* New York: Routledge.

García, Bernardo. 1998. *The Development of a Latino Gay Identity.* New York: Garland Publishing.

García, Ignacio M. 1989. *United We Win: The Rise and Fall of La Raza Unida Party.* Tucson: University of Arizona Press/Mexican American Studies Research Center.

———. 1996. "Juncture in the Road: Chicano Studies since 'El Plan de Santa Barbara.'" In *Chicanas/Chicanos at the Crossroads: Social, Economic, and Political Change*, David R. Maciel and Isidoro D. Ortíz, eds., 181–203. Tucson: University of Arizona Press.

———. 1997. *Chicanismo: The Forging of a Militant Ethos among Mexican Americans.* Tucson: University of Arizona Press.

García, Ramón. 1994. "Miss Primavera Contest." *Americas Review* 22 (3–4): 71– 72.

Gilroy, Paul. 1991. "Sounds Authentic: Black Music, Ethnicity, and the Challenge of a Changing Same." *Black Music Research Journal* 2 (2): 111–36.

———. 1992. "Discussant's Comments." In *Black Popular Culture*, ed. Gina Dent, 325–31. Seattle: Bay Press.

———. 1993a. *The Black Atlantic: Modernity and Double Consciousness.* Cambridge, Mass.: Harvard University Press.

———. 1993b. "It's a Family Affair: Black Culture and the Trope of Kinship." In *Small Acts: Thoughts on the Politics of Black Cultures*, 192–207. London: Serpent's Tail Press.

Gilroy, Paul, Lawrence Grossberg, and Angela McRobbie, eds. 2000. *Without Guarantees: In Honor of Stuart Hall.* London: Verso.

Goldstein, Steve. 2000. "By Any Means Necessary: Spike Lee on Video's Viability." *Res: The Future of Filmmaking* 3 (4): 49.

Gómez-Quiñones, Juan. 1990. *Chicano Politics: Reality and Promise, 1940–1990.* Albuquerque: University of New Mexico Press.

Gonzales, Rodolfo "Corky." 1972. *I am Joaquín/Yo soy Joaquín.* New York: Bantam.

———. 1973. "Chicano Nationalism: The Key to Unity for La Raza." In *Chicano: The Evolution of a People*, Renato Rosaldo, Robert A. Calvert, and Gustav L. Seligmann, eds., 420–35. Minneapolis, Minn.: Winston Press.

———. 2001. *Message to Aztlán: Selected Writings*, ed. Antonio Esquibel. Houston: Arte Público Press.

Gonzales, Sylvia Alicia. 1975. "National Character vs. Universality in Chicano Poetry." *De Colores* 1 (4): 10–21.

González, Cesar A. 1982. " 'La Familia' de Joaquín Chiñas." *De Colores* 6 (1/2): 146–49.

González, Deena J. 1991. "Malinche as Lesbian: A Reconfiguration of 500 Years of Resistance." *California Sociologist* (14): 90–97.

González, John M. 1996. "Romancing Hegemony: Constructing Racialized Citizenship in María Amparo Ruíz de Burton's *The Squatter and the Don*." In *Recovering the U.S. Hispanic Literary Heritage*, vol. 2, Erlinda Gonzáles Berry and Chuck Tatum, eds., 23–39. Houston: Arte Público Press.

González, Ray, ed. 1996. *Muy Macho: Latino Men Confront Their Manhood*. New York: Doubleday.

González, Rigoberto. 2006. *Butterfly Boy: Memories of a Chicano Mariposa*. Madison: University of Wisconsin Press.

Grajeda, Rafael. 1980. "The Pachuco in Chicano Poetry: The Process of Legend-Creation." *Revista Chicano-Riqueña* 8 (autumn): 45–59.

Gray, Herman. 2004. *Watching Race: Television and the Struggle for Blackness*. Minneapolis: University of Minnesota Press.

———. 1996. "Is Cultural Studies Inflated?: The Cultural Economy of Cultural Studies in the United States." In *Disciplinarity and Dissent in Cultural Studies*, Cary Nelson and Dilip Parameshwar Gaonkar, eds., 203–16. New York: Routledge.

Griswold del Castillo, Richard. 1984. *La Familia: Chicano Families in the Urban Southwest, 1848 to the Present*. Notre Dame, Ind.: University of Notre Dame Press.

Grossberg, Lawrence. 1997. "Cultural Studies, Modern Logics, and Theories of Globalisation." In *Back to Reality?: Social Experience and Cultural Studies*, ed. Angela McRobbie, 9–35. Manchester: Manchester University Press.

Grossberg, Lawrence, Cary Nelson, and Paul Treichler, eds. 1992. *Cultural Studies*. New York: Routledge.

Guevara, Nancy. 1987. "Women Writin' Rappin' Breakin'." In *The Year Left II, Toward a Rainbow Socialism: Essays on Race, Ethnicity, Class, and Gender*, Mike Davis, et al., eds., 160–75. New York: Verso.

Gupta, Sunil. 1989. "Black, Brown and White." In *Coming On Strong: Gay Politics and Culture*, Simon Shepherd and Mick Wallis, eds., 163–79. London: Unwin Hyman.

Gutiérrez, Eric-Steven. 1992. "Latino Issues: Gay and Lesbian Latinos Claiming La Raza." In *Positively Gay: New Approaches to Gay and Lesbian Life*, ed. Betty Berzon, 240–46. Berkeley: Celestial Arts Publishing.

Gutiérrez, José Angel. 1985. "Ondas y Rollos (Wavelengths and Raps): The Ideology of Contemporary Chicano Rhetoric." In *A War of Words: Chicano Protest in the 1960s and 1970s*, John C. Hammerback, Richard J. Jensen, and José Angel Gutiérrez, eds. 121–62. Westport, Conn.: Greenwood Press.

Gutiérrez, Ramón A. 1993. "Community, Patriarchy and Individualism: The Politics of Chicano History and the Dream of Equality." *American Quarterly* 45 (March): 44–72.

———. 1996. "The Erotic Zone: Sexual Transgression on the U.S.-Mexican Border." In *Mapping Multiculturalism*, Avery F. Gordon and Christopher Newfield, eds., 253–62. Minneapolis: University of Minnesota Press.

Gutiérrez-Jones, Carl. 1995. *Rethinking the Borderlands: Between Chicano Culture and Legal Discourse*. Berkeley: University of California Press.

Guzmán, Manuel. 1997. "'Pa La Escuelita con Mucho Cuida'o y por la Orillita': A Journey through the Contested Terrains of the Nation and Sexual Orientation." In *Puerto Rican Jam: Essays on Culture and Politics*, Frances Negrón-Muntaner and Ramón Grosfoguel, eds., 209–28. Minneapolis: University of Minnesota Press.

Halberstam, Judith. 1997. "Mackdaddy, Superfly, Rapper: Gender, Race, and Masculinity in the Drag King Scene." *Social Text* 52–53 (fall–winter): 104–31.

———. 1998. *Female Masculinity*. Durham, N.C.: Duke University Press.

Hall, Doug, and Sally Jo Fifer, eds. 1990. *Illuminating Video: An Essential Guide to Video Art*. New York: Aperture/BAVC.

Hall, Stuart. 1981. "Notes on Deconstructing the Popular." In *People's History and Socialist Theory*, ed. Raphael Samuel, 227–49. London: Routledge.

———. 1990. "The Emergence of Cultural Studies and the Crisis of the Humanities." *October* 53 (summer): 11–23.

———. 1996. "What Is This 'Black' in Black Popular Culture?" In *Stuart Hall: Critical Dialogues in Cultural Studies*, David Morley and Kuan-Hsing Chen, eds., 465–75. New York: Routledge.

Hall, Stuart, and Tony Jefferson, eds. 1976. *Resistance through Rituals: Youth Subcultures in Post-war Britain*. London: Routledge.

Harlow, Barbara. 1987. *Resistance Literature*. New York: Methuen.

Haro, Juan. 1998. *The Ultimate Betrayal: An Autobiography*. Pittsburgh: Dorrance Publishing Co.

Hawkeswood, William G. 1996. *One of the Children: Gay Black Men in Harlem*, ed. Alex W. Costley. Berkeley: University of California Press.

Hayden, Tom. 2004. *Street Wars: Gangs and the Future of Violence*. New York: New Press.

Heath, Stephen. 1981. *Questions of Cinema*. Bloomington: Indiana University Press.

Hebdige, Dick. 1988. "Hiding in the Light: Youth Surveillance and Display." In *Hiding in the Light: On Images and Things*, 17–41. New York: Routledge.

Hennessy, Rosemary. 2000. *Profit and Pleasure: Sexual Identities in Late Capitalism*. New York: Routledge.

Hernández, Benjamin Francisco. 1981a. "Note from the Publisher." *Firme Magazine* 1 (2): 7.

———. 1981b. "Note from the Publisher." *Firme Magazine* 1 (5): 5.

Hernández, Carlos. 1981. "A Gay Life Style (Only if La Familia Approves)." *Firme Magazine* 1 (5): 18–19.

Hernández, Robb. 2006. "Performing the Archival Body in the Robert "Cyclona" Legorreta Fire of Life/El Fuego de la Vida Collection." *Aztlán: A Journal of Chicano Studies* 31 (fall): 113–25.

Hidalgo-de la Riva, Teresa "Osa." 2004. "Mujerista Moviemaking: Chicana Filmmakers Sylvia Morales and Lourdes Portillo." Ph.D. diss., University of Southern California.

———, ed. 2006. "Chicana Spectators and Mediamakers: Imagining TransCultural Diversity." Special issue, *Spectator: The University of Southern California Journal of Film and Television Criticism* (spring).

Hinojosa, Rolando. 1985. "*I Am Joaquín*: Relationships between the Text and the Film." In *Chicano Cinema: Research, Reviews, and Resources*, ed. Gary D. Keller, 142–45. Binghamton, N.Y.: Bilingual Review/Press.

Hirsch, Marianne. 1997. *Family Frames: Photography, Narrative, and Postmemory*. Cambridge, Mass.: Harvard University Press.

Hocquenghem, Guy. 1993. "Capitalism, the Family, and the Anus." *Homosexual Desire*, trans. Daniella Dangoor, 93–112. Durham, N.C.: Duke University Press.

Holling, Michelle A. 2006. "*El Simpático* Boxer: Underpinning Chicano Masculinity with a Rhetoric of *Familia* in *Resurrection Blvd.*" *Western Journal of Communication* 70 (April): 91–114.

Holston, Mark. 1993. "The Straight Rap." *Hispanic* (Jan./Feb.): 130–36.

Hoobler, Dorothy and Thomas. 1994. *The Mexican American Family Album*. New York: Oxford University Press.

Huaco-Nuzum, Carmen. 1998. Review of *Mi Familia/My Family* (New Line Cinema movie). *Aztlán: A Journal of Chicano Studies* 23 (spring): 141–52.

Hurtado, Aida. 1996. *The Color of Privilege: Three Blasphemies on Race and Feminism*. Ann Arbor: University of Michigan Press.

Jagger, Gill, and Caroline Wright, eds. 1999. *Changing Family Values*. New York: Routledge.

James, David E. 2005. *The Most Typical Avant-Garde: History and Geography of Minor Cinemas in Los Angeles*. Berkeley: University of California Press.

Kelley, Robin D. G. 1994. "Kickin' Reality, Kickin' Ballistics: 'Gangsta Rap' and Postindustrial Los Angeles." In *Race Rebels: Culture, Politics, and the Black Working Class*, 183–227. New York: The Free Press.

Kelly, Raegan. 1993a. "Aztlán Underground." In *It's Not About a Salary: Rap, Race, and Resistance in Los Angeles*, ed. Brian Cross (with Raegan Kelly and T-Love), 263–67. New York: Verso.

———. 1993b. "Hip Hop Chicano: A Separate but Parallel Story." In *It's Not About a Salary: Rap, Race, and Resistance in Los Angeles*, ed. Brian Cross (with Raegan Kelly and T-Love), 65–76. New York: Verso.

King, Wayne. 1981. "Low Riders Are Becoming Legion among Chicanos." *New York Times*, May 9, 8.

Kitwana, Bakari. 1994. *The Rap on Gangsta Rap*. Chicago: Third World Press.

Kogawa, Tetsuo. 1996. "Video: The Access Medium." In *Resolutions: Contemporary Video Practices*, Michael Renov and Erika Suderburg, eds., 51–60. Minneapolis: University of Minnesota Press.

Kun, Josh. 1997. "Against Easy Listening: Audiotopic Readings and Transnational Soundings." In *Everynight Life: Culture and Dance in Latin/o America*, eds. Celeste Fraser Delgado and José Esteban Muñoz, eds., 288–309. Durham, N.C.: Duke University Press.

———. 2004. "What Is an MC If He Can't Rap to Banda? Making Music in Nuevo L.A." *American Quarterly* 56 (September): 741–58.

Lasch, Christopher. 1977. *Haven in a Heartless World: The Family Besieged*. New York: Norton.

Lazarus, Neil. 1999. *Nationalism and Cultural Practice in the Postcolonial World*. New York: Cambridge University Press.

Leo, John. 1989. "The Familialism of 'Man' in American Television Melodrama." In *Displacing Homophobia: Gay Male Perspectives in Literature and Culture*, Ronald R. Butters, John M. Clum, and Michael Moon, eds., 31–51. Durham, N.C.: Duke University Press.

León-Portilla, Miguel. 1963. *Aztec Thought and Culture: A Study of the Ancient Nahuatl Mind*, trans. Jack Emory Davis. Norman: University of Oklahoma Press.

Lewels Jr., Francisco J. 1974. *The Uses of the Media by the Chicano Movement: A Study in Minority Access*. New York: Praeger.

Limón, José E. 1992. *Mexican Ballads, Chicano Poems: History and Influence in Mexican-American Social Poetry*. Berkeley: University of California Press.

Lloyd, David. 1993a. *Anomalous States: Irish Writing and the Post-Colonial Moment*. Durham, N.C.: Duke University Press.

———. 1993b. "Adulteration and the Nation." In *Anomolous States: Irish Writing and the Post-Colonial Moment*, 88–124.

———. 1997. "Nationalisms against the State." In *The Politics of Culture in the Shadow of Capital*, Lisa Lowe and David Lloyd, eds., 173–97. Durham, N.C.: Duke University Press.

Longeaux y Vásquez, Enriqueta. 1975. "The Woman of La Raza." In *Chicano Voices*, ed. Carlota Cárdenas de Dwyer, 167–72. Boston: Houghton Mifflin Company.

López, Sonia A. 1977. "The Role of the Chicana within the Student Movement." In *Essays on La Mujer*, ed. Rosaura Sánchez, 16–29. Los Angeles: UCLA Chicano Studies Center.

López Sáenz, Lionila. 1972. "Machismo, No! Igualdad, Si!" *La Luz* 1 (May): 19–24.

Loza, Steve. 1993. *Barrio Rhythm: Mexican American Music in Los Angeles.* Urbana: University of Illinois Press.

Lubiano, Wahneema. 1992a. "Black Ladies, Welfare Queens, and State Minstrels: Ideological War by Narrative Means." In *Race-ing Justice, En-gendering Power*, ed. Toni Morrison, 323–63. New York: Pantheon.

———. 1992b. "Discussant's Comments." In *Black Popular Culture*, ed. Gina Dent, 325–31. Seattle: Bay Press.

———. 1997. "Don't Talk with Your Eyes Closed: Caught in the Hollywood Gun Sights." In *Queer Representations: Reading Lives, Reading Cultures*, ed. Martin Duberman, 139–45. New York: New York University Press.

Lucero Trujillo, Marcela. 1978. "The Terminology of Machismo." *De Colores* 4 (3): 34–42.

Maciel, David R., Isidro D. Ortíz, and María Herrera-Sobek, eds. 2000. *Chicano Renaissance: Contemporary Cultural Trends.* Tucson: University of Arizona Press.

Madsen, William. 1973. *The Mexican-Americans of South Texas*, 2nd ed. New York: Holt, Rinehart, and Winston.

Márez, Curtis. 1996. "Brown: The Politics of Working-Class Chicano Style." *Social Text* 48 (fall): 109–32.

Marín, Christine. 1977. *A Spokesman for the Mexican American Movement: Rodolfo "Corky" Gonzáles and the Fight for Chicano Liberation, 1966–1972.* San Francisco: R&E Research Associates.

Mariscal, George (Jorge). 2002. "Left Turns in the Chicano Movement, 1965–1975." *Monthly Review* 59 (July/August): 59–68.

———. 2005. *Brown-Eyed Children of the Sun: Lessons from the Chicano Movement, 1965–1975.* Albuquerque: University of New Mexico Press.

Martínez, Eliud. 1980. "*I am Joaquín* as Poem and Film: Two Modes of Chicano Expression." *Journal of Popular Culture* (spring): 505–15.

Martínez, Elizabeth. 1998. *De Colores Means All of Us: Latina Views for a Multi-Colored Century.* Cambridge, Mass.: South End Press.

Martínez, Rubén. 1992. "East Side, West Side." *Los Angeles Times Magazine*, May 3, 12.

McClintock, Anne. 1995. *Imperial Leather: Race, Gender, and Sexuality in the Colonial Contest.* New York: Routledge.

McFarland, Pancho. 2002. "'Here Is Something You Can't Understand . . .': Chicano Rap and the Critique of Globalization." In *Decolonial Voices: Chicana and Chicano Cultural Studies in the 21st Century*, Arturo Aldama and Naomi H. Quiñonez, eds., 297–315. Bloomington: Indiana University Press.

McLaren, Peter. 1995. "Gangsta Pedagogy and Ghettoethnicity: The Hip-Hop Nation as Counterpublic Sphere." *Socialist Review* 25 (2): 9–55.

McPeek Villatoro, Marcos. 1994. "Rap and La Raza." *Request*, August, 44–47, 80–83.

McRobbie, Angela. 1991. *Feminism and Youth Culture: From Jackie to Just Seventeen.* London: Macmillan.

Melendez, Miguel "Mickey." 2003. *We Took the Streets: Fighting for Latino Rights with the Young Lords.* New York: St. Martin's Press.

Melville, Margarita B., ed. 1980. *Twice a Minority: Mexican American Women.* St. Louis: C.V. Mosby Company.

Mercer, Kobena. 1990. "Black Art and the Burden of Representation." *Third Text* 10 (spring): 61–78.

Miller, Mary, and Karl Taube. 1993. *An Illustrated Dictionary of the Gods and Symbols of Ancient Mexico and the Maya.* London: Thames and Hudson.

Mirandé, Alfredo. 1979. "A Reinterpretation of Male Dominance in the Chicano Family." *Family Coordinator* 28 (4): 473–97.

——. 1982. "Machismo: Rucas, Chingasos, y Chingaderas." *De Colores: Journal of Chicano Expression and Thought* 6 (1/2): 17–31.

——. 1997. *Hombres y Machos: Masculinity and Latino Culture.* Boulder, Colo.: Westview Press.

Moddelmog, Debra. 1999. *In Pursuit of Desire: Reading Ernest Hemingway.* New York: Cornell University Press.

Modleski, Tania. 1991. *Feminism without Women: Culture and Criticism in a "Postfeminist" Age.* New York: Routledge.

Montiel, Miguel. 1970. "The Social Science Myth of the Mexican American Family." *El Grito* 3 (summer): 56–63.

Moon, Michael. 1991. *Disseminating Whitman: Revision and Corporeality in "Leaves of Grass."* Cambridge, Mass.: Harvard University Press.

Moraga, Cherríe. 1983. *Loving in the War Years: Lo que nunca pasó por sus labios.* Boston: South End Press.

——. 1989. "Writing Is the Measure of My Life . . . : An Interview with Cherríe Moraga" (with Dorothy Allison, Tomás Almaguer, and Jackie Goldsby). *Out/Look* 4 (winter): 53–57.

——. 1993a. *The Last Generation.* Boston: South End Press.

——. 1993b. "Queer Aztlán: The Re-formation of Chicano Tribe." In *The Last Generation*, 145–74.

———. 1997. *Waiting in the Wings: Portrait of a Queer Motherhood*. Ithaca, N.Y.: Firebrand Books.

Morales, Ed. 2003. *The Latin Beat: The Rhythms and Roots of Latin Music, from Bossa Nova to Salsa and Beyond*. Cambridge, Mass.: Da Capo Press.

Morales, Iris. 1998. "¡Palante, Siempre Palante!: The Young Lords." In *The Puerto Rican Movement: Voices from the Diaspora*, Andrés Torres and José E. Velázquez, eds., 210–27. Philadelphia: Temple University Press.

Morales, Sylvia. 1979. "Filming a Chicana Documentary." *Somos* 2 (June): 42–45.

Mosse, George L. 1985. *Nationalism and Sexuality: Middle-Class Morality and Sexual Norms in Modern Europe*. Madison: University of Wisconsin Press.

Muñoz Jr., Carlos. 1989. *Youth, Identity, Power: The Chicano Movement*. New York: Verso.

Muñoz, José Esteban. 1996. "Ephemera as Evidence: Introductory Notes to Queer Acts." *Women and Performance: A Journal of Feminist Theory* 8 (2): 5–17.

———. 1999. *Disidentifications: Queers of Color and the Performance of Politics*. Minneapolis: University of Minnesota Press.

———. 2000. "Feeling Brown: Ethnicity and Affect in Ricardo Bracho's *The Sweetest Hangover (and Other STDs)*." *Theatre Journal* 52 (March): 67–79.

Muñoz, Manuel. 2003. *Zigzagger*. Evanston, Ill.: Northwestern University Press.

———. 2007. *The Faith Healer of Olive Avenue*. Chapel Hill, N.C.: Algonquin Books.

Murillo, Nathan. 1971. "The Mexican American Family." In *Chicanos: Social and Psychological Perspectives*, Nathaniel N. Wagner and Marsha J. Haug, eds., 97–108. Saint Louis: C.V. Mosby Company.

Nardi, Peter M. 1999. *Gay Men's Friendships: Invincible Communities*. Chicago: University of Chicago Press.

Navaro, J. L. 1969. "To a Dead Lowrider." *Con Safos* 3 (March): 26–27.

Navarrete Jr., Ruben. 1993. *A Darker Shade of Crimson: Odyssey of a Harvard Chicano*. New York: Bantam Books.

Navarro, Armando. 1995. *Mexican American Youth Organization: Avant-Garde of the Chicano Movement in Texas*. Austin: University of Texas Press.

———. 2000. *La Raza Unida Party: A Chicano Challenge to the U.S. Two-Party Dictatorship*. Philadelphia: Temple University Press.

"Nava's New Line Deal." 1999. *Latin Heat* (February/March): 5.

Nelson, Hilde Lindemann, ed. 1997. *Feminism and Families*. New York: Routledge.

Newton, Huey P. 1995. "The Women's Liberation and Gay Liberation Movements." In *To Die for the People*, ed. Toni Morrison, 152–55. New York: Writers and Readers Publishing.

Nieto Gómez, Anna. 1976. "Chicana Feminism." *Caracol* 2 (5): 3–5.

Nieves, Santiago, and Frank Algarín. 1997. "Two Film Reviews: *My Family/Mi Familia* and *The Pérez Family*." In *Latin Looks: Images of Latinas and Latinos in the U.S. Media*, ed. Clara E. Rodríguez, 221–24. Boulder, Colo.: Westview Press.

Noriega, Chon A. 1996a. "Imagined Borders: Locating Chicano Cinema in America/América." In *The Ethnic Eye: Latino Media Arts*, Chon A. Noriega and Ana M. López, eds., 3–21. Minneapolis: University of Minnesota Press.

———. 1996b. "Talking Heads, Body Politic: The Plural Self of Chicano Experimental Video." In *Resolutions: Contemporary Video Practices*, Michael Renov and Erika Suderburg, eds., 207–28. Minneapolis: University of Minnesota Press.

———. 1998. "No Introduction." In *Urban Exile: Collected Writings of Harry Gamboa Jr.*, ed. Chon A. Noriega, 1–22. Minneapolis: University of Minnesota Press.

———. 2000. *Shot in America: Television, the State, and the Rise of Chicano Cinema*. Minneapolis: University of Minnesota Press.

———. 2002a. "'American Family': Mi Casa Es Su Casa." *Chronicle of Higher Education*, March 8, B15.

———. 2002b. "Ready for Prime Time: Minorities on Network Entertainment Television." *Latino Policy and Issues Brief. No. 2*. Los Angeles: UCLA Chicano Studies Research Center (May). http://www.chicano.ucla.edu/press/briefs/archive.asp (accessed October 24, 2008).

Nutter, Chris. 2000. "Ill Communication." *Vibe*, October, 80.

Olvera, Joe. 1980. "Gay Ghetto District." In *Flor y Canto IV and V: An Anthology of Chicano Literature*, José Armas and Bernice Zamora, eds., 111. n.p.: Pajarito Publications/Flor y Canto Committee.

Omi, Michael, and Howard Winant. 1994. *Racial Formation in the United States: From the 1960s to the 1990s*, 2nd ed. New York: Routledge.

Oropeza, Lorena. 2005. *¡Raza Sí!, ¡Guerra No!: Chicano Protest and Patriotism during the Viet Nam War Era*. Berkeley: University of California Press.

Oropeza, Lorena, and Dionne Espinoza, eds. 2006. *Enriqueta Vasquez and the Chicano Movement: Writings from "El Grito del Norte."* Houston: Arte Público Press.

Ortíz, Ricardo L. 1993. "Sexuality Degree Zero: Pleasure and Power in the Novels of John Rechy, Arturo Islas, and Michael Nava." *Journal of Homosexuality* 2 (summer): 111–26.

Padilla, Beverly. 1997. "Chicanas and Abortion." In *Chicana Feminist Thought: The Basic Historical Writings*, ed. Alma García, 120–21. New York: Routledge.

Padilla, Genaro. 1989. "Myth and Comparative Cultural Nationalism: The Ideological Uses of Aztlán." In *Aztlán: Essays on the Chicano Homeland*, Rudolfo Anaya and Francisco Lomelí, eds., 111–34. Albuquerque: University of New Mexico Press.

Paredes, Américo. 1993a. *Folklore and Culture on the Texas-Mexico Border*, ed. Richard Bauman. Austin: University of Texas/CMAS Publications.

———. 1993b. "The United States, Mexico, and *Machismo*." In *Folklore and Culture on the Texas-Mexican Border*, ed. Richard Bauman, 215–34. Austin: University of Texas/CMAS Publications.

Parker, Andrew, Mary Russo, Doris Sommer, and Patricia Yaeger, eds. 1991. *Nationalisms and Sexualities.* New York: Routledge.

Patterson, Sylvia. 2000. "Our Music Makes You Wanna Do Push-ups and Fight. It's Fuuuhn-eee!" *NME: New Musical Express*, April 1, 24–27.

Perea, Juan F., ed. 1997. *Immigrants Out!: The New Nativism and the Anti-Immigrant Impulse in the United States.* New York: New York University Press.

Pérez, Emma. 1999. *The Decolonial Imaginary: Writing Chicanas into History.* Bloomington: Indiana University Press.

Pérez, Laura E. 1999. "*El desorden*, Nationalism, and Chicana/o Aesthetics." In *Between Woman and Nation: Nationalism, Transnational Feminisms, and the State*, Caren Kaplan, Norma Alarcón, and Minoo Moallem, eds., 19–46. Durham, N.C.: Duke University Press.

Pérez, Patrick. 2000. "Image Is Everything: Simón Silva's Fresh Perspective on Art and Ideals." *Oye* 1 (winter): 48–51.

Pérez-Torres, Rafael. 1995. *Movements in Chicano Poetry: Against Myths, Against Margins.* New York: Cambridge University Press.

———. 1997. "Refiguring Aztlán." *Aztlán: A Journal of Chicano Studies* 22 (fall): 15–41.

———. 2006a. *Mestizaje: Critical Uses of Race in Chicano Culture.* Minneapolis: University of Minnesota Press.

———. 2006b. "Popular Music and Postmodern Mestizaje." In *Mestizaje: Critical Uses of Race in Chicano Culture*, 85–113. Minneapolis: University of Minnesota Press.

Perkins, William Eric, ed. 1996. *Droppin' Science: Critical Essays on Rap Music and Hip Hop Culture.* Philadelphia: Temple University Press.

Pesquera, Beatriz M., and Denise Segura. 1993. "There Is No Going Back: Chicanas and Feminism." In *Chicana Critical Issues*, Norma Alarcón, et al., eds., 95–115. Berkeley: Third Woman Press.

Pettit, Arthur G. 1980. *Images of the Mexican American in Fiction and Film.* College Station: Texas A&M University Press.

Pino, Frank. 1973. "Chicano Poetry: A Popular Manifesto." *Journal of Popular Culture* 6 (spring): 718–30.

Plascencia, Luis F. B. 1983. "Low Riding in the Southwest: Cultural Symbols in the Mexican Community." In *History, Culture and Society: Chicano Studies in the 1980's*, Mario T. García, et al., eds., 141–75. Ypsilanti, Mich.: Bilingual Press/Editorial Bilingüe.

Portillo, Lourdes. 1995. "On Chicanas and Filmmaking—A Commentary." In *Chicana (W)rites: On Word and Film*, María Herrera-Sobek and Helena María Viramontes, eds., 279–82. Berkeley: Third Woman Press.

Powers, Lloyd D. 1973. "Chicano Rhetoric: Some Basic Concepts." *Southern Speech Communication Journal* 3 (summer): 340–46.

Quinn, Eithne. 2005. *Nuthin' but a "G" Thang: The Culture and Commerce of Gangsta Rap.* New York: Columbia University Press.

Ramírez, John. 1995. "The Chicano Homosocial Film: Mapping the Discourses of Sex and Gender in *American Me.*" PRE/TEXT: *A Journal of Rhetorical Theory* 16 (fall-winter): 260–74.

Rashkin, Elissa J. 1997. "Historic Image/Self Image: Re-Viewing *Chicana.*" In *Sex Positives? The Cultural Politics of Dissident Sexualities*, Thomas Foster, Carol Siegel, and Ellen E. Berry, eds., 97–119. New York: New York University Press.

Rendón, Armando. 1996. *Chicano Manifesto.* Berkeley: Ollin and Associates, Inc.

Reyes, David, and Tom Waldman. 1998. *Land of a Thousand Dances: Chicano Rock 'n' Roll from Southern California.* Albuquerque: University of New Mexico Press.

Reyes, Rodrigo. 1981. "Latino Gays: Coming Out and Coming Home." *Nuestro* 5 (3): 42–45, 64.

Reyes, Rodrigo, Francisco X. Alarcón, and Juan Pablo Gutiérrez. 1985a. *Ya Vas, Carnal.* San Francisco: Humanizarte Publications.

———. 1985b. "Carnal Knowledge." In *Ya Vas, Carnal*, 8–9. San Francisco: Humanizarte Publications.

Rincón, Bernice. 1971. "La Chicana: Her Role in the Past and Her Search for a New Role in the Future." *Regeneración* 1 (10): 15–18.

Rivera, Raquel Z. 2003. *New York Ricans from the Hip Hop Zone.* New York: Palgrave.

Ro, Ronin. 1996. *Gangsta: Merchandising the Rhymes of Violence.* New York: St. Martin's Press.

———. 1998. *Have Gun Will Travel: The Spectacular Rise and Violent Fall of Death Row Records.* New York: Doubleday.

Roberts, John Storm. 1999. *The Latin Tinge: The Impact of Latin American Music on the United States*, 2nd ed. New York: Oxford University Press.

Rodríguez, Eugene. 1998. Personal interview. July 22.

———. 1999. Artist's Statement. n.p.

Rodríguez, Juana María. 2003. *Queer Latinidad: Identity Practices, Discursive Spaces.* New York: New York University Press.

Rodríguez, Pebo. 1993. "Reality Rappers at the Crossroads." *Lowrider Magazine*, June, 62.

Rodríguez, Richard T. 2000. "Reimagined Communities: Family, Masculinity, and Nationalism in Chicano Cultural Production." Ph.D. diss., University of California, Santa Cruz.

——. 2002. "Serial Kinship: Representing La Familia in Early Chicano Publications." *Aztlán: A Journal of Chicano Studies* 27 (spring): 123–38.

——. 2006. "Queering the Homeboy Aesthetic." *Aztlán: A Journal of Chicano Studies* 31 (fall): 127–37.

——. 2007. Review of *¡Gaytino! Theatre Journal* 59 (May): 309–10.

Romano-V., Octavio Ignacio. 1968. "The Anthropology and Sociology of the Mexican-Americans." *El Grito* 2 (fall): 13–26.

——. 1970. "Social Science, Objectivity, and the Chicanos." *El Grito* 4 (fall): 4–16.

Roque Ramírez, Horacio N. 2003. " 'That's *My* Place!': Negotiating Racial, Sexual, and Gender Politics in San Francisco's Gay Latino Alliance, 1975–1983." *Journal of the History of Sexuality* 12 (April): 224–58.

——. 2004. "Rodrigo Reyes." In *Encyclopedia of Lesbian, Gay, Bisexual, and Transgender History in America*, vol. 3, ed. Marc Stein, 33–34. New York: Charles Scribner's Sons/Thomson Gale.

Rosaldo, Renato. 1986. "When Natives Talk Back: Chicano Anthropology since the Late 60s." *Renato Rosaldo Lecture Series Monograph* 2 (spring): 3–20.

——. 1989. *Culture and Truth: The Remaking of Social Analysis*. Boston: Beacon Press.

Rose, Tricia. 1992. "Black Texts/Black Contexts." In *Black Popular Culture*, ed. Gina Dent, 223–27. Seattle: Bay Press.

——. 1994. *Black Noise: Rap Music and Black Culture in Contemporary America*. Hanover, N.H.: Wesleyan University Press.

Rosen, David, and Peter Hamilton. 1990. *Off-Hollywood: The Making and Marketing of Independent Films*. New York: Grove Weidenfeld.

Roth, Benita. 2003. *Separate Roads to Feminism: Black, Chicana, and White Feminist Movements in America's Second Wave*. New York: Cambridge University Press.

Rubel, Arthur J. 1966. *Across the Tracks: Mexican-Americans in a Texas City*. Austin: University of Texas Press.

Rubin, Gayle. 1975. "The Traffic in Women: Notes on the 'Political Economy' of Sex." In *Toward an Anthropology of Women*, ed. Rayna R. Reiter, 157–210. New York: Monthly Review Press.

Ruíz, Alfonso. 1996. "No Longer a Kid." *Frontera Magazine* (2): 28.

Ruíz, Vicki L. 1987. *Cannery Women/Cannery Lives: Mexican Women, Unionization, and the California Food Processing Industry, 1930–1950*. Albuquerque: University of New Mexico Press.

——. 1998. *From Out of the Shadows: Mexican Women in Twentieth-Century America*. New York: Oxford University Press.

Saldívar, José David. 1990. "The Limits of Cultural Studies." *American Literary History* 2 (summer): 251–66.

———. 1997. *Border Matters: Remapping American Cultural Studies.* Berkeley: University of California Press.

Saldívar-Hull, Sonia. 2000. *Feminism on the Border: Chicana Gender Politics and Literature.* Berkeley: University of California Press.

Sánchez, Félix. 1999. "Combating the Network 'Brownout.'" *Hispanic Business*, October, 46.

Sánchez, George J. 1993. *Becoming Mexican American: Ethnicity, Culture, and Identity in Chicano Los Angeles, 1900–1945.* New York: Oxford University Press.

Sandoval, Denise Michelle. 2003. "Cruising through Low Rider Culture: Chicana/o Identity in the Marketing of *Low Rider Magazine*." In *Velvet Barrios: Popular Culture and Chicana/o Sexualities*, ed. Alicia Gaspar de Alba, 179–96. New York: Palgrave Macmillan.

Sandoval-Sánchez, Alberto. 1999. *José, Can You See?: Latinos On and Off Broadway.* Madison: University of Wisconsin Press.

Santisteban, Ray. 1999. "A Program for Change: Chicano Media into the Next Millennium." *Aztlán: A Journal of Chicano Studies* 24 (fall): 121–29.

Savage, Fernando. 1990a. "Kid Frost: A 'Hispanic' Spreading Panic." *Lowrider Magazine*, September, 38.

———. 1990b. "Kid Frost: Interview." *Lowrider Magazine*, November, 10.

———. 1992. "An East Side Story: Kid Frost." *Lowrider Magazine*, May, 20.

Schneider, David. 1997. "The Power of Culture: Notes on Some Aspects of Gay and Lesbian Kinship in America Today." *Cultural Anthropology* 12 (2): 270–82.

Sedano, Michael Victor. 1980. "Chicanismo: A Rhetorical Analysis of Themes and Images of Selected Poetry from the Chicano Movement." *Western Journal of Speech Communication* 44 (summer): 177–90.

Shaw, William. 2000. *West Side: Young Men and Hip Hop in L.A.* New York: Simon and Shuster.

Sinfield, Alan. 1998. *Gay and After.* London: Serpent's Tail.

Sir Dyno. 1999. *Midst of My Confusion.* Tracy, Calif.: DarkRoom Publishing.

Small, Michael. 1992. *Break It Down: The Inside Story from the New Leaders of Rap.* New York: Citadel Press.

Smith, Lynn. 1995. "*My Family* Offers Different Perspective." *Los Angeles Times*, May 11, D18.

Soja, Edward W. 1989. *Postmodern Geographies: The Reassertion of Space in Critical Social Theory.* New York: Verso.

———. 1996. *Thirdspace: Journeys to Los Angeles and Other Real-and-Imagined Places.* Cambridge, Mass.: Blackwell.

Sommer, Doris. 1991. *Foundational Fictions: The National Romances of Latin America.* Berkeley: University of California Press.

Sosa Riddell, Adaljiza. 1974. "Chicanas in El Movimiento." *Aztlán* 5 (spring/fall): 155–65.

Stacey, Judith. 1990. *Brave New Families: Stories of Domestic Upheaval in Late Twentieth Century America.* New York: Basic Books.

———. 1996. *In the Name of the Family: Rethinking Family Values in the Postmodern Age.* Boston: Beacon Press.

Stancell, Steven. 1996. *Rap Whoz Who: The World of Rap Music.* New York: Schirmer Books.

Steiner, Stan. 1970. *La Raza: The Mexican Americans.* New York: Harper and Row.

Stephens, Gregory. 1992. "Interracial Dialogue in Rap Music: Call-and-Response in a Multicultural Style." *New Formations* 16 (spring): 62–79.

Sternad, Jennifer Flores. 2006. "Cyclona and Early Chicano Performance Art: An Interview with Robert Legorreta." *GLQ* 12 (3): 475–90.

Stone, Michael Cutler. 1990. "'Bajito y Suavecito': Low Riding and the 'Class' of Class." *Studies in Latin American Popular Culture* 9: 85–126.

Swedenburg, Ted. 1992. "Homies in the 'Hood: Rap's Commodification of Insubordination." *New Formations* 18 (winter): 53–66.

Tafolla, Carmen. 1985. *To Split a Human: Mitos, Machos y La Mujer Chicana.* San Antonio, Texas: Mexican American Cultural Center.

Tapia, Micael. 1976. "Machismo, Class, and National Oppression." *Brother* 14–15 (summer): 20.

Thorne, Barrie. 1992. "Feminism and the Family: Two Decades of Thought." In *Rethinking the Family: Some Feminist Questions*, Barrie Thorn and Marilyn Yalom, eds., 3–30. Boston: Northeastern University Press.

Thorne, Barrie, and Marilyn Yalom, eds. 1992. *Rethinking the Family: Some Feminist Questions.* Boston: Northeastern University Press.

Tijerina, Reies López. 2000. *They Called Me "King Tiger": My Struggle for the Land and Our Rights*, trans. José Angel Gutiérrez. Houston: Arte Público Press.

Toop, David. 1991. *Rap Attack 2: African Rap to Global Hip Hop.* London: Serpent's Tail Press.

Torres, Edén E. 2003. *Chicana without Apology: The New Chicana Cultural Studies.* New York: Routledge.

Treviño, Jesús Salvador. c. 1974. Interview with Francisco X. Camplis. Transcript in Jesús Salvador Treviño Collection, M624, Box 13, Folder 10. Department of Special Collections, Stanford University.

———. 1984. "Chicano Cinema Overview." *Areíto* 37: 40–43.

———. 2001. *Eyewitness: A Filmmaker's Memoir of the Chicano Movement.* Houston: Arte Público Press.

Trillin, Calvin, and Ed Koren. 1978. "Low and Slow, Mean and Clean." *New Yorker*, July 10, 70–74.

Turner, Graeme. 1992. *British Cultural Studies: An Introduction*, 2nd ed. London: Routledge.

Ugarte, Sandra. 1997. "Chicana Regional Conference." In *Chicana Feminist Thought: The Basic Historical Writings*, ed. Alma M. Garcia, 153–55. New York: Routledge.

Vaca, Nick. 1970. "The Mexican-American in the Social Sciences, 1912–1970." *El Grito* 3 (summer): 17–51.

Valdez, Luis. 1972. "La Plebe." In *Aztlán: An Anthology of Mexican American Literature*, Luis Valdez and Stan Steiner, eds., xiii–xxxiv. New York: Vintage.

Vidal, Mirta. 1971. "New Voice of La Raza: Chicanas Speak Out." *International Socialist Review*, October, 7–9, 31–33.

Viego, Antonio. 1999. "The Place of Gay Male Chicano Literature in Queer Chicana/o Cultural Work." *Discourse* 21 (3): 111–31.

Viesca, Victor Hugo. 2004. "The Battle of Los Angeles: The Cultural Politics of Chicana/o Music in the Greater Eastside." *American Quarterly* 56 (3): 719–39.

Vigil, Ernesto B. 1999. *The Crusade for Justice: Chicano Militancy and the Government's War on Dissent*. Madison: University of Wisconsin Press.

Vigil, James Diego. 1991. "Car Charros: Cruising and Lowriding in the Barrios of East Los Angeles." *Latino Studies Journal* 2 (2): 71–79.

Villanueva, Tino. 1972. "Pachuco Remembered." *Con Safos* (8): 12–13.

Villarreal, José Antonio. 1959. *Pocho*. New York: Doubleday.

Voss, Karen. 1998. "Replacing L.A.: *Mi Familia, Devil in a Blue Dress*, and Screening the Other Los Angeles." *Wide Angle* 20 (3): 157–81.

Wallace, Michele. [1978]. 1999. *Black Macho and the Myth of the Superwoman*. London and New York: Verso.

Warner, Michael. 2005. *Publics and Counterpublics*. New York: Zone Books.

Watkins, S. Craig. 2005. *Hip Hop Matters: Politics, Pop Culture, and the Struggle for the Soul of a Movement*. Boston: Beacon Press.

Weeks, Jeffrey. 1991. *Against Nature: Essays on History, Sexuality, and Identity*. London: Rivers Oram Press.

West, Dennis. 1995. "Filming the Chicano Family Saga: An Interview with Gregory Nava." *Cineaste* 21 (4): 26–28.

Weston, Kath. 1992. "The Politics of Gay Families." In *Rethinking the Family: Some Feminist Questions*, Barrie Thorn and Marilyn Yalom, eds., 119–39. Boston: Northeastern University Press.

Wexman, Virginia Wright. 1993. *Creating the Couple: Love, Marriage, and Hollywood Performance*. Princeton, N.J.: Princeton University Press.

Wible, Scott. 2004. "Media Advocates, Latino Citizens and Niche Cable: The Limits of 'No Limits' TV." *Cultural Studies* 18 (January): 34–66.

Williams, Norma. 1990. *The Mexican American Family: Tradition and Change*. Dix Hills, N.Y.: General Hall.

Williams, Shirley Anne. 1992. "Two Words on Music: Black Community." In *Black Popular Culture*, ed. Gina Dent, 164–72. Seattle: Bay Press.

Wong, Deborah. 1994. "'I Want the Microphone': Mass Mediation and Agency in Asian-American Popular Music." *Drama Review* 38 (3): 152–67.

Wright, Les. 1999. "San Francisco." In *Queer Sites: Gay Urban Histories since 1600*, ed. David Higgs, 164–89. New York: Routledge.

Yarbro-Bejerano, Yvonne. 1997. "Crossing the Border with Chabela Vargas: A Chicana Femme's Tribute." In *Sex and Sexuality in Latin America*, Daniel Balderston and Donna J. Guy, eds., 33–43. New York: New York University Press.

Ybarra, Lea. 1977. "Conjugal Role Relationships in the Chicano Family." Ph.D. diss., University of California, Berkeley.

———. 1982. "Marital Decision-Making and the Role of Machismo in the Chicano Family." *De Colores* 6 (1/2): 32–47.

Ybarra-Frausto, Tomás. 1977. "The Chicano Movement and the Emergence of a Chicano Poetic Consciousness." *New Scholar* 6 (1/2): 81–109.

———. 1992. "Chicano Art: Text and Context." In *Different Voices: A Social, Cultural, and Historical Framework for Change in the American Art Museum*, ed. Marcia Tucker, 17–29. New York: Association of Art Museum Directors.

Zamora, Bernice. 1977. "Notes from a Chicana 'Coed.'" *Caracol* 3: 19.

Zavella, Patricia. 1987. *Women's Work and Chicano Families: Cannery Workers of the Santa Clara Valley*. Ithaca, N.Y.: Cornell University Press.

Zheutlin, Barbara, and David Talbot. 1978. "Jesús Salvador Treviño." In *Creative Differences: Profiles of Hollywood Dissidents*, 344–52. Boston: South End Press.

Zook, Kristal Brent. 1992. "Reconstructions of Nationalistic Thought in Black Music and Culture." In *Rockin' the Boat: Mass Music and Mass Movements*, ed. Reebee Garofalo, 255–66. Boston: South End Press.

———. 2001. "La Vida Local: With 'Resurrection Blvd.', Showtime Aims to Reverse an L.A. Vanishing Act." *Washington Post*, June 25, C1.

Discography

Alfaro, Luis. 1993. *Down Town.* New Alliance Records.

Brown Pride. 1993. *Livin' in the Barrio.* Familia Records.

Chicano Brotherhood. 1991. "Cruising Bristol." Troop Town Records.

———. 1994. "G.T.A./That's What It's Like." Troop Town Records.

———. 1995. "The Finished Product/Way of Life." Troop Town Records.

Conejo. 1999. *City of Angels.* BGM/U.S. Latin.

Cypress Hill. 1991. "Latin Lingo." *Cypress Hill.* Ruffhouse/Columbia.

———. 1999. *Los Grandes Éxitos en Español.* Ruffhouse/Columbia.

Darkroom Familia. 1998. *Penitentiary Chances.* Dogday Records.

Jae-P. 2004. "Latinos Unidos." *Esperanza.* Univisión Records.

———. 2006. "Pa Mi Raza." *Pa Mi Raza.* Univisión Records.

JV. 1994. *Nayba' Hood Queen.* Thump Records.

(Kid) Frost. 1990. "La Raza." *Hispanic Causing Panic.* Virgin Records.

———. 1992. *East Side Story.* Virgin Records.

———. 1995. "La Familia." *Smile Now, Die Later.* Ruthless/Relativity.

———. 1995. "La Raza II." *Smile Now, Die Later.* Ruthless/Relativity.

———. 1999. *That Was Then, This Is Now, Vol. 1.* Celeb Entertainment.

Lil Bandit. 2005. "Dedication to My Family." *Let It Be Known.* Aries Music Entertainment.

M.C. Blvd. 1994. *I Remember You, Homie.* Beckwood Records.

Proper Dos. 1992. "Mexican Power." *Mexican Power.* Skanless Records.

Rage Against the Machine. 1996. "Bulls on Parade." *Evil Empire.* Epic.

Sister Sledge. 1979. "We Are Family." *We Are Family.* Cotillion/Atlantic Records.

Slow Pain with Cisco. 1999. "Hustling Ain't Dead." Thump Records.

Various Artists. 1999. *Brown Eyed Soul: The Sound of East L.A.* Rhino.

Various Artists. 1992. *Rap Declares War.* Rhino.

Various Artists. 1995. *Latin Lingo: Hip-Hop from the Raza.* Rhino.

Filmography

Agueda Martínez: Our People, Our Country (Esperanza Vásquez, 1977)

American Me (Edward James Olmos, 1992)

The American Tapestry (Gregory Nava, 2000)

Baby Kake (Harry Gamboa Jr., 1984)

La Bamba (Luis Valdez, 1987)

Blanx (Harry Gamboa Jr., 1984)

Born in East L.A. (Richard "Cheech" Marín, 1987)

Bound by Honor/Blood In, Blood Out (Taylor Hackford, 1993)

Buried and Unseen: Chiaroscuro (Eugene Rodríguez, 1998)

Chicana (Sylvia Morales, 1979)

Chismoso y Manteca en Jealousy (Aurora Sarabia, 2005)

Cholo Joto (Augie Robles, 1993)

Colors (Dennis Hopper, 1988)

Cruel Profit (Harry Gamboa Jr., 1973)

De Colores (Peter Barbosa and Garrett Lenoir, 2001)

Entelequía (Juan Salazar, 1978)

Fear and Learning at Hoover Elementary (Laura Angélica Simón, 1995)

Good Soldier II (Johnny Skandros Reyes, 2006)

Heroes of Latin Hip Hop (Joe Ritter and Fred Sherman, 2002)

Hip Hop Homos (Dave O'Brien, 2004)

I Am Joaquín (El Teatro Campesino/Luis Valdez, 1969)

Imperfecto (Harry Gamboa Jr., 1983)

Insultan (Harry Gamboa Jr., 1983)

L.A. Familia (Harry Gamboa Jr., 1993)

Low 'n' Slow: The Art of Lowriding (Rick Tejada-Flores, 1983)

Marginal Eyes (Osa Hidalgo de la Riva, 1999)

Mi Familia/My Family (Gregory Nava, 1995)

Mi Vida Loca/My Crazy Life (Allison Anders, 1994)

Mujería: Primitive and Proud (Osa Hidalgo de la Riva, 1992)

No Supper (Harry Gamboa Jr., 1987)

El Norte (Gregory Nava, 1983)

The Olmeca Rap (Osa Hidalgo de la Riva, 1992)

Pass the Mic! (Richard Montes, 2002)

Pick Up the Mic (Alex Hinton, 2005)

Price of Glory (Carlos Avila, 2000)

La Raza Unida (Jesús Salvador Treviño, 1972)

Real Women Have Curves (Patricia Cardoso, 2002)

Requiem for a Heavyweight (Ralph Nelson, 1962)

Right Cross (John Sturges, 1950)

The Ring (Kurt Neumann, 1952)

S&M in the Hood (Al Lujan, 1998)

Seguín (Jesús Salvador Treviño, 1982)

Selena (Gregory Nava, 1997)

Star Maps (Miguel Arteta, 1997)

Vaporz (Harry Gamboa Jr., 1984)

¡Viva 16! (Augie Robles and Valentín Aguirre, 1994)

Walkout (Edward James Olmos, 2006)

Wanted Alive: Teresita, La Campesina (Valentín Aguirre, 1997)

What Is Art? (Aurora Sarabia, 1989)

Why Do Fools Fall In Love? (Gregory Nava, 1998)

Yo Soy (Jesús Salvador Treviño, 1985)

Yo Soy Chicano (Jesús Salvador Treviño, 1972)

Zoot Suit (Luis Valdez, 1981)

TV PROGRAMS

¡Ahora! (KCET-TV, 1969–70), public affairs.

Resurrection Blvd. (Showtime Cable Network, 2000–2002), dramatic series.

The Brothers Garcia (Nickelodeon Cable Network, 2000–2004), situation comedy.

The George Lopez Show (American Broadcasting Company, 2002–2007), situation comedy.

An American Family (Public Broadcasting Service, 2002, 2004), dramatic series.

Index

Page numbers in italics refer to illustrations

Arteaga, Alfred, 31–32, 203n50
Arteta, Miguel, 187n1
Asco, 16, 58, 81–82, 185n22, 192 nn. 30, 32
Asian-American rap, 107
Assimilationism, 16, 148
Avila, Carlos: as Peruvian, 187n1. *See also Price of Glory* (Avila)
Avila, Ricardo, 128–29
Aztlán: An Anthology of Mexican American Literature (Valdez and Steiner), 59
Aztlán: International Journal of Chicano Studies Research, 36–37, 38
Aztlán Underground, 101, 108–10

Baby Kake (Gamboa), 83–85; alternative view of family dynamics in, 16, 56; gender roles undermined by, 84; in second phase of Asco, 83; social norms uprooted by, 85
Baca, Walter, 183n16
Baca Zinn, Maxine, 24, 179 nn. 4, 5, 180n7, 184n18
Baka Boyz, 99
Ballis, George, 62
Bamba, La (Valdez), 190n15
Bandit, 199n33
Benmayor, Rina, 171
Bersani, Leo, 145, 210n10
Black Atlantic: Modernity and Double Consciousness (Gilroy), 10
Black Cultural Studies, 10
Blanx (Gamboa), 83
Borderlands/La Frontera: The New Mestiza (Anzaldúa), 14
Border Matters: Remapping American Cultural Studies (Saldívar), 13, 106
Border studies, 13
Botello, David Rivas, 41

Bound by Honor/Blood In, Blood Out (Hackford), 106, 120, 201n41
Boxing, 91, 92, 193n39
Boyd, Todd, 196n17
Brah, Avtar, 172
Bravmann, Scott, 170
Bright, Brenda Jo, 196n12
Brothers García (television series), 56, 193n38
Brother to Brother (collection), 166
"Brown pride," 118, 120
Brown Pride (rap group), 201n44
"Brown Pride" web site, 100
Brownside, 123, 199n31
Bruce-Novoa, Juan, 137–38
Bryant, Anita, 143
Buchanan, Patrick J., 8–9
Bullfight, 205n11
Buried and Unseen: Chiaroscuro (Rodríguez), 160
Butchlalis de Panochtitlan (BdP), 51
Butler, Judith, 6, 82, 175, 210n10

Camacho Contreras, Andres, 171
Candelaria, Cordelia, 142
Cantú, Lionel, 204n9
Caracol (journal), 37–38, *39*
Carby, Hazel, 10
Cárdenas de Dwyer, Carlota, 35
Cardoso, Patricia, 187n1
Carnalismo: as bond between gay men, 141; in Chicanismo, 109; Chicanismo promoting interests of *carnales*, 141; Chicano gay men in recasting of, 17, 136; Chicano student activists on commitment to, 21; in *La Familia de La Raza*, 26–27; "la familia" in rap as metaphor for, 127; in Reyes's work, 164, 165–66
"Carnal Knowledge" (Reyes), 165–66

Carrasco, Barbara, 84, 204n4

Castañeda, Omar S., 44

Castillo, Ana, 50–51, 187n30

Castrellón, Clara Gloria, 180n7, 192n34

Chabram-Dernersesian, Angie, 13, 29, 45, 114, 178n9, 183n16

Charlie Chase (Carlos Mandes), 99

Chatterjee, Partha, 2

Chávez, César E., 22–23, 65, 140, 204n4

Chavoya, C. Ondine, 82

Chicana (Morales), 62–64; as feminist critique of *I Am Joaquín*, 62; live-action shots at end of, 63–64; recasts roles of women, 63; shoots back at patriarchal governance, 15–16, 94; on women ensconced in heterosexual family, 63, 77

"Chicana, La: Her Role in the Past and Her Search for a New Role in the Future" (Rincón), 46

Chicana feminism: counternarrative of Chicano movement of, 141; on *la familia de la raza*, 24–25; ideal family challenged by, 1–2; machismo and, 45–46; as not contradictory to be Chicana and feminist, 48; this study guided by critical efforts of, 14

Chicana lesbians: butch and femme identities, 51; Chicano gay men's male privilege and, 169, 175; kinship networks as defined by, 5, 6; literary work by, 136, 137, 138; as macha, 47; machismo and, 49–51; as *marimacha*, 50–51; metropolitan identities of, 170–71; objecting women written off as dykes, 151; rappers, 128; reclamation of the family by, 18; shared marginalization with Chicano gay men, 169–70

Chicana Lesbians: The Girls Our Mothers Warned Us About (Castillo), 50–51

"Chicana/o Cultural Representations: Reframing Alternative Critical Discourses" (*Cultural Studies*), 13

"Chicana/o Latina/o Transnational and Transdisciplinary Movements" (*Cultural Studies*), 13

Chicana Regional Conference (1971), 25

Chicanas: brotherhood often excludes, 141; Chicano Liberation Youth Conference on, 24–25; Chicano rap and, 96, 116, 127–28, 201n44; childrens' demands on, 84, 192n34; fail to challenge patriarchy, 25, 180n7; in liberation movement, 33–34; machismo and, 45–51; macho, 47, 50, 147; "protection" of, 14; provocative photographs in magazines, 150–51, 207n20; in *Regeneración*, 81; resistance to patriarchy among, 141; self-identification as members of *la familia de la raza*, 184n18; woman-headed families, 5–6. *See also* Chicana feminism; Chicana lesbians

Chicana without Apology: The New Chicana Cultural Studies (Torres), 13

Chicanismo: Chicano gay men and, 17; in Chicano rap, 16, 103, 109, 112, 131; familia principle as pivotal for, 26; *flor y canto* festivals convey, 142; gay-affirmative, 158; machismo as anchor of, 145; masculinity associated with, 141; *Mi Familia/My Family* and, 70–71; patriarchy and, 19; persistence into 1980s and 1990s, 147–48

"Chicanismo: A Rhetorical Analysis of Themes and Images of Selected Poetry from the Chicano Movement" (Sedano), 112–13

Chicano, El, 119, 121

Chicano/a studies, 9–14; on Chicano gay male literary production, 136, 139; connection to community, 5, 6; cultural nationalism made enemy in, 7; in dialogue with cultural studies, 12–13

Chicano Brotherhood, 117–18, *118*

"Chicano Cinema Overview" (Treviño), 59

Chicano gay men, 135, 143–44, 146–47, 149, 165–66; alternative kinship networks of, 159–60; brotherhood often excludes, 141; *carnal* as bond between, 141; cast in antifamily terms, 17; Chicano rap and, 96; as fetish for straight men, 156; *Firme Magazine*'s "Gay Life Style (Only if La Familia Approves)," 17, 148, 151–56, 206n16, 207n21; *Firme Magazine*'s homophobic impulse, 150, 151; homo-hop, 17, 128–30; literary production by, 136–40; male privilege of, 169, 175; metropolitan identities of, 170–71; *Mi Familia/My Family* and, 76; nontraditional documents of, 141–42; pachucos and, 198n23; penetrator versus penetrated in gay sex, 145; reclamation of the family by, 18; recovery work on cultural production of, 139, 203n3; in *Resurrection Blvd.*, 93–94, 194n42; seen as failed men, 156; sexism of, 14, 169; shared marginalization with Chicana lesbians, 169–70; visual cultural representations of, 156–64; web site of antigay rap lyrics, 202n45

Chicano Manifesto (Rendón), 44–45

Chicano nationalism. *See* Nationalism

Chicano rap: Chicanas and, 96, 116, 127–28, 201n44; cross-cultural exchange with black rappers, 110–11; dismissive views of, 101; ethnic diversity within, 103; family in, 116–27, 132–33; gangs and, 96–97, 116–24; gangsta rap, 123, 127; history and characteristics of, 99–105; homo-hop, 17, 128–30; "I am Joaquín" as influence on, 31; internet distribution of, 102; invisibility of, 95, 194n4; kinship discourse in, 95–96, 98; list of lesser-known performers, 195n9; masculinist protocols in, 16–17, 96, 106, 107, 114–18, 124–25; movement poetry compared with, 112–13, 197n21; nationalism in, 96, 97, 98, 105–10, 111–16, 130–32; as never specifically Chicano, 107; popularity of, 101–2; as resistance narratives, 113; valorization of mothers in, 200n39; working-class consciousness in, 108, 131

Chicano Rap Magazine, 95, 103

Chicano Renaissance: Contemporary Cultural Trends (Maciel, Ortíz, and Herrera-Sobek), 140–41

Chicanos: as "all-encompassing" identity, 209n4; pachucos, 75, 114, 150, 198 nn. 23, 24, 207n18, 208n26. *See also* Chicanas; Chicano gay men; Chicano rap; Machismo; Nationalism

Chicano Time Trip series, 41

Chicano Youth Liberation Conference: brings people together, 113; on Chicanas, 24–25; Crusade for Justice as sponsor of, 28. *See also El Plan Espiritual de Aztlán* (Chicano Liberation Youth Conference)

¡Gaytino! (Guerrero), 204n5

Gender: Asco challenges gender roles, 82; *Baby Kake* undermines gender roles, 84; Chicano rap and relations of, 97; distinguishing sexuality from, 14; feminism and gay and lesbian struggles as challenge to conventional roles, 140; kinship discourse's impact on, 97, 98; men as fettered by gender roles, 14; national difference compared with gender difference, 4. *See also* Femininity; Masculinity

Genealogy, 3, 11

George López Show, 56, 193n38

G-Fellas, 123

Gilroy, Paul: on accumulation of families, 116; *The Black Atlantic: Modernity and Double Consciousness*, 10; in black cultural studies, 10, 97; on Chicano and black rap, 110; exchange with Lubiano, 125–26; on the family and nationalism, 12; foundationalism attributed to, 11; "It's a Family Affair: Black Culture and the Trope of Kinship," 12, 97, 125; Kid Frost's music and, 106, 111; on kinship discourse among African Americans, 119

Gómez, Ignacio, 38, *40*, 41

Gómez-Quiñones, Juan, 16–17, 20

Gonzales, Rodolfo "Corky": in authorship of *El Plan Espiritual de Aztlán*, 20, 28; as boxer, 91; on Chicana leadership, 186n26; in Crusade for Justice, 23, 28, 30, 112; "I am a revolutionary," 113; on machismo, 44; nationalism of, 30, 31; *Yo Soy Chicano* on, 64. *See also* "I am Joaquín" (Gonzales)

González, Cesar A., 32, 35, 183n16

González, John M., 196n15

González, Ray, 43–44

Grajeda, Rafael, 114

Gray, Herman, 73

Gronk, 81, 82–83, 84, 192 nn. 30, 32

Grossberg, Lawrence, 9, 10

Guerrero, Andre, 30

Guerrero, Dan, 204n5

Guevara, Nancy, 115

Gupta, Sunil, 168–69

Gutiérrez, Eric-Steven, 157

Gutiérrez, José Angel, 23, 64, 147–48

Gutiérrez, Juan Pablo, 165

Gutiérrez, Ramón, 141, 191n21, 199n32

Gutiérrez-Jones, Carl, 138

Guzmán, Manuel, 139, 173–74, 210n9

Hackford, Taylor, 106, 120

Halberstam, Judith, 51, 202n47

Hall, Stuart, 9, 10, 13, 56, 104–5

Harlow, Barbara, 197n21

Healy, Wayne Alaniz, 41

Hemingway, Ernest, 146, 205n11

Hennessy, Rosemary, 208n24

Hernández, Benjamin Francisco, 149, 152, 154, 155

Hernández, Carlos, 152–53, 155

Hernández, Judithe Elena, 37, *38*

Herón, Willie, 81

Herrera-Sobek, María, 140–41

Heteronormativity: in Chicano rap, 96, 98, 115, 128, 129, 130; in familial/nationalist politics, 148; feminism and gay and lesbian struggles as challenge to, 140, 146; in *Firme Magazine*'s "A Gay Life Style (Only if La Familia Approves)," 154, 156; gay male bond that extends beyond, 165; of lowrider culture, 158; in *Mi Familia/My Family*, 76; nonheteronormative attempts at collectivity, 176; Rodríguez's work and, 162, 163; women ensconced in heterosexual family, 63, 77

Heteropatriarchy, 2; in *American Family*, 93; family associated with, 20, 176; family seen as site of resistance to, 7; in Hollywood film industry, 74; machismo associated with, 45; in *Mi Familia/My Family*, 16; Morales challenges, 94; nationalism associated with, 3, 12; in *Price of Glory*, 93; queer family for contesting, 167, 168; "shoots back" at stereotypes, 72, 75

Hidalgo-de la Riva, Teresa "Osa," 188n3, 189 nn. 9, 10

Hinton, Alex, 128

Hip hop. *See* Rap

"Hip Hop Chicano: A Separate but Parallel Story" (Kelly), 113

Hirsch, Marianne, 160

Hispanic Causing Panic (Kid Frost), 106, 112, 115

"Historic Images of the Chicana" (Nieto-Gómez), 63

Hocquenghem, Guy, 145

Hoggart, Richard, 10

Holling, Michelle A., 92, 94

Hombres y Machos: Masculinity and Latino Culture (Mirandé), 52, 198n23

Homo-hop, 17, 128–30

"Homo/Latino" (Avila), 128–29

Homosexuality: biblical prohibition of, 153; ethnic infighting over, 186n24; gay artists in Asco, 192n30; Newton on, 205n12; queer reconfiguration of the family, 167–76; Sister Sledge's "We Are Family" claimed by queer community, 200n40; Tijerina's homosexual baiting, 179n3. *See also*

Chicana lesbians; Chicano gay men; Gay and lesbian movement

"Homosexuality and the Chicano Novel" (Bruce-Novoa), 137–38

Huaco-Nuzum, Carmen, 76–78, 84

Huerta, Dolores, 62, 63–64, 65, 140, 189n10

Hurtado, Aída, 187n29

"I am Joaquín" (Gonzales), 28–32; Aztlán and, 29, 181n12; call for family-based network in, 15; Chicano student movement influenced by, 29; as companion piece to *El Plan Espiritual de Aztlán*, 28–29; exemplifies Chicano subject, 29; on *la familia de la raza*, 23; *La Familia de La Raza* quotes, 27; family spirit in, 31–32; film *I Am Joaquín* based on, 58, 60–61; as first Chicano poem, 59; influence of, 112; Kid Frost's work compared with, 113, 120; last lines of, 61; masculinist autobiographical "I" in, 116–17; pre-Columbian references in, 29; publication of, 181n11; as rebellion against *corridos*, 31; on urbanization process, 30; on women, 182n14

I Am Joaquín (Valdez), 58–62; *Chicana* as feminist critique of, 62–64; Chicano-based counterimagery in, 15–16, 56, 60; completion of, 59; dating of, 188n5; family photograph in, 61–62; as first Chicano film, 57, 59–60, 188n6; Huerta as depicted in, 62; influence of, 60; last lines of, 61; masculinist tendencies of, 61, 189n9; United Farm Workers show, 60

Ice-T, 99, 107, 112

Identity politics, 8

Illegals, 71, 191n21

Lasch, Christopher, 1, 5

Latin Hustle, 158

Latin Lingo: Hip-Hop from La Raza (CD), 115

Latino Cultural Citizenship (Flores and Benmayor), 171

"Latino Gays: Coming Out and Coming Home" (Reyes), 157

"Latino Rap Scene: Chicanos' Time for Rhythm and Rhyme" (Alvarez), 100

Latin Rap Magazine, 123

Latin Tinge: The Impact of Latin American Music on the United States (Roberts), 110–11

Lazarus, Neil, 107

Lee, Spike, 74

Leoni, Dennis E., 90, 193n39

Lesbians. *See* Chicana lesbians

LeShan, Nina, 191n21

Lewels, Francisco J., Jr., 57

Lighter Shade of Brown, A, 101, 102, 107, 108, 127

Lil Bandit, 95, 200n39

Lil Rob (Robert Flores), 102, 114, 126, 200n36

"Limits of Cultural Studies" (Saldívar), 13

Limón, José E., 31, 182n14

Lloyd, David, 131, 198n28

Longeaux y Vásquez, Enriqueta, 33–34, 183n17

López, Sonia A., 24–25

Low 'n' Slow (Tejada-Flores), 148

Lowrider Magazine, 110, 123, 149, 151, 157, 207 nn. 17, 20

Lowriders, 109, 110, 148, 157

Loza, Steve, 100

Lubiano, Wahneema, 73, 97, 123, 125–26

Lujan, Al, 17, 158

Machismo, 43; Armas on, 46–47, 146, 206n13; Chicana feminists and, 45–46; Chicana lesbians and, 49–51; Chicanas and, 45–51; in Chicanismo, 145; Chicano male scholars fail to thoroughly scrutinize, 180n5; as essentialist, 147; in *La Familia de La Raza*, 26–27; family ideal promoted by, 1–2; of Hemingway, 146, 205n11; in Moraga's assessment of cultural nationalism, 8; nationalism associated with, 44–45; positive versus negative aspects of, 46; in Western academic view of family, 23; what is to be done with the term, 51–54; white men can and want to be macho, 44, 146; in women, 47, 50, 147; women's and gay liberation movements on, 145–46

"Machismo" (Armas), 17, 145, 146, 205n11

"Macho Man" (Village People), 44

Maciel, David R., 140–41

Madsen, William, 23, 30

Maize: Notebooks of Xicano Art and Literature, 38, 40

Márez, Curtis, 101, 108–10, 127

Marín, Christine, 31

Marín, Richard "Cheech," 191n23

Mariscal, Jorge, 8

Martínez, Angie, 202n44

Martínez, Eliud, 58

Martínez, Rubén, 101

Masculinity: Chicanismo associated with, 141; in Chicano rap, 16–17, 96, 106, 107, 114–18, 124–25; as depicted in *Resurrection Blvd.*, 92; family associated with, 4, 14, 20; lesbian butch identity, 51; *Mi Familia/My Family*'s masculinism, 76; in

Masculinity (*cont.*)

nationalism, 53, 97; reconfigurations of, 52; seen as a problem, 14. *See also* Machismo; Patriarchy

Master OC (Oscar Rodríguez Jr.), 99

MC Blvd., 111, 114, 124, 200n40

McClintock, Anne, 4

McFarland, Pancho, 101, 105, 108, 196n16

McPeek Villatoro, Marcos, 132

MECHA (Movimiento Estudiantil Chicano de Aztlán), 8–9

Mellow Man Ace (Ulpiano Sergio Reyes), 101, 107, 127, 128

Melville, Margarita B., 184n18

Mercer, Kobena, 10–11, 13

"Mexican American Family" (Murillo), 29–30

"Mexican Power" (Proper Dos), 103, 111, 131

Mi Familia/My Family (Nava): as redemption, 72; breaks with conventions of Chicano cinema, 69–70; breaks with cultural nationalism, 16, 56, 187n2; Catholic aspects of, 190n20; commercial success of, 68–69, 190n19; crossover appeal of, 75; East Los Angeles setting of, 69, 75; film industry context of, 73–75; *The Godfather* compared with, 69; good son/bad son theme in, 78; *L.A. Familia* contrasted with, 85, 88–89; pedagogical aspect of, 75, 191n25; pre-Columbian mythic structure of, 16, 70; promotional material for, 76, 77; Sánchez family in, 69; as taking back culture and family from the media, 71–72

¡Mira! (Rodríguez), 161–62, *162*

Mirandé, Alfredo, 52–53, 198n23

"Miss Primavera Contest" (García), 18, 174–75

Mi Vida Loca/My Crazy Life (Anders), 119, 199n30

Montes, Richard, 101, 128

Montiel, Miguel, 187n33

Montoya, José, 114

Moon, Michael, 27

Moraga, Cherríe: assessment of cultural nationalism by, 7–8; on Chicano gay male literary production, 136–37, 138; on family as site of resistance, 7, 55; on family as where we learn how to love, 1; on heterosexual Chicanos learning about masculinity from gays, 162; leaves country, 206n16; on machismo, 53–54; "Queer Aztlán: The Re-formation of the Chicano Tribe," 8, 168, 169, 173; on reclamation of the family, 17, 168–70; on silence of Chicano gay men, 207n16; in struggle against homophobia, 141; tribute to Reyes, 164

Morales, Ed, 100

Morales, Iris, 52

Morales, Sylvia: cultural nationalism challenged by, 57; directs episodes of *Resurrection Blvd.*, 91, 93, 94; in Ethno-Communications Program, 57; heteropatriarchy challenged by, 94; on Huerta appearing in *Yo Soy Chicano*, 65. *See also Chicana* (Morales)

Morgan, Joan, 97, 128

Mozo: An Introduction into the Duality of Orbital Indecision (Pérez), 188n6

Mr. Cartoon, 96, 199n34

MSMs, 208n23

Muñoz, Carlos, Jr., 113, 179n2

Muñoz, José Esteban, 141, 157, 203n2, 208n24
Muralism, 41, 42, 58, 62, 185n22
Murillo, Nathan, 29–30
Murs Murs (Varda), 192n32
Muy Macho: Latino Men Confront Their Manhood (González), 43–44
My Family (Nava). *See Mi Familia/My Family* (Nava)
My Trip in a '52 Ford (Palamino), 188n6

Nationalism: Aztlán in, 29; Chicana counternarrative of Chicano movement, 141; Chicano gay men confront homophobia in, 157; in Chicano rap, 96, 97, 98, 105–10, 111–16, 130–32; of *La Familia de La Raza*, 26–27; family associated with, 4, 12, 29, 31–32, 168; family ideal promoted by, 1–2; film and television in movement, 57; of Gonzales, 30, 31; heteropatriarchy associated with, 3, 12; machismo associated with, 44–45; on masculinity, 53, 97; Moraga's assessment of, 7–8; multiple ideologies in, 8; the national-popular, 104–5; pachuco as symbol of, 114; *El Plan Espiritual de Aztlán* as call for, 20; pre-Columbian history and, 70. *See also* Chicanismo
National Latino Media Council, 90
Nava, Gregory: *American Family* series directed by, 74, 91–93; *The American Tapestry*, 68; Asco artists contrasted with, 81; background of, 68; on media representation of Latinos, 72–73; New Line Cinema deal of, 68, 74, 190n16; *El Norte*, 68, 190n17; other work of, 190n18; *Selena*, 56, 68, 92; *Why Do Fools Fall in Love?*, 68. *See also Mi Familia/My Family* (Nava)
Nava, Michael, 138
Navarrette, Ruben, Jr., 186n24
Navarro, J. L., 114
Nelson, Cary, 9
New Communicators Incorporated, 58
New Harvest Christian Fellowship flyer, *43*
New Line Cinema, 68, 74, 90, 190n16
Newton, Huey, 205n12
New West (magazine), 38, *40*, 41
Nieto-Gómez, Anna, 24, 62–63
Nieves, Santiago, 75
No-Movies, 58, 82–83
Noriega, Chon, 57, 59, 66, 67, 74, 80, 188n5, 192n31, 193n38
Norte, El (Nava), 68, 190n17
No Supper (Gamboa), 81
"Notes from a Chicana 'Coed'" (Zamora), 47
Nuestra Familia, La, 126, 201n41
Nuestro (magazine), 157

Official nationalism, 7
Olmos, Edward James: in *American Family*, 92; *American Me*, 106, 197n17, 201n41; in *Mi Familia/My Family*, 76; *Walkout*, 181n12
Olvera, Joe, 17, 142–44, 145, 156
Ometeotl, 70, 190n20
Omi, Michael, 11–12
Ortíz, Isidro D., 140–41
Ortíz, Ricardo L., 138
Osuña, Gloria, 37–38, *39*, 185n21

Pachucos, 75, 114, 150, 198 nn. 23, 24, 207n18, 208n26
Padilla, Genaro, 203n50
Palacios, Procopio, 37

193n40. *See also Yo Soy Chicano*
(Treviño)

Ugarte, Sandra, 25
United Farm Workers, 22, 36, 60,
    204n4
Univision, 103
*Uses of the Media by the Chicano
    Movement: A Study in Minority
    Access* (Lewels), 57

Vaca, Nick, 121
Valdez, Daniel, 59
Valdez, Luis: Asco artists contrasted
    with, 81; *La Bamba*, 190n15; as
    director of *I Am Joaquín*, 188n4; "La
    Plebe," 59; as prominent television
    director, 67, 190n15; on recovering
    Mexican heritage, 58–59; in El
    Teatro Campesino, 57; *Zoot Suit*,
    106, 190n15. *See also I Am Joaquín*
    (Valdez)
Valdez, Patssi, 81, 192n32
Values: traditional, 27. *See also* Family
    values
Vaporz (Gamboa), 83
Varda, Agnes, 192n32
Vargas, Chavela, 51
Vargas, Roberto, 186n24
Vásquez, Esperanza, 189n12
Vásquez, Tre (Rigomortis), 128
Vidal, Eric, and Nick, 99
Vidal, Mirta, 24, 45
Video: accessibility of, 79–80; in Chi-
    cano gay men's cultural production,
    157–58; the family in, 15–16, 79–90;
    relationship to film, 79
Viego, Antonio, 136, 137, 138–39
Viesca, Victor Hugo, 196n14
Villa, Pancho, 58, 64

Village People, 44
Villanueva, Tino, 114
Villarreal, José Antonio, 138
Virgen de Guadalupe, La, 62, 127,
    129, 171
Visual media: Chicano gay men gay
    in, 156–64; grapples with family
    principles, 15–16, 32–43. *See also*
    Film; Television; Video
¡Viva 16! (Robles and Aguirre), 18,
    171–76, 209n4
Voss, Karen, 191n25

Waldman, Tom, 100, 110
Walkout (Olmos), 181n12
War (music group), 107, 110
Warner, Michael, 173
Watkins, S. Craig, 101
"We Are Family" (Sister Sledge), 124,
    200n40
Weeks, Jeffrey, 176
West, Danny, 70
Weston, Kath, 18, 167
Wexman, Virginia Wright, 74
Why Do Fools Fall in Love? (Nava), 68
Wible, Scott, 91–92, 193n40
Williams, Raymond, 10, 13
Williams, Shirley Anne, 96
Willis, Paul, 13
Winant, Howard, 11–12
Wino (Manuel Moreno), 117–18, *118*,
    199n29
Women: misogynist sentiment in
    rap, 123, 201n43; nationalism
    disregards experiences of, 4. *See
    also* Chicanas
"Women's Liberation and Gay Lib-
    eration Movements" (Newton),
    205n12
Wong, Deborah, 107

Wood, Brenton, 111

Wright, Les, 143

Yano, Steve, 107

Yarbro-Bejarano, Yvonne, 51

Ya Vas, Carnal (poetry collection), 165

Ybarra, Lea, 179n4

Ybarra-Frausto, Tomás, 28

Yoatl (Orozco), 101, 109–10, 195n6

Yo Soy Chicano (Treviño), 64–65;

Huerta depicted in, 64, 65; need to shoot patriarch in, 15–16

Young Lords, 51–52

Zamora, Bernice, 47, 142

Zapata, Carmen, 62, 63

Zapata, Emiliano, 58, 64

Zavella, Patricia, 179n5

Zoot Suit (Valdez), 106, 190n15

Zoot suit riots, 75

Richard T. Rodríguez is an associate professor of English and Latina/Latino studies at the University of Illinois, Urbana-Champaign.

Library of Congress Cataloging-in-Publication Data
Rodríguez, Richard T., 1971–
Next of kin: the family in Chicano/a cultural politics/Richard T. Rodríguez.
p. cm. — (Latin America otherwise: languages, empires, nations)
Include bibliographical references and index.
ISBN 978-0-8223-4525-1 (cloth: alk. paper)
ISBN 978-0-8223-4543-5 (pbk.: alk. paper)
1. Mexican American families. 2. Chicano movement. I. Title. II. Series: Latin America otherwise.
E184.M5R588 2009
306.868'72073—dc22   2009003601